Remaking the Rust Belt

AMERICAN BUSINESS, POLITICS, AND SOCIETY

Series editors:
Andrew Wender Cohen, Pamela Walker Laird,
Mark H. Rose, and Elizabeth Tandy Shermer

Books in the series American Business, Politics, and Society explore
the relationships over time between governmental institutions and
the creation and performance of markets, firms, and industries large
and small. The central theme of this series is that politics, law, and
public policy—understood broadly to embrace not only lawmaking but
also the structuring presence of governmental institutions—has been
fundamental to the evolution of American business from the colonial era
to the present. The series aims to explore, in particular, developments
that have enduring consequences.

A complete list of books in the series
is available from the publisher.

Remaking the Rust Belt

The Postindustrial Transformation of North America

Tracy Neumann

PENN

UNIVERSITY OF PENNSYLVANIA PRESS

PHILADELPHIA

Published by
University of Pennsylvania Press
Philadelphia, Pennsylvania 19104-4112
www.upenn.edu/pennpress

Printed in the United States of America on acid-free paper
1 3 5 7 9 10 8 6 4 2

Library of Congress Cataloging-in-Publication Data
ISBN 978-0-8122-4827-2

CONTENTS

Cities and the Postindustrial Imagination

In 1968, shortly after Jack Moore became Hamilton, Ontario's, first economic development commissioner, he took a trip to Pennsylvania. Concerned about industrial decentralization, suburban migration, and central city decline, Hamilton's municipal officials had replaced the city's Industrial Development Commission with an Economic Development Commission and initiated a series of urban renewal projects intended to reinvent their drab steel town as a bustling regional service center. Pittsburgh, Hamilton's steel-producing neighbor to the south, offered them a successful model, and Moore went down to investigate. Hiram Milton, president of Pittsburgh's Regional Industrial Development Corporation, and John J. Grove, executive director of the Allegheny Conference on Community Development, took Moore on a tour of the city's redevelopment sites. But Moore was more interested in learning the details of how the corporate-led Allegheny Conference had worked with public officials to turn the city's smoke-filled downtown into a modern commercial center. "My principal reason for visiting Pittsburgh," he had written to Grove when arranging his trip, "is not just to look at industrial development but to learn a good deal more about how your organization was successful in spearheading the redevelopment of downtown Pittsburgh. I am particularly interested in knowing how you can demand and get active participation from your top business executives."[1]

For Moore and the city officials he represented, reproducing Pittsburgh's public-private partnership looked like the best route to making Hamilton something more than a steel town. Public officials in other manufacturing centers had the same idea. In the 1950s and 1960s, more than seventy national and international delegations of urban policy tourists who hoped to replicate the "Renaissance," as the city's urban renewal program was known, arrived in Pittsburgh to see first-hand how Democratic mayors and Republican businessmen had worked together to scrub clean the streets and skies of the dirty, polluted, and flood-prone city. Visitors from Dayton and Detroit wanted to know more about Pittsburgh's urban renewal program and the public-private partnership behind it; so did officials from Australia, Brazil, Belgium, Germany, and Scotland. Canadian policymakers were especially interested in the Renaissance, sending a stream of urban specialists to Pittsburgh from Quebec, Ontario, and Manitoba.[2] International consulting firms, too, recommended that their clients visit Pittsburgh. In fact, the year before Moore's trip, Hamilton's Economic Development Commission had hired Boston-based Arthur D. Little and Company to study Hamilton's lackluster commercial development. Citing successful downtown renewal efforts in U.S. cities, and especially Pittsburgh, the consultants urged Hamilton's city officials to diversify the regional economy by working with local businessmen through a civic organization that was separate from but worked closely with local government.[3] In response, the Economic Development Commission sent Moore to Pittsburgh.

When Moore arrived in Pittsburgh, pundits, politicians, and policymakers did not yet describe the city's physical redevelopment as "post-industrial"— that term would not gain widespread usage until the 1970s, when a wave of plant closings devastated communities in the U.S. manufacturing belt. But what Moore observed on his visit was, indeed, the beginning of postindustrialism: the social and physical redevelopment of manufacturing centers that accompanied economic transitions from heavy industry to finance, services, and research in heavily industrialized North Atlantic cities in the second half of the twentieth century.[4] Postindustrialism included a pervasive ideology that privileged white-collar jobs and middle-class residents, as well as a set of pragmatic tactics designed to remake urban space, including financial incentives, branding campaigns, and physical redevelopment, typically carried out by public-private partnerships.

Beginning in the early twentieth century and accelerating after World War II, the distribution of functions between cities and the suburbs and hinterlands that composed their metropolitan regions changed as production moved out of central cities to less expensive land, first in outlying areas and eventually to countries in the global South.[5] Manufacturing, of course, did not entirely disappear from cities. Instead, between the 1950s and the 1990s, "smokestack" industries like steel and automotive gave way to smaller-scale, more technologically advanced production. As industry decentralized, management functions and professional services became centralized in downtown skyscrapers. Corporations increasingly enlisted the professional services of well-paid ad men, bankers, accountants, lawyers, and real estate agents, whose activities were likewise centralized. Managers, over the course of their workday, also relied on the labor of other kinds of service work-ers—the janitors who cleaned their offices, the waitresses who brought their business lunches, the maids who cleaned the hotel rooms when colleagues came to town—who typically earned at or just above minimum wage. In the United States, the lower wages that accompanied the shift from manufactur-ing to services meant that average hourly pay fell by 7.5 percent between 1973 and 1993.[6]

Contemporary narratives of the inexorable decline of basic industry in North America and Western Europe make the postindustrial transformation of national economies and old manufacturing centers seem like a historical inevitability, the product of natural business cycles and neutral market forces. This book tells a different story, one in which growth coalitions composed of local political and business elites set out to actively create postindustrial places. They hired the same international consultants and shared ideas about urban revitalization on study tours, at conferences, and in the pages of pro-fessional journals. Growth coalitions narrowly focused on creating the jobs, services, leisure activities, and cultural institutions that they believed would attract middle-class professionals. In doing so, local officials abandoned social democratic goals in favor of corporate welfare programs, fostering an increasing economic inequality among their residents in the process.

Pittsburgh and Hamilton are exemplary of postindustrialism, but they are not exceptional. The stories of the two steel towns are local variants of larger social, political, and economic processes that affected many North Ameri-can and Western European cities. The changing geography of production made the industrial crises of the 1970s and 1980s a decidedly North Atlantic, rather than strictly national or truly international, phenomenon. Cities in the North Atlantic coal and steel belts had been seats of industrial power in the early twentieth century. By the 1970s, the economic and political might of the North American heartland, Germany's Ruhr Valley, and the English Black Country had been significantly diminished by newly industrializing regions in the global South, from the U.S. Sunbelt and Mexico to Latin America, Asia, and the Middle East.[7]

The late twentieth-century decline of manufacturing and the transition to service- and finance-sector economies that seemed to come as a shock to manufacturing workers, corporate executives, and elected officials through-out the North Atlantic were decades in the making. Industrial restructuring was a spatially and temporally uneven process, taking place in different ways,

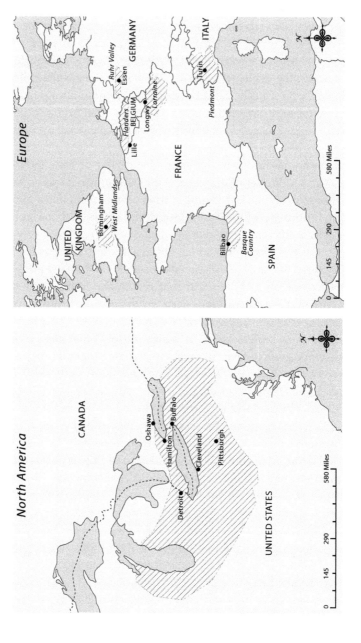

Figure 1. The North Atlantic Rust Belt.

at different times, in different regions. It was in the North American heart-land, however, where the combination of declining infrastructure and indus-trial restructuring first took its toll. The precipitous decline of Pittsburgh, Hamilton, and other mature steel centers served as a bellwether for aging manufacturing cities around the world.

From the vantage point of the 1950s, the Great Lakes manufacturing belt had seemed impervious to rust. The region had long been a site of mate-rial and symbolic significance to the North Atlantic economy. Its factories produced the tanks and planes that helped the Allies win World War II and later turned out the consumer goods that expanded American markets into physically and economically devastated postwar Europe. The Detroit-cen-tered automotive and rubber industries spawned boomtowns in Ohio and Ontario, and the steel and coal belts ranged north from the Ohio border through Western Pennsylvania and into Southern Ontario. Great Lakes man-ufacturing centers in the early postwar decades projected an image of invul-nerability to the boom-and-bust cycles that affected other economic sectors. At midcentury, the hulking factories that punctuated the regional landscape lent an air of permanence to industries like steel and automotive and to the hundreds of thousands of jobs they created.[8] Within a few decades, however, trade liberalization, U.S. subsidies for foreign manufacturers, and successful industrial attraction schemes in the South and the Sunbelt had reduced Great Lakes manufacturers' shares of international markets, and increasingly glo-balized manufacturing and labor flows diminished executives' commitments to the communities in which their companies were headquartered. By 1984, Democratic presidential candidate Walter Mondale lamented "the vast Rust Bowl with tragic unemployment and broken dreams all through the great industrial Midwest."[9]

Mondale failed to coin a term with "Rust Bowl," but with the populariza-tion of the Rust Belt appellation, as historian Steven High has noted, "the problem became imaginatively contained, tied to one place."[10] Accepted his-torical wisdom tells us that the Rust Belt is an American phenomenon, an economically devastated region stretching from New York to Chicago. This book expands the geography of the Rust Belt across the northern border of the United States to the manufacturing centers of the Canadian heartland. The Rust Belt may have been discursively situated in North America, but by the 1980s Western Europe's steel and coal country, from Lille to the Ruhr to Sheffield and Glasgow, was corroding as well.[11] And if the crisis of North Atlantic manufacturing was symbolically tied to the North American Rust Belt, solutions to the problems facing those manufacturing centers were tied to one city: Pittsburgh. For public officials and civic-minded businessmen from the middle of the twentieth century into the twenty-first, postindustrial Pittsburgh represented a phoenix that rose from the ashes of the steel industry with a revived downtown; a lively cultural district; expansive university, medical, and technological complexes; and vibrant residential neighborhoods. From St. Louis to Birmingham to Dortmund, city officials' and civic leaders' imaginations swelled with similar visions for postindustrial futures. They imagined gleaming headquarters buildings and luxury housing designed to meet the needs of the financial and commercial service sectors, residential neighborhoods scrubbed free of industrial detritus, state-of-the-art sports stadiums and conference centers, and culture and leisure activities that would appeal to tourists and suburbanites.[12]

Hamilton's elected officials and civic leaders were no exception, even as Pittsburgh and Hamilton's manufacturing bases contracted in very different ways. In Pittsburgh, the steel industry collapsed, leading to the eventual shutdown of all but one of the region's steel mills and countless steel-related manufacturers. In Hamilton, the steel industry restructured, which allowed the mills to remain profitable but eliminated a quarter of the city's well-paid manufacturing jobs. In the 1980s, the Pittsburgh region's shuttered plants, legions of unemployed steelworkers, and bankrupt mill towns became emblems of an emerging Rust Belt. Hamilton also faced high unemployment rates, aging infrastructure, and a declining tax base, but its mills continued to churn out steel, and the Golden Horseshoe—the cluster of industry around Lake Ontario stretching from Niagara Falls to Oshawa—remained a manufacturing center. Popular imagery of postindustrial cities may evoke shuttered factories, but, in places like Hamilton, postindustrialism was a utopian planning model that did not require the collapse of manufacturing. Even as plumes continued to rise from Hamilton's smokestacks, its growth coalition doggedly pursued schemes intended to produce postindustrial space.

While Pittsburgh features prominently in the literature on postwar U.S. cities, it was in many ways an atypical place. Its physical geography and robust philanthropic foundations made it unique among North Atlantic manufacturing centers, and its relatively small African American population made it unlike other major northern U.S. cities.[13] Hamilton, on the other hand, has not achieved Pittsburgh's rarefied status among urban scholars, in part because it is overshadowed by nearby Toronto and in part because its postindustrial redevelopment was halting and incomplete.[14] Nevertheless, the growth coalitions in both cities acted in similar ways. Hamilton's elected officials and civic leaders, like Pittsburgh's, sought to stem the flow of businesses to the suburbs, to attract corporate headquarters and service sector jobs, and to draw suburban residents and their spending power into the city. But the ad hoc coalition between Hamilton's mayors and local businessmen could not control the activities of urban planners to the same extent as its counterpart in Pittsburgh, where collaboration between political and business elites limited political contestation.

The structure of this book reflects the uneven development across space and time evident in Pittsburgh and Hamilton.[15] On one level, it provides case studies of two cities in transition within the larger context of North Atlantic economic restructuring. On a second level, it explains the relationship between local redevelopment strategies in Pittsburgh and Hamilton and broader shifts in regional and national public policies. On a third level, it considers how exchanges between the two cities reflected policy circulation in the North Atlantic. Events in Pittsburgh and Hamilton highlight the primacy of local place in understanding how the global and national social, political, and economic processes that constituted postindustrialism were worked out on the ground. Yet national policy orientations and regional politics constrained local political and civic leaders' abilities to adopt redevelopment models that they believed would allow them to realize their goals. In Pittsburgh, entrepreneurial mayors and university presidents, corporate elites, state government officials, local foundations, and community development corporations worked together to pursue a shared vision for an expansive postindustrial transformation facilitated by state and federal policy. In Hamilton, municipal officials partnered with small business owners and the local Chamber of Commerce on an ad hoc basis to carry out development projects, but their postindustrial imaginations were constrained more often than they were supported by federal and provincial regulations. Hamilton's municipal officials sought to reproduce Pittsburgh's partnership structure and its public subsidies for private developers, but they were largely unsuccessful in achieving either goal because provincial political institutions barred municipal financial incentives for private development. And as Hamilton's public officials pursued redevelopment projects and a new urban image, their visions for a postindustrial future were limited by a provincial growth policy that required the city to remain a manufacturing center and by the continued presence of heavy industry near the downtown core.

But these were not foregone conclusions when Jack Moore arrived in Pittsburgh in 1968. By that point, local and national policymakers in heavily industrialized North Atlantic nations had been concerned with diversifying their economies and hastening the transition to services for nearly twenty years.[16] It was only after the 1973 publication of Harvard sociologist Daniel Bell's *The Coming of Post-Industrial Society*, however, that they had a common grammar with which to describe their activities. In the book, Bell described post-industrial society as one in which the basis of the economy had shifted from the production of goods to the provision of services. He argued that knowledge industries had replaced manual labor as the most important social force in advanced capitalist nations, and that a technical-professional class had supplanted the working class as the largest and most significant occupational group. For Bell, this marked progress toward a more just future characterized by shorter workdays, more leisure time, and a more equitable distribution of resources.[17]

Bell had rehearsed his ideas in a few scholarly articles in the late 1960s, but they gained little attention outside the academy.[18] *The Coming of Post-Industrial Society*, however, hit bookshelves just as the golden age of postwar capitalism wound to an end, and Bell's utopian prognostications resonated with popular audiences. Shortly after the book's publication, Amherst sociologist Norman Birnbaum lamented Bell's outsized influence in the academy and among the more "sophisticated in public affairs and business," complaining, "when Daniel Bell declares society has changed, it does not follow that it has done so. But it does follow that many people will think it has."[19]

Birnbaum was right. Journalists, pundits, and politicians eagerly embraced Bell's book, and "post-industrial society" rapidly became part of the popular and professional lexicon. Bell's influence in urban planning circles was cemented when Robert Cassidy, the editor of the American Planning Association's professional journal, penned a glowing review for the *Chicago Tribune*. Unlike Birnbaum, who worried that Bell's intellectual stature would garner more attention than his work deserved, Cassidy fretted that the book would be ignored because of its turgid prose. Bell was unlikely to make the best-seller list or *The Dick Cavett Show*, Cassidy joked, but *The Coming of Post-Industrial Society* advanced a theoretical framework that let "us know not only where we are, but where we may be headed."[20] Cassidy's concerns that Bell's work would slide into oblivion were unfounded: by the end of the decade, widely circulating popular discourses of postindustrialism reflected Bell's optimism that the relative decline of manufacturing and the increase in services in the United States and other industrialized nations heralded an economic transition that would eventually lead to unprecedented social and economic stability.

When Bell predicted that manufacturing would decline and that professional services and technology industries would become increasingly important to industrialized economies, he was not telling planners and politicians in Detroit, Manchester, and the Ruhr Valley anything they did not already know. In those places, economic trends away from manufacturing and toward increased service sector employment had been clear for a decade or more—Bell, in fact, identified 1956 as a "symbolic turning point," because that was the first year that white-collar workers outnumbered blue-collar workers in U.S. occupational rankings.[21] His forecast for employment trends turned out to be correct. In advanced industrial economies such as the United States, Canada, the UK, Germany, Austria, Italy, France, Belgium, and Spain, manufacturing employment declined between 1970 and 2000, while service-sector employment increased. The United States, the UK, and Belgium shed around half their manufacturing jobs; Germany lost 40 percent; Canada and France more than a third; and Italy 20 percent. In those countries, employment in services and the public sector increased by 10 to 20 percent over the same period.[22]

For Bell, the shift from goods-producing to service-producing industries was a logical outcome of social democratic impulses embedded in postwar state-building projects. After World War II, in an effort to stave off the conditions for another depression, North American and Western European governments had embraced a form of political-economic organization variously described as growth liberalism, embedded liberalism, or Keynesian liberalism, the essential characteristics of which were the use of Keynesian fiscal and monetary policy to dampen business cycles and ensure full employment, a business-labor accord, and the creation or expansion of social welfare programs. Under growth liberalism, business elites accepted varying degrees of regulation and redistribution because Keynesian policies increased consumer demand and facilitated high levels of industrial growth. By the end of the 1960s, however, growth rates fell while inflation and unemployment rates climbed, causing stagflation and a series of fiscal crises in national and local economies. In response, national governments and a shifting constellation of business leaders worked together to dismantle growth liberalism and replace it with a new international political economic order.[23]

Bell's post-industrial society thesis both reflected and shaped political and business leaders' responses to structural change throughout the North Atlantic. As his critics pointed out, however, it did not actually explain the historical processes at work. Bell's detractors and political opponents of growth coalitions' urban redevelopment plans included labor leaders, rank-and-file workers, and some academics on the Left. As they confronted political and economic restructuring, they struggled to develop a language adequate to explain the uneven social, spatial, and economic changes underway. On the ground in economically troubled cities, "deindustrialization" and "post-industrial society" functioned as rhetorical devices through which urban constituencies articulated competing visions for cities after the decline of manufacturing. Planners and politicians embraced the positive connotations of the forward-looking "post-industrial society." Labor activists preferred the term "deindustrialization," which evoked powerful place-based imagery of abandoned factories and boarded-up buildings in a way that "post-indus-trial" did not.[24] Scholars, however, have been exceedingly skeptical of both terms, contending that neither convincingly explains the social relations of the economic transition from basic manufacturing to the dominance of other types of economic activity.[25]

Within the academy, critics on the Left instead described the related pro-cesses of remaking the geography of state power and the social, cultural, and economic geography of cities in the late twentieth century first as "postmod-ern," then as "post-Fordist," and most recently as "neoliberal."[26] No matter which they term they employed, critics of contemporary capitalism argued that a crisis in the 1970s led to disinvestment in the industrial mode of pro-duction and the emergence of flexible production models and service- and finance-based economies.[27] After neoliberalism supplanted postmodernism and post-Fordism as the lingua franca of social criticism, scholars commonly associated policy tactics such as deregulation, privatization, devolution, and the evisceration of the welfare state with the implementation of neoliberal political projects.[28] Under neoliberalism, state retrenchment occurred in some policy areas, such as social welfare provision, while at the same time state involvement expanded in other areas, such as military spending, corpo-rate tax incentives, and the repression of labor unions.

Contemporary scholars of neoliberalism tend to fall into one of two groups: those who are interested in the intellectual history of the term and its progenitors, the economists of the Mont Pèlerin Society; and those who engage neoliberalism as an analytical framework to explain the features of contemporary capitalism. Members of the first group, composed primarily but not solely of historians, have charted the political and economic influence between the 1930s and the 1980s of ideas first advanced by "market advo-cates" such as Friedrich Hayek, Ludwig von Mises, and Milton Friedman. Academics on the Left and social critics in the second group began to use neoliberalism broadly to refer to market fundamentalism and the unmak-ing of North Atlantic welfare states. They adopted neoliberalism as rhetorical shorthand for their outrage over the hollowing out of the middle class and the widespread acceptance of inequality that accompanied economic shifts.[29]

Critics have pointed out that scholars tend to invoke neoliberalism without defining the term and often fail to differentiate between its historical and contemporary meanings. One scholar characterized neoliberalism as "one of the boom concepts of our time," an "all-purpose descriptor" for wide-ranging phenomena.[30] Another quipped that "neoliberalism" is used so imprecisely in many texts "that one is tempted to pencil one's objections in the margins as one might in a student essay."[31] Historians, on the whole, have objected to anachronistic uses of the term, pointing out that, unlike liberals, conservatives, or neoconservatives, the historical actors typically labeled neoliberal—Augusto Pinochet, Margaret Thatcher, and Ronald Reagan among them—would not have used the term to describe themselves.[32] Even as historians caution against too-broad invocations of neoliberalism, however, they agree that, in the 1970s, the liberal order broke down without a clear successor.[33]

The rapidly proliferating scholarship on the subject amply demonstrates that actually existing neoliberalism did not have a single germinal moment. It did not spring forth, fully formed, like a Venus of Mont Pèlerin. There were instead many overlapping paths to neoliberalism—through routes as diverse as international development organizations and financial institutions, U.S. foreign policy initiatives, and welfare state reforms—which began at different times and in different places. In the global South, neoliberalism often followed aid packages from the World Bank and the International Monetary Fund (IMF), which required developing countries to implement wrenching social and economic reforms. If the strings attached to IMF loans pulled Calcutta, Mexico City, and Lagos to neoliberalism, postindustrialism forged the path for Pittsburgh, Essen, and Rennes.[34]

Postindustrialism thus represented one trajectory to neoliberalism among many, and urban sociologists and geographers have argued that cities quickly became testing grounds for neoliberal policy experiments. Scholars cite capital subsidies, place promotion, supply-side intervention, central-city makeovers, and place branding as the urban manifestations of the widespread privatization and devolution that accompanied market orthodoxy.[35] They describe public-private partnerships as an essential marker of neoliberal urbanism and the primary mechanism through which privatization and devolution took place. Public-private partnerships took varied forms, all of which involved marshaling the powers of the local state in service of business interests, usually through a public subsidy for private development designed to serve individual or corporate, rather than collective or public, interests.[36]

The social and political processes at work in postwar Pittsburgh and Hamilton illustrate the range of ideas about political realignment, spatial change, and urban citizenship that social scientists now call neoliberal. They also demonstrate that the institutional arrangements for privatization (particularly through public-private partnerships) and devolutionary urban policy were not developed in response to a break or rupture in the 1970s. Instead, they were in place well before social scientists argue that neoliberalism became ascendant in North Atlantic nations.

The decline of manufacturing and rise of services that Bell predicted would yield a socially just post-industrial society instead turned out to be harbingers of the rising inequality critics associated with neoliberalism. Yet, in troubled manufacturing centers, the late twentieth-century changes to local economies, to the built environment, and to social relations are best understood as an acceleration and intensification of processes that began in the early postwar period. The people involved did not, of course, use the term "neoliberal." Instead, they described their activities in the narrower context of "economic diversification" in the 1950s and 1960s and, after Bell's book was published, adopted his rhetoric of post-industrial society. They began to talk, too, of an emerging "knowledge economy" or "information society," in which the production of knowledge and the manipulation of information would replace basic manufacturing's central role in advanced capitalist economies.[37]

Neoliberalism has supplied scholars with a framework through which to make sense of disparate tactics with broad and diverse constituencies that were implemented for a host of pragmatic reasons over several decades that by the 1980s had become commonsense. Policies originally intended to revive declining cities were used to justify government retrenchment from the urban sphere in the United States, Canada, and other advanced industrial economies, especially the UK. A consensus emerged among policymakers across partisan and political boundaries that public incentives for private-sector economic and urban redevelopment projects were not just one way but, instead, the only way to confront urban problems. Planners, elected officials, and corporate elites in declining manufacturing centers around the world shared common understandings of the problems facing their cities and sought to create similar institutional arrangements to address those problems, most often through public-private partnerships modeled on those developed in the United States.[38] There was nothing essentially neoliberal, or even particularly new, about such policies—most had long histories as urban development tactics. They were merely deployed in new ways, with different intentions, and in changing institutional settings, at a time when liberals and conservatives increasingly came to share the same sense of political possibilities.

Postindustrialism and neoliberalism may seem like arcane subjects, but the public policies and political actions taken in support of or opposition to them have shaped the material possibilities and daily lives of urban dwellers for more than half a century. Local politicians and policymakers confronted with industrial decline and urban crises incrementally rejected options that were not predicated on devolution and privatization—tactics that later became central to scholars' conceptions of neoliberal urbanism—out of pragmatism rather than hubris. As public resources dwindled, city officials made harsh calculations about whose needs they would no longer meet, rather than seeking to better meet the needs of all residents. In the 1970s and 1980s, mayors and planners sought to attract middle-class taxpayers back to hollowed-out central cities, not to hollow out the middle class by diminishing their political and economic power. They faced difficult choices and, seeing no other way forward, made decisions about how to allocate resources in a way that exacerbated inequality and sacrificed the well-being of large portions of urban populations in order to "save" cities. As the stories of Pittsburgh and Hamilton demonstrate, local officials in rusting manufacturing centers may have helped lay the foundation for what scholars call "neoliberal urbanism," but their complicity was the unintentional outcome of limited resources and an inability to see beyond postindustrialism as a planning model.

CHAPTER ONE

—————

The Roots of Postindustrialism

In declining manufacturing centers throughout the North Atlantic, public-private partnerships that allowed political and civic leaders to provide public subsidies for private development were vital to postindustrialism. Such partnerships flourished in U.S. cities like Pittsburgh in the 1950s and 1960s but emerged more slowly in other parts of the world. In Canada, for instance, public development corporations were "difficult to form," according to the U.S. consultants who had advised Hamilton Mayor Vic Copps to look to Pittsburgh for a redevelopment model.[1] Yet when Copps sent Jack Moore to Pittsburgh to study the Allegheny Conference in 1968, neither the mayor nor the economic development commissioner appeared to give much thought to why that was the case. This was perhaps because the consultants had cavalierly assured city officials that there was "nothing to prevent the Hamilton Economic Development Commission or some other body from encouraging interested private citizens to form a development corporation."[2]

While it may have been true that Canadian laws did not prohibit formation of a private development corporation, Arthur D. Little's "Lunchpail Report," as local officials referred to it, ignored the influence of national political frameworks on when and where public-private partnerships formed and how they functioned. The consultants instead stressed the importance of strong mayoral leadership and the participation of "highly influential private citizens" in U.S. cities after World War II. In Pittsburgh, they wrote, the city's famed Renaissance could not have occurred "unless well intentioned men decided to act."[3] They overlooked the fact that securing the long-term cooperation of those "well intentioned men," in Pittsburgh and elsewhere, rested on changing state and federal laws to create an institutional framework for public-private cooperation that allowed business leaders to profit handsomely from their participation in publicly sponsored urban redevelopment plans.[4]

Public-private partnerships had a long history in North America by the time Arthur D. Little submitted the Lunchpail Report. In U.S. cities, ad hoc booster relationships established in the early nineteenth century transformed into informal partnerships around 1850, when businessmen formed civic associations and clubs through which to rationalize the urban landscape and create new opportunities for real estate development.[5] Nineteenth-century U.S. and Canadian public works projects were often public-private ventures. Boosters on both sides of the border assembled subsidies and loans to attract private railroad companies in a way that foreshadowed the interurban competition for jobs common among North Atlantic cities by the 1970s.[6] In Europe, Louis Napoléon's reconstruction of Paris in cooperation with Crédit Mobilier was a nineteenth-century forerunner of the partnerships that implemented urban renewal projects in the 1950s and 1960s. And in the United States the federal government began to underwrite locally led partnerships through New Deal housing and public works programs.[7]

From the ground, public-private cooperation often looked like a purely local affair, negotiated between a city's political and business elites. But the power of public-private partnerships to make postindustrial places was shaped and constrained, materially and discursively, at the metropolitan, national, and global scales. National governments handled demands for resources from ascendant and declining regions in different ways, which limited local government budgets as well as the policy options available to urban growth coalitions. Within metropolitan regions, municipal officials' autonomy over allocation of public resources for urban development varied, as did local executives' interest in directing civic projects. In Pittsburgh and Hamilton, distinctions between the city's position in its metropolitan region, national political institutions, and growth coalitions' abilities to harness internationally circulating ideas about how to remake manufacturing centers meant that postindustrialism unfolded in spatially and temporally uneven ways.

Public-Private Partnerships for Urban Redevelopment

Postindustrialism opened a new chapter in a long history of idea sharing among municipal officials and city planners in the North Atlantic region. The mid-nineteenth-century industrialization of the same cities that sought shared solutions to the decline of manufacturing a hundred years later led boosters, social reformers, and policymakers to develop a network of people, institutions, and frameworks that facilitated the exchange of urban planning and policy ideas between North American, Western European, and colonial cities from Calcutta to Nairobi to Fez. In the late nineteenth century, boosters intensified these informal international transfers through selective borrowing among (or imperial imposition by) the elected officials, national policymakers, and bureaucrats tasked with solving the problems of modern industrial cities. Their fertile intellectual exchange continued into the early twentieth century, when urban experts in specialized institutions, philanthropic foundations, and nongovernmental organizations established formal exchange organizations to disseminate what contemporary planners might call "best practices" for urban social and physical development.[8]

As a result of shared ideas and policy circulation, early twentieth-century plans for U.S. and Canadian cities replicated the grand boulevards of European capitals, while London and Paris adopted skyscrapers, industrial architecture, and technological innovations from the United States. In the interwar period, Americans traveled to Berlin to study zoning, to Birmingham to investigate municipal ownership of utilities, and to Vienna to visit social housing. British and German planners, in turn, kept a close eye on New Deal housing and infrastructure programs. In the 1940s, modernist design aesthetics pioneered in France and Germany influenced planners and architects in the United States and Canada, even as American planning ideas and discourses increasingly permeated European cities.[9]

After World War II, urban renewal programs occupied planners on both sides of the Atlantic. The ad hoc public-private partnerships that had built railroads across the United States and Canada and remade nineteenth-century Paris began to transition to more formal partnerships in the 1940s and 1950s.[10] In the midwestern and northeastern United States, cities emerged from the Depression and war with decayed downtowns, deteriorated residential neighborhoods, and severe housing shortages. New Deal programs had laid the groundwork for federally funded housing programs, and subsidies for suburban development and for industrial decentralization to the suburbs and the Southwest threatened manufacturing centers' tax revenues. To secure the economic futures of the cities in which their enterprises operated, local businessmen and corporate elites joined forces with municipal officials to make over troubled downtowns, protect their capital investments, and restore investor confidence in industrial centers. Federal, state, and local officials used public funds to "leverage" private investment, typically under the auspices of federal urban renewal programs. Federal housing acts passed in 1949 and 1954, together with the 1956 Highway Act and various pieces of state legislation dating to the 1940s, provided the legal foundation for urban renewal. State and federal programs for the first time formally embedded public-private partnerships into government funding structures for urban development conceived during the New Deal.[11]

In the United States, urban renewal was ostensibly intended to address urban housing shortages after World War II and provide decent shelter for all Americans. Coalitions of Democratic politicians, Republican businessmen, real estate developers, and unionists from the construction trades lobbied for renewal legislation and the federal funding that made it possible. Federal urban renewal funds required cities to use their powers of eminent domain to acquire land and transfer it to private developers at low or no cost; once they had done so, federal funds could be used for clearance and development subsidies. Making funds contingent on public-private partnerships was a new requirement, but the redevelopment partnerships that carried out federally sponsored urban renewal programs in the 1950s and 1960s often had much longer histories. In places such as Pittsburgh, Chicago, and St. Louis, mayors and local businessmen collaborated on large-scale slum removal and downtown redevelopment projects before federal urban renewal funds became available. State and local enabling legislation passed to support downtown redevelopment in those cities became models for federal renewal programs.[12] Whether using state or federal programs, however, the private-sector members of redevelopment partnerships typically took the lead, because urban renewal funds could not be released until a private developer signed on to a project.[13]

From the perspective of chambers of commerce boardrooms and mayors' offices, the institutional arrangements of urban renewal were mutually beneficial for the public and private sectors. City officials expected new development to improve their tax bases and make downtowns more appealing to potential investors. Private-sector partners received public subsidies to enhance their property values and expand their activities. Government officials and civic leaders imbued their activities with a sense of public purpose by describing urban renewal as a way to meet public needs for adequate housing and commercial development. In practice, however, the benefits of urban renewal primarily accrued to a small number of local elites and blue-collar workers in the construction trades. The burdens of renewal fell most heavily on low-income, predominantly African American residents, who were displaced from aging central city neighborhoods and only occasionally provided with suitable replacement housing. Instead of affordable, high-quality housing for all, in the United States, redevelopment partnerships most often produced poorly maintained public housing complexes, office buildings, luxury residences, sports stadiums, and convention centers.[14]

Canadian, Latin American, German, and British cities also established expansive urban renewal programs after World War II, but, in those places, redevelopment partnerships were typically state led and managed, and public-private cooperation remained ad hoc.[15] In Canada, as in the United States, urban renewal programs required a private-sector partner, but federal funds were contingent only on securing advance cooperation between municipal, provincial, and federal governments, rather than between public agencies and private developers.[16] Under this scenario, local urban renewal authorities could use federal funds to acquire land through eminent domain and clear it before identifying a site developer, which gave public officials significantly greater freedom to direct where and what kind of investment took place. In the UK, too, public partners had greater control over the nature of redevelopment. Local governments determined redevelopment sites and, in the case of central city commercial regeneration, required developers to include features that public officials had identified as serving a pressing public need, such as a library or a bus station.[17]

Differences in the institutional arrangements of urban renewal between nations reflected a long tradition of privatism in the United States that was comparatively weak elsewhere in the North Atlantic. The central assumption of privatism—that serving private interests and public welfare was one and the same—was well suited to the political economy and social organization of the early American towns out of which the tradition developed.[18] By the twentieth century, however, privatism had come to signify a shared belief between policymakers and business leaders that cities were engines for economic growth through unencumbered individual participation in free markets. Privatist ideology made it difficult for municipalities to allocate resources or regulate growth and development as public officials increasingly came to see the role of government as facilitating the production of private wealth rather than seeking to impose order or control over markets.[19]

Midcentury urban renewal programs reflected varying degrees of privatism between countries, but, by 1968, the transatlantic urban renewal order foundered in all of them. Trenchant critiques of modernist planning and design by American social critic Jane Jacobs and German-born Harvard professor Herbert Gans circulated internationally. Citizens' organizations in the United States, Canada, the UK, and Germany successfully mobilized against urban renewal programs and highway projects that displaced residents and destroyed neighborhoods.[20] At the same time, privatism's more pragmatic corollary, privatization, began to gain wide currency as a tactic of governance. In the United States, all levels of government began to outsource public provision of goods and services to the private sector. Over the next two decades, U.S., Canadian, and British governments began to transfer state-owned businesses, agencies, utilities, services, and sites to for-profit or nonprofit enterprises.[21]

When urban renewal programs collapsed in the late 1960s and early 1970s, the redevelopment partnerships that had carried them out were left in flux. In the United States and Canada, public-private partnerships had relied heavily on federal money to conduct their activities, but both federal governments terminated urban renewal funding in the 1970s. In response to federal retrenchment, some existing partnerships fell apart, others retooled, and new partnerships emerged. Formal partnerships were written into public policy for urban development in the United States, Canada, and England; for economic development in Italy and Holland; and for industrial development in Germany and France. In North Atlantic manufacturing centers, urban development strategies increasingly became predicated on postindustrialism, which had a different kind of public-private partnership at its center. In the 1970s and 1980s, more flexible and more complex growth partnerships supplanted redevelopment partnerships. They took a range of forms, from business-led coalitions to local government-led collaboration to public-private organizations run by a national government. At all levels of government, public officials increased the powers of redevelopment authorities and encouraged entrepreneurial mayors to engage in international interurban competition for jobs.[22]

Redevelopment partnerships of the urban renewal era laid the foundation for postindustrial urbanism, but in the 1970s and beyond growth partnerships facilitated the wholesale remaking of former manufacturing centers for service- and finance-dominated local economies. Growth partnerships were born out of multiple currents: national governments' disinvestment in cities, privatization, deregulation, and the devolution of authority over and the responsibility of paying for urban development to the local level. Public officials no longer rhetorically justified government subsidies for private redevelopment by describing individual projects as meeting pressing public needs for decent housing or reduced central city congestion. Entrepreneurial mayors from across the political spectrum, instead, came to believe that free markets, rather than liberal social programs, would allocate resources in a socially just manner.[23] In the United States, where growth partnerships first formed, their members sought to create good "business climates" in distressed regions by adopting tactics from successful businessmen's campaigns that had lured jobs and residents to the rising Sunbelt since the 1930s.[24] To attract private investment, growth coalitions incorporated new partners, expanded their activities to include economic development and the physical redevelopment of areas beyond downtown, and offered a broad array of financial inducements to attract development. They expanded local, state, and federal financial inducements for private investment, such as personal tax reductions, discretionary business tax incentives, changes in corporate and banking regulations, and technology development programs.[25]

As privatist policy orientations and postindustrial planning tactics—sometimes ideological, sometimes pragmatic—traveled together through the North Atlantic, their implementation was contingent on the historical and geographical particularities of cities and regions and on the political, institutional, and cultural differences between nations. In the United States, public incentives to the private sector moved beyond direct federal subsidies. Entrepreneurial mayors combined programs like Richard Nixon's Community Development Block Grants and Jimmy Carter's Urban Development Action Grants with federal, state, and local tax incentives, bond issues, and loan guarantees.[26] In Britain, changes to the national Town and Country Planning Act in 1968 authorized local public authorities to partner directly with private developers on commercial projects. Under the new regulations, Birmingham subsidized a shopping center and hotel by securing a loan for the developer at public sector loan rates, and subsequently secured government grants to expand the project.[27] The mayor of Rennes formalized a decade-old ad hoc partnership in 1984 when he formed CODESPAR, a consortium of unions, business representatives, and public officials, to develop a regional strategic plan for the French city. CODESPAR reoriented economic development around advanced technology and health services and eventually built a high-tech office park.[28] Similarly, Hamburg's Chamber of Commerce and major banks established the Hamburg Business Development Corporation in 1985, a semi-public corporation that used public and private funds to channel investment into the city.[29]

Canadian municipalities were a bit slower to adopt U.S.-style growth partnerships. Historically, Canadian urban policy emphasized collective over individual good, while a stronger culture of privatism in the United States meant that urban policy was more commonly designed to encourage private consumption and corporate gain. This was due in part to different constitutional understandings of property rights: in the United States, property rights lay with the individual, while in Canada, property rights were vested in the Crown. One result was that Canadian cities were comparatively more public than U.S. cities.[30] The nature of federalism in the United States and Canada also shaped the range of tactics available to municipal officials who sought to adopt postindustrialism as an urban development model. Among the North Atlantic nations with declining basic industry, only the United States, Canada, and Germany had federal systems, a decentralized form of government in which the national government shared power with regional governments (states in the United States and Germany and provinces in Canada). Under the U.S. and Canadian constitutions, states and provinces held the exclusive power to establish local governments—municipal, county, regional, or otherwise—and local governments could only exercise powers delegated to them by state constitutions or provincial legislation.

In the United States, national and state governments shared a broad range of powers that affected the social, spatial, and economic development of cities. These included the powers to tax, borrow money, build highways, charter banks and corporations, take private property, and spend public money for the general welfare. After World War II, U.S. cities were highly dependent on federal funding for urban and economic development. With the exception of highway construction, U.S. states typically delegated powers that allowed municipal officials to direct urban and economic development, often with significant financial support but little oversight from state agencies. In the 1950s and 1960s, big city mayors formed close relationships with federal officials and agencies such as the Federal Housing Authority; after 1964, the Department of Housing and Urban Development (HUD) had substantial influence over urban development.

Canadian municipalities shared fewer direct relationships with the federal government than did U.S. cities in the postwar period. The national and provincial governments only shared authority over immigration, agriculture, and pensions. Provinces held sole authority over direct taxation, anything local or private in nature, business, transportation, banking, health, education, and welfare. Typically, provincial governments devised, funded, and administered urban and economic development programs and delegated fire protection, street maintenance, sewage systems, taxation of land and buildings, and land use regulation to municipalities. Canada's substantially different system of intergovernmental relations meant that its federal government provided far fewer cost-sharing, grants-in-aid, or conditional programs for urban development than did the United States. When Canadian municipalities did receive federal money, it was subject to provincial oversight. As a result, the Canadian federal government had far less influence over urban social and physical development than the U.S. federal government, where relationships between federal agencies and mayors often bypassed state houses altogether. The very different relationships between the U.S. and Canadian federal governments and their cities created very different sets of political possibilities for growth coalitions in Pittsburgh and Hamilton.

The Urban Renewal Era

As policy discourses and tactics crossed national borders and postindustrial solutions to the social and economic problems in declining manufacturing centers became commonsense in North Atlantic nations, national politics and institutions framed the options available to local growth coalitions. So did metropolitan history and geography. The activities of steel mills and steel-related industries substantially shaped Pittsburgh's and Hamilton's social and economic geographies, but neither place had ever truly been a single-industry town. Both had more diverse industrial bases than Great Lakes auto centers like Detroit, Flint, or Oshawa, or smaller steel towns like Youngstown and Weirton.

Pittsburgh had the dubious distinction of being Pennsylvania's only "second-class city." A gateway to the Midwest, Pittsburgh was located more than 250 miles west of Philadelphia, the state's largest metropolis and most important commercial and banking center. Pittsburgh functioned as the administrative center of a sprawling industrial agglomeration, as well as an important regional financial center, home to the headquarters of several Fortune 500 corporations. Historically, it was the urban core of an industrial region, surrounded by mill towns, mining villages, scattered rural development, and the administrative centers of rural hinterlands. Mesta Machine in West Homestead, Dravo Shipyards on Neville Island, Union Switch and Signal in Pittsburgh, and Westinghouse Air Brake Company in Wilmerding all provided inputs to the steel industry as part of their production processes. Westinghouse's electrical and, after World War II, nuclear facilities operated in Pittsburgh's eastern suburbs, and coke production took place in Westmoreland and Fayette Counties.

While Pittsburgh was the commercial and financial center of a heavily industrialized region, Hamilton was a heavily industrialized city in the middle of a predominantly agricultural region. The self-proclaimed "Ambitious City," the heart of Canada's Golden Horseshoe, was located a mere forty miles south of Toronto, the provincial capital and the commercial, financial, and cultural hub of Anglophone Canada. Most of Hamilton's manufacturing industries, including Canada's two largest steel companies, Stelco and Dofasco, were concentrated in four square miles along Hamilton Harbor.

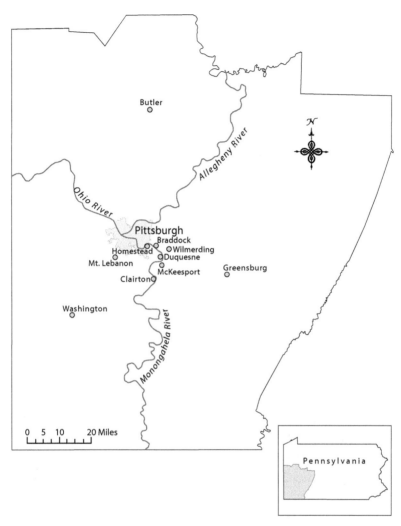

Figure 2. Pittsburgh and Southwestern Pennsylvania.

Other local manufacturing generally reflected national ownership patterns of U.S. branch plants and wholly owned subsidiaries of U.S. corporations. Pittsburgh-based Westinghouse, long the Hamilton region's second-largest employer after Stelco, established its first of several plants in Hamilton in 1896. International Harvester, Otis Elevator, Proctor and Gamble, Hoover, Firestone, and the Beech-Nut Packing Company followed suit in the first half of the twentieth century.[31]

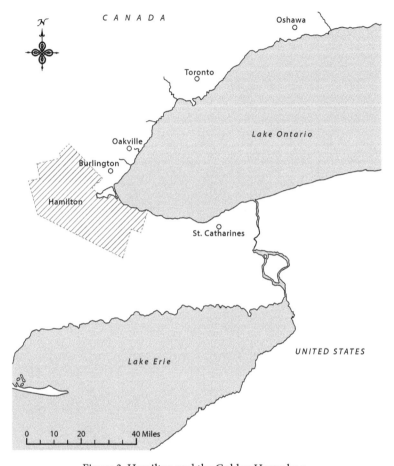

Figure 3. Hamilton and the Golden Horseshoe.

Pittsburgh, Hamilton, and their metropolitan regions were, at the end of World War II, at a moment of transition. Suburbanization was underway but had not yet drained urban tax bases.[32] In 1950, 31 percent of the Pittsburgh region's residents still lived in the city; forty years later, only 16 percent did.[33] Hamilton, with its less densely populated region, did not experience such a dramatic change: nearly three-quarters of the region's residents lived in Hamilton in 1951, down to just over half in 1991.[34] At midcentury, Southwestern Ontario was a racially homogeneous place. Most of Hamilton's residents were Canadian-born of British or French descent. Its small population of recent immigrants, primarily from western and southern Europe, tended to live near and work in the North End industrial area. Canada eased immigration restrictions in the 1960s, and, by 1996, a quarter of Hamilton's residents were foreign-born; still, the majority of residents were white, with only 14 percent classified as "visible minorities." Only 2 percent of those were black.[35] Pittsburgh in 1950 was more heterogeneous. The city's African American population more than doubled between 1900 and midcentury, from around 5 percent to 12 percent. Far fewer African Americans moved to Pittsburgh during the Great Migration than to other northern industrial centers such as Chicago, Detroit, and Cleveland, cities whose black populations increased from under 2 percent in 1900 to between 14 and 16 percent in 1950. By 1990, only a quarter of Pittsburgh's residents were African American, compared to 39 percent in Chicago, nearly half in St. Louis, and three-quarters in Detroit.[36]

Visitors to Pittsburgh and Hamilton at midcentury would have encountered similar physical landscapes: dirty, smoky cities with visibly aging downtown cores and residential areas. Steel production continued apace in Pittsburgh's South Side and Hazelwood neighborhoods and in Hamilton's North End. In 1950, nearly 38 percent of the Pittsburgh region's workers held manufacturing jobs, and almost half of those were in iron and steel.[37] Most of those jobs were located in the mill towns along the along the Monongahela, Ohio, and Allegheny Rivers. Four decades later, only 12 percent of the region's jobs were in manufacturing.[38] In Hamilton, more than half of the labor force worked in manufacturing in 1951, and the majority of those jobs were located within the city limits.[39] By 1991, only 15 percent of Hamiltonians were manufacturing workers.[40]

In 1950, neither city was yet equipped with the world-class universities that would later become central to postindustrial knowledge economies. The Carnegie Institute of Technology and the Mellon Institute had not merged to form Pittsburgh's prestigious Carnegie Mellon University (they did so in 1967), and the University of Pittsburgh had not become a major research university. In a coup against Hamilton's nearby rival, the Chamber of Commerce successfully convinced a Baptist college, McMaster University, to relocate from Toronto to Hamilton's West End in 1927. When McMaster held its first classes in Hamilton in 1930, it offered only two professional programs: theology and nursing. During and after World War II, the university administration came under tremendous pressure from the province to develop a specialization in technical and scientific fields, but it would take until 1957 for McMaster to do so, when it dissolved its religious affiliation and become eligible for federal funding.[41]

Such were the conditions that elected officials and civic leaders faced at midcentury. Despite long-standing economic diversity in both Pittsburgh and Hamilton and hints of the change to come in ensuing decades, both cities were popularly perceived as smoky, decaying steel towns. It was that association mayors and civic leaders set out to shed, first through urban renewal and later through postindustrialism. At the scale of the metropolitan region, establishing public-private partnerships through which to offer a range of subsidies to private developers was the most important indicator of growth coalitions' ability to do so. In Pittsburgh, the exceptional degree of public-private cooperation after World War II had deep roots in regional planning efforts dating back to the 1920s.[42] In this context, in 1944, Pittsburgh's civic leaders formed the Allegheny Conference on Community Development (Allegheny Conference) to revitalize the city after postwar reconversion. Banking scion Richard King (R.K.) Mellon helmed the organization, which formed an archetypal redevelopment partnership with Democratic Mayor David Lawrence and the Allegheny County Commissioner to direct Pittsburgh's urban development for the next fifty years. The press-shy and exceptionally private Mellon served in both World Wars and spent a year and a half at Princeton before dropping out to take a position at the family firm. He was the longtime chairman of the banking dynasty founded by his grandfather in the 1860s and expanded by his father, Richard, and uncle, Andrew, in the early twentieth century.

Pittsburgh was home to several prominent industrialists, but none was so nationally important as Mellon, who, with his sister Sarah Mellon Scaife and his cousins Paul Mellon and Ailsa Mellon Bruce, was heir to one of the largest family fortunes in the United States. In 1957, *Fortune* listed the four Mellons among the eight richest people in the nation, estimating the family's combined wealth at $3 billion—just a few billion shy of J. Paul Getty, the richest man in America. While Mellon's better-known cousin Paul rejected the family business, relocated to Virginia, and, with wife Bunny, became a well-known philanthropist, R.K. lived most of his life forty miles from Pittsburgh on an estate in pastoral Ligonier and took an active role in regional civic affairs.[43]

Under Mellon's leadership, the Allegheny Conference's institutional structure concentrated power in the hands of corporate elites, who ensured that it had the financial resources and political influence to carry out their development plans. The organization had more than a hundred members, but a smaller Executive Committee set an agenda carried out by an executive director and permanent staff. The Allegheny Conference's bylaws required Executive Committee members, typically the directors of Pittsburgh's largest corporations, to be physically present for meetings and prohibited them from delegating their responsibilities to subordinates. Allegheny Conference members had strong ties to the state legislature and city government, and the organization worked closely with groups such as the Pennsylvania Economy League and the Pittsburgh Regional Planning Association (PRPA). The Allegheny Conference was also instrumental in establishing and then directing the activities of Pittsburgh's Urban Redevelopment Authority, a quasi-public corporation authorized by the state of Pennsylvania in 1946 to carry out urban renewal activities; the Regional Industrial Development Corporation (RIDC), formed in 1955 to attract industrial investment to the Pittsburgh region; and Penn's Southwest, created in 1972 to market Southwestern Pennsylvania.[44]

Mellon and Lawrence's efforts to remake Pittsburgh reflected the shared concerns of political and corporate elites that Pittsburgh's reputation as a smoke-filled industrial city would slow its postwar growth and deter new investment in the city and region, worries common to mayors and businessmen in aging manufacturing centers around the world.[45] Most visibly and most importantly, projects undertaken by the city's redevelopment partnership improved Pittsburgh's environmental conditions through smoke, pollution, and flood controls.[46] Lawrence touted Pittsburgh's partnership as a possible model for other cities at national conferences. "This is a new kind of blending of public and private enterprise," he told the National Association of Housing Officials in 1951. "It has novelty. It has untried phases. It has pioneering. . . . It is the most promising and rewarding program in our public life today."[47]

The primary goal of the Renaissance was to revitalize Pittsburgh's central business district, known as "the Golden Triangle," and "blighted" areas nearby. Private sector partners added office space to the downtown business district through skyscraper construction, while city officials undertook massive slum clearance projects and used public funds to subsidize Jones & Laughlin Steel's expansion within the city limits. An industrial district at the Point, the confluence of the Monongahela, Allegheny, and Ohio Rivers, was reborn as Point State Park. The extent to which Pittsburgh's massive urban renewal program benefited city residents was highly dependent on their race and class. The largely African American Hill District was partially destroyed to make way for a new convention center. On the city's North Side, a working-class white ethnic neighborhood was torn apart for commercial development and a new sports stadium.[48]

The Renaissance produced uneven development between Pittsburgh and steel- and coal-producing towns in its metropolitan region, as well between neighborhoods within city limits. Lawrence once described urban renewal as "another kind of soil conservation," in which "the soil is the fantastically valuable kind that is measured in square feet instead of square miles—the heartland of our cities—the areas where we concentrate the population, the wealth, the productive capacity, and the leadership of our Nation."[49] His analogy may have resonated with Pittsburgh's industrialists and financiers, but it surely confounded workers in the strip mines in Pittsburgh's hinterlands. By the early 1960s, Pennsylvania's coal miners were permanently out of work and riverside factories stood empty.[50] Even as the PRPA praised the growth coalition for facilitating "a significant rearrangement of functions" within the city itself, in 1963 its planners issued a dire economic forecast for the region. In coming decades, the PRPA warned, increased corporate investment, job training programs, and additional government intervention and planning would be necessary to manage a coming economic transition from manufacturing to service and finance industries. That transition, they (correctly) predicted, would be more difficult in the Pittsburgh region than in other areas of the country because the regional economy and labor force were shaped "to an exceptional extent" by coal and steel specialization. "Nineteenth century industrial development patterns," the PRPA cautioned, had to be jettisoned to make Pittsburgh more appealing to a postwar populace with greater spending power and more leisure time.[51]

The PRPA study anticipated the economic transition that Daniel Bell described a decade later in *The Coming of Post-Industrial Society*. Pittsburgh's regional planners forecast that, faced with international competition, manufacturing in general and primary metals in particular would continue to decline in importance in the regional economy. In response, they contended, Pittsburgh's public officials and business leaders needed to diversify the regional economy by attracting jobs in light industry, advanced manufacturing, and commercial services. Certainly, planners were not so prescient in the 1960s that they sought to redevelop the Strip District's warehouses as live-work space, nor did they imagine that the South Side, then primarily home to steelworkers, would some day house the financial district's young, white-collar workforce. Instead, planners predicted in general terms the types of economic activity that would come to dominate the urban and regional economy in the last quarter of the twentieth century. They offered suggestions in broad strokes for moving away from development patterns associated with industrial cities toward a spatial organization of social and economic functions that would attract service, finance, and light industry, exhibiting early

evidence of the postindustrial imagination shared among planners throughout the North Atlantic within the next few decades.[52]

The mayor's office and the Allegheny Conference's board showed limited
interest in regional development in the 1960s, delegating development beyond
city limits to county governments and the RIDC. The RIDC acquired its first
parcel for redevelopment in rural O'Hara Township the year the PRPA study
came out and in 1966 began renting space in one of the nation's first planned
industrial parks to area companies for light manufacturing. Two years later,
the organization began construction on a second industrial park at the edge
of Allegheny County, eventually securing a U.S. post office sorting facility
as a tenant and attracting the Society of Automotive Engineers away from
their New York City headquarters. By 1971, the RIDC was so pleased with
its economic diversification efforts that it issued a self-congratulatory report,
"Transition of a Region: Southwestern Pennsylvania's Changing Economy."
Its glossy cover juxtaposed images of steelworkers and the Golden Triangle.
In case the symbolism was lost on readers, the RIDC staffers pointedly noted
that the cover celebrated "the transition in the economic structure of the
Pittsburgh and Southwestern Pennsylvania region. The region appears to be
moving from a mature heavy industry economy toward one with a balance of
material goods-producing industries and service industries." A presidential
note at the outset cited National Planning Association data that indicated
that service-producing industries had increased their share of regional jobs.
The RIDC predicted that the Pittsburgh region would achieve a "balanced"
economy by 1980.[53]

In the early 1970s, heavy industry still formed the material basis of the
declining regional economy, but urban renewal had laid the spatial and institutional foundations for a postindustrial rebirth in the city. Mayor Joseph
Barr had symbolically marked the end of the Renaissance with the 1969 dedi-
cation of a new headquarters for Westinghouse, the last building completed
in the Golden Triangle. "It's hard to believe that less than twenty years ago
this area where we now are standing was blighted industrial and commercial
slum," Barr said at the event, praising the $200 million downtown facelift that
had, the *Washington Post* enthusiastically reported, "transformed one of the
nation's worst eyesores into a cluster of dazzling skyscrapers."[54] Coal miners in the hinterlands may have been out of work, but downtown, modernist
glass-and-steel skyscrapers had replaced the "nineteenth-century" architecture that the growth coalition believed forestalled new investment.

Hamilton was a different story. It did not share Pittsburgh's long history of corporate welfare, and, because of its greater reliance on publicly

Figure 4. Downtown Pittsburgh before the Renaissance with industry still visible
at the Point, ca. 1950. Reprinted with the permission of the Allegheny
Conference on Community Development and its Affiliates.

funded, planned, and managed projects, postwar urban redevelopment
moved more slowly there than it did in Pittsburgh.[55] The city had established a master plan in 1944, drafted by Toronto planning consultant E. G.
Faludi. When city officials hired Faludi, Hamilton did not have a planning
department. The city council appointed an ad hoc town planning committee composed of local politicians, civic leaders, and representatives from
labor, industry, and women's organization to assist Faludi. Faludi's findings
were worrisome for political and civic leaders: he and the town planning
committee determined that more than three-quarters of Hamilton's residences were blighted or in decline, and the report recommended that the
city use the slum clearance provision of Canada's 1944 National Housing
Act to replace some of them with affordable housing. The master plan outlined an ambitious slum clearance program that led city officials to formally

Figure 5. Downtown Pittsburgh after the Renaissance, showing corporate headquarters buildings and Point State Park, ca. 1969. Reprinted with the permission of the Allegheny Conference on Community Development and its Affiliates.

establish a planning department in 1947, but it would be more than a decade before public opinion and political will made a large-scale redevelopment program feasible.[56]

In Pittsburgh and other U.S. cities, redevelopment partnerships went hand-in-hand with central business district redevelopment. Hamilton's city officials, too, were eager to implement a downtown urban renewal program in the early 1960s. In 1962, Vic Copps made downtown revitalization a central feature of his mayoral campaign. Copps won in a major upset, unseating thirteen-year incumbent Lloyd D. Jackson. Within months of taking office, Copps made overtures to local businessmen and corporate leaders to ensure their cooperation with his redevelopment plans. But his efforts were stymied: in 1962, Canada's federal government only subsidized low- and moderate-income housing, not commercial development.[57]

The ambitious Copps held office for nearly twenty-five years and was the patriarch of what would become Hamilton's Liberal political dynasty—his wife Geraldine was a city councilor in the 1980s and 1990s; his daughter Sheila served in provincial and national parliament and as deputy prime minister under Jean Chrétien. A journalist by trade, Copps had moved to Hamilton shortly after World War II to pursue a career as a sportscaster. Riding on his popularity as a radio personality, he entered politics in 1960, winning more votes than any other candidate in a Board of Control election. As a councilor, Copps earned the loyalty of Hamilton's pensioners through bus fare reductions and secured support from workers by introducing job retraining programs for the unemployed. By the time Copps ran against Jackson, Jackson and local labor leaders were in open conflict. The Hamilton and District Labor Council declined to endorse either candidate, but union officials and rank-and-file workers backed Copps and led him to victory.[58]

Copps may have styled himself as a labor mayor, but he was eager to work with Hamilton's businessmen and industrialists to realize his urban redevelopment goals. During his campaign, he presented his lack of experience as an asset, telling voters that it meant he was not "bogged down with a lot of political affiliations." It also meant that he was not bound by patronage. "I was something like a frontbencher in Parliament," he recalled of his time in council shortly after becoming mayor. "I could criticize freely and it wasn't so important to seek harmony with those around me." As mayor, he said, "I am trying to foster a real spirit of co-operation so that we can get a few things done around here." That cooperative spirit extended to courting businessmen who had campaigned against him. Four months into his first term, Copps proudly reported, "A great many people who didn't support me and weren't too keen on seeing me as mayor have come forward with offers of help and have helped already."[59]

By the time the Canadian government amended its urban renewal legislation to include commercial development in 1964, Copps had established a congenial relationship with Hamilton's businessmen. He did not, however, have a private-sector partner with the stature of Pittsburgh's R.K. Mellon or an Allegheny Conference-style civic organization with which to work. Hamilton's businessmen instead organized through the more traditional arena of the Hamilton and District Chamber of Commerce. Copps personally ensured the cooperation of individual executives and business owners on a project-by-project basis, but Hamilton's corporate and business leaders were not particularly concerned with urban planning or economic development in the 1960s. Jack Moore intimated as much when he wrote to John Grove to arrange his 1968 Pittsburgh trip. He told Grove he was especially interested in learning how the Allegheny Conference secured the active participation of local executives. In Hamilton, Moore groused, "We can get ours to agree to serve but their attendance at meetings is not always of the best."[60]

Even if Hamilton's business leaders had shown greater interest in attending meetings about civic projects, Copps's ability to enter into a partnership with the private sector was limited by the province. In contrast with the Commonwealth of Pennsylvania, which had little direct influence over urban development, Ontario was the final arbiter of land use and economic development in the province. Ontario's 1946 Planning Act required all municipalities to develop a comprehensive plan, which had to be approved by the Ontario Municipal Board (OMB). Any subsequent amendments were also subject to prior approval by the OMB. This meant that private developers could appeal local land use decisions to the OMB, which sometimes overturned municipal regulations. Ontario also precluded local governments from offering wide-ranging economic incentives for industrial or commercial expansion, preferring instead to coordinate those activities at the provincial level. For these reasons, when Copps secured approval for a downtown urban renewal program in 1965, the formal "partnership" that supported it included only the provincial and federal governments, not the private sector.

Compounding Copps's difficulties, a year after he unveiled an ambitious new plan to remake downtown Hamilton as a commercial and service center, the province launched a regional planning initiative that mandated Hamilton's continued development as a regional manufacturing hub that would support, rather than compete with, Toronto's role as Ontario's service and finance center. The regional development initiative stemmed from Progressive Conservative Premier John Robarts's concerns about Ontario's competitive position.[61] After taking office in 1961, Robarts established two agencies to advise him on economic issues, the Department of Economics and Development (a provincial ministry) and the Ontario Economic Council (OEC, an independent advisory committee). Staffed by economists and businessmen, the OEC advocated for provincial reforms that would benefit business interests. The OEC commissioned research reports from economic experts in the universities and private sector, who typically recommended that Ontario should reduce the social safety net, institute business-friendly tax reforms, and pursue various forms of deregulation and decentralization.[62]

In 1965, on the advice of his economic policy advisors from the OEC and the Department of Economics and Development, Robarts held two international conferences. He invited experts from the United States, Canada, and the UK to address regional development in Ontario as well as Canada's changing economic structure. A popular consensus in favor of government-led regional planning and development emerged from the conferences. A year later, Ontario Department of Municipal Affairs Minister Darcy McKeough announced a comprehensive regional planning initiative, Design for Development, which launched what scholars later described as Ontario's "golden age of planning."[63] Robarts, despite his conservative economic views, thought centralized planning was the best way to ensure regional economic stability. He and McKeough explicitly linked provincially led regional planning to private sector initiatives. To achieve Design for Development's goals, McKeough called for "a partnership relationship between the Provincial Government, municipalities, and private enterprise in bringing about the quality and pattern of development that we all want and that we are confident can be achieved." He praised private developers, noting that, while most of the planning beyond the scale of individual projects would be carried out by the provincial and municipal governments, "by the quality of its performance this development industry has earned the right to be accepted into the partnership that will develop this region along the lines we are drawing here today."[64] In contrast to local redevelopment partnerships in the United States, Ontario officials sought private-sector partners who would help the province carry out development projects initiated by public officials.

Design for Development created a series of economic development regions, through which provincial officials planned to decentralize industry out of Southern Ontario to the "underdeveloped" northern and eastern reaches of the province. The industrial belt around Lake Ontario with Hamilton at its center was the only exception.[65] Hamilton would remain a manufacturing hub. Hamilton's supporting role in what provincial officials deemed the "Toronto-centered region" vexed municipal officials who wanted to develop their city as a regional commercial center. In response, Hamilton's Economic Development Commission prepared a study that forecast the increasing importance of service sector jobs, while tacitly accepting that Hamilton would likely house a greater share of regional manufacturing due to industrial decentralization out of Toronto. Like Pittsburgh's PRPA earlier in the decade, Hamilton planners proposed a regional development pattern that would "accommodate increasing preoccupation with leisure-time activities" and promote "a pattern of urbanization that is amenable to social changes based on future economic and technological developments." They predicted intensified professional, cultural, and educational activities and recommended land uses that would encourage rather than hinder that intensification. This translated, for the planners, into zoning changes and public investment geared toward establishing new nodes of development around specialized industry, outside both the city center and the traditional industrial areas along the harbor. In apparent defiance of Design for Development, Hamilton's planners argued that the city's place in Ontario's urban system should remain flexible.[66]

Though they shared the postindustrial imagination of Pittsburgh's growth coalition, Hamilton's public officials and civic leaders were constrained by national regional development programs that privileged underdeveloped provinces, a lack of federal funds for commercial revitalization, provincial growth policies that protected Toronto's regional supremacy, and a local business class with little interest in urban development. The expensive study Copps commissioned from Arthur D. Little and Moore's subsequent trip to Pittsburgh to figure out how to create a redevelopment partnership did not change those facts. As the 1960s drew to a close, Hamilton had not replicated the redevelopment partnership that facilitated Pittsburgh's Renaissance, and its proposed downtown renewal program was stalled.

Decentralization and Regional Development

Pittsburgh and Hamilton's growth coalitions found themselves at a crossroads at the end of the 1960s, caught between optimistic downtown revitalization schemes and dire regional economic forecasts. In Ontario, provincial officials had taken steps to formalize public-private cooperation, which should have been a boon to Copps's and Moore's efforts to form a partnership. The designation of a "Toronto-centered region," however, made Copps's vision of Hamilton as a serious competitor to Toronto untenable. In Pittsburgh, the Allegheny Conference shifted course as the first Renaissance wound to an end, leaving the city's future development up in the air. The U.S. and Canadian federal systems, too, were approaching a crossroads. In the United States, federal housing policies dating back to the New Deal had promoted uncontrolled suburban expansion and deindustrialization and created racially segregated metropolitan areas through redlining and other discriminatory real estate practices. Urban renewal programs carried out under the auspices of redevelopment partnerships destroyed African American and working-class white neighborhoods, displaced long-time residents, and lined the pockets of real estate developers. These practices provoked urban uprisings that tore apart central cities, devastated urban tax bases, accelerated middle-class relocation to the suburbs, and led pundits to describe northeastern and mid-western cities as in the throes of an urban crisis.[67] By contrast, Canadian central city housing markets were not redlined, and residents could more easily get mortgages and home improvement loans than could residents of U.S. central cities. In the 1960s, Canadian cities did not burn. Instead, when Canadian policymakers talked about a looming urban crisis, they referred to an aging urban infrastructure insufficient to meet the demands of a projected population boom in the next decade.[68]

To address its urban crisis, the U.S. government focused more attention and greater resources on central cities through Lyndon Johnson's Great Society programs; the Canadian government instead turned to regional development. Canada's federal transfers to other levels of government generally took the form of unconditional equalization payments that, beginning in 1957, redistributed revenue from wealthier to poorer provinces to ensure that all provinces could provide similar services to their citizens at reasonably comparable levels of taxation, regardless of each province's ability to generate revenue—a program for which there was no analogue in the United States.[69] Federal agencies like the Tennessee Valley Authority (1933) and the Appalachian Regional Commission (1965) funneled federal funds for infrastructure projects to distressed regions, while the more ambitious but short-lived Area Redevelopment Administration (1961–1965) encouraged economic development primarily in Appalachia and the South.[70] None of these federal agencies, however, redistributed wealth at a national scale.

At the national scale, distinctions in U.S. and Canadian urban and regional development policy shaped the political possibilities for public-private partnership and postindustrial redevelopment in Pittsburgh and Hamilton. Canada's stronger commitment to regional development and social welfare spending became increasingly evident as national policy orientations toward privatization and decentralization intensified steadily, if unevenly, in the United States and Canada after the political watershed of 1968. On both sides of the Great Lakes, newly elected leaders faced urban crises in cities in the East and the industrial heartland. At the same time, political and economic elites in North American boom regions—the U.S. Sunbelt and the Canadian West—exerted pressure on their national governments to stem what boosters in places like Phoenix and Calgary saw as undue federal aid for troubled manufacturing centers. U.S. president Richard Nixon and Canadian Prime Minister Pierre Trudeau set out to quell the simmering tensions between declining and ascendant regions by renegotiating the relationship between components of the federal system. As centers of the old economy and beneficiaries of liberal social programs, Pittsburgh and Hamilton stood to lose their relatively privileged positions in their respective national urban funding hierarchies.

Nixon and Trudeau were often politically and personally at odds—Nixon intemperately called Trudeau a "son of a bitch," a "pompous egghead," and an "asshole"—but, by the early 1970s, both had implemented bureaucratic reforms intended to temper regional conflict.[71] Trudeau tried and failed to centralize power in the national government, while Nixon sought from the outset to decentralize power to state governments. Their original intentions notwithstanding, both leaders ultimately reconfigured intergovernmental relations in a way that pointed to increased decentralization and public-private partnerships for urban development in the 1970s. Pittsburgh's growth coalition was well positioned to flourish under these conditions, while Hamilton's political and civic leaders struggled to form a durable partnership that would allow them to respond to a rapidly changing policy environment.

"Trudeaumania" swept the nation after the handsome young Quebecois Liberal formed a government in 1968. Shortly after taking office, Trudeau said he dreamed of a society that provided "individual freedoms, and equality of opportunity, health, and education."[72] He believed it was the government's responsibility to ensure equal opportunity and fair treatment for all Canadians, and he staunchly defended liberal social programs such as national health insurance, equalization payments, and centralized planning. Trudeau had reason to think his goals would find wide support. In contrast to the United States, where small-government conservatives gained control of the national Republican Party in the 1960s, Canada's Progressive Conservative party was not particularly concerned with reducing the size of the government or attacking unions. Compared to Democrats and Republicans, the Liberals and Progressive Conservatives, Canada's two largest political parties, differed more on cultural issues than on the role of government in society. The viability of the New Democratic Party, Canada's labor party, in regional and national elections meant that neither the Liberals nor the Progressive Conservatives could afford to alienate business, labor, or welfare state supporters if they hoped to win elections.

Trudeau's critics, however, attacked his liberal economic programs. They complained about federal overreach in relation to provincial governments when Trudeau sought to fund redistributive social programs with oil money from the western provinces—including those programs designed to address the so-called urban crisis.[73] In an effort to rationalize urban growth patterns, Trudeau established the Department of Regional Economic Expansion

(DREE) in 1969 and the Ministry of State for Urban Affairs (MSUA) in 1971. Through his new agencies, Trudeau embarked on a decade-long effort to centralize urban and economic policy and direct growth from Ottawa. DREE and MSUA were met with substantial resistance from provincial officials, particularly in economically strong Ontario and the western provinces, who thought Trudeau had overstepped his constitutional purview. Undeterred, Trudeau appointed his old friend Jean Marchand, former trade unionist and fellow Liberal Quebecois, head of DREE. Marchand, along with Trudeau and Gérard Pelletier, had been one of Quebec's "three wise men" hand-selected by the Liberal party to run for national office in the hope that their elections would curtail mounting discontent stirred by the separatist Parti Québécois. Like Trudeau, Marchand believed regional economic disparity stemmed from the uneven development of urban areas across Canada.[74]

Toronto and Hamilton provided employment opportunities for migrants from Northern Ontario, but the Atlantic provinces lacked dynamic metropolitan areas, and residents often had to leave the region to find work. Instead of targeting small towns and rural areas, as had been the goal of earlier economic development initiatives, DREE sought to stimulate manufacturing enterprises in "growth centers." The agency designated "Special Areas" in cities and regional centers in disadvantaged provinces, particularly in eastern Canada, to which it funneled federal funds to support development activities. DREE's industrial incentive programs nominally funded distressed areas in all ten provinces, but Marchand's focus on the Atlantic provinces stirred resentment in other regions, particularly heavily industrialized Southern Ontario.[75] When DREE provided the Montreal region with a substantial two-year subsidy under the Special Areas program beginning in 1970, officials in Ontario and the West were incensed: if Montreal was eligible for federal aid, why not Vancouver, Calgary, or Hamilton? Trudeau and Marchand thought that Montreal could counter sluggish growth with limited federal assistance and, in the process, address some of the economic concerns of separatists, who believed that Quebec's economy had been hindered by decades of federal policy. To observers outside Ottawa, however, DREE appeared to be using its funds to ensure that only selected regions would grow.[76]

The Liberals lost seats in the West in the 1972 federal elections, where provincial leaders accused Trudeau of focusing too heavily on eastern Canada at the expense of other regions. As part of his effort to placate voters, Trudeau replaced Marchand with Donald Jamieson, a Newfoundlander who had worked in that province's Department of Rural Reconstruction in the 1940s and served as Trudeau's minister of defense production and minister of transport before taking over DREE in 1972. Jamieson quickly tried to pacify irate provincial and municipal leaders in Ontario and the western provinces. In 1973, he eliminated the Special Areas program and introduced General Development Agreements (GDAs) and, in an unprecedented move, decentralized DREE's administration to provincial and regional offices.[77] A "flexible" new joint federal-provincial administrative mechanism driven by provincial initiative rather than centralized planning, GDAs became a politically popular model for federal-provincial cooperation in economic development. GDAs also created a national institutional framework for the type of local public-private partnerships that Hamilton's civic leaders and elected officials wanted to establish. DREE was legally precluded from working directly with the private sector or municipalities, but the terms of individual GDAs often created public corporations for which municipal governments served as agents. The arrangement gave municipal officials the authority either to undertake projects on their own, using federal and provincial funding, or to hire private developers to carry out publicly funded projects. In this way, municipalities had significant authority over the management of development projects, making GDAs popular with local as well as provincial governments.[78]

Bureaucratic decentralization and the implementation of GDAs represented a sharp break from Trudeau's plan to use centralized planning to redistribute wealth between provinces or regions within provinces. DREE's new structure initially benefited wealthy Ontario and heavily industrialized areas like Hamilton. Under Jamieson, Canada's economic development activities shifted toward provincially led development projects that leveraged federal incentives to entice private investment.[79] Jamieson announced in 1974 that "the process of regional development should not limit itself to rather narrow programs focused on solving problems." Instead, he said, it should "include the process of identifying and pursuing in a flexible and imaginative manner the many existing development opportunities."[80] The federal government began to use its regional development policy to stimulate private investment in distressed areas through federally financed demonstration projects, infrastructure improvements, and in some cases the relocation of federal offices, rather than to redistribute wealth from more prosperous to less prosperous regions. For municipal officials in cities like Hamilton who hoped to attract private-sector partners, DREE's decentralization created tantalizing possibilities.

MSUA, too, quickly landed on public-private partnerships as a tool to achieve national urban development goals. Trudeau created MSUA to

determine policy options for dealing with population forecasts that predicted an influx of new immigrants in the 1970s and 1980s. Federal and provincial policymakers agreed that people and economic activity should be
decentralized out of the primary population centers of Toronto, Montreal,
and Vancouver to less-developed areas in those metropolitan regions and
to smaller cities throughout the country, such as Hamilton. In contrast to
DREE's redistributive impulses in its early years, from the outset, MSUA
officials rejected efforts to reduce population disparity or regional under-
development as an "explicit intrusion into the market" that might threaten
business interests. Perhaps with the conflicts over DREE's Special Areas program in mind, MSUA officials worried that the newly prosperous western
provinces or economically weak regions in the East might begin to believe
that they were at "some sort of serious disadvantage" relative to the industrial heartland and consider leaving the confederation. They were also concerned that population redistribution along the Windsor-Quebec corridor
might agitate domestic and American-owned corporations that relied on
proximity to the U.S. market.[81]

As the political climate shifted after the 1972 elections and the Trudeau
administration sought to mollify western voters, MSUA officials, like those
at DREE, began to look to provincial and private sector partners rather than
centralized planning to achieve national urban development goals. By the
middle of the decade, MSUA officials viewed public-private partnerships
as a mechanism through which to secure private sector buy-in to Trudeau's
national planning agenda and to help finance urban development projects.
DREE was prohibited from entering into direct agreements with municipalities or the private sector, but MSUA's officials had greater freedom to facilitate
joint ventures between the public and private sectors.[82] They did so with a
wary eye on similar partnerships in the United States and mandated that in
Canada public-private partnerships must "satisfy the principles of responsible government," which meant that no public agency involved in a partnership could relinquish its statutory duties to the private sector.[83] While
MSUA officials acknowledged the need to provide an "attractive climate"
for private developers, they also insisted that "no private agency should be
able to profit from the public purse unduly" and that the government should
"get a fair social return" for its investments.[84] Public-private partnerships
were a fledgling enterprise in Canada in the 1970s, but thanks to DREE and
MSUA, public officials at all levels of government were cautiously optimistic
that partnerships might be part of the solution to the country's urban and
regional development problems. Hamilton's elected officials had reason to

believe that the Allegheny Conference-style partnership they desired might be on the horizon.

In the United States, as in Canada, tensions over urban and economic development simmered in the late 1960s within the federal system and between ascendant and declining regions. Four months after Trudeau was sworn in as prime minister, Nixon accepted the Republican presidential nomination. Nixon, like Trudeau, took office intending to restructure the relationship between national and subnational governments. Unlike Trudeau, Nixon did not see centralized planning as a vehicle through which to solve social problems. Instead, he argued that federal intervention exacerbated social problems. His predecessor's Great Society programs had not ended poverty or the urban crisis, but they had dramatically expanded the federal bureaucracy and increased the complexity of federal aid to city and state governments. Democrats criticized Johnson for underfunding social programs, while Republicans denounced them as too expensive, civil rights leaders demanded a Marshall Plan for cities, community groups complained about increased red tape, and urban violence rose rather than fell. These circumstances allowed Nixon to take office with substantial bipartisan support for his plan to return control over urban affairs to lower levels of government, a proposal that found a receptive audience in the nation's state houses.[85]

During his first year in office, Nixon reminded Americans that the nation faced "an urban crisis, a social crisis—and, at the same time, a crisis of confidence in the capacity of government to do its job." These crises, he said, were the legacy of three decades of failed social experiments emerging from New Deal. The government institutions established under Franklin Delano Roosevelt and expanded under successive Democratic presidents, Nixon explained, had become a "bureaucratic monstrosity," whose "entrenched" social programs were no longer relevant. His solution was simple: Nixon would restore to the states the autonomy Roosevelt had taken from them. It was time, he declared, for "a New Federalism," a devolutionary program intended to decentralize authority away from the federal government and return power and money to the "states and the people."[86]

Nixon intended to decentralize federal power through revenue-sharing programs. He introduced a new program, general revenue sharing, designed to transfer a portion of federal revenue back to state and local governments. The week after announcing his New Federalism agenda, Nixon sent a message to Congress outlining a plan for general revenue sharing "to be used as the States and their local governments see fit—without Federal strings." In his Congressional message, Nixon pointed particularly to the problems

facing cities. Under Johnson, he argued, the federal government had promised too much and provided too little, which had created an urban crisis and
led Americans to lose faith in the federal government. "Ultimately, it is our
hope to use this mechanism to so strengthen State and local government
that by the end of the coming decade, the political landscape of America
will be visibly altered," Nixon advised Congress, "and States and cities will
have a far greater share of power and responsibility for solving their own
problems."[87]

Nixon portentously described revenue sharing as a "turning point in
Federal-State relations, the beginning of decentralization of governmental
power, the restoration of a rightful balance between the State capitals and
the national capital."[88] He used the programs to direct federal aid away from
socially and economically distressed central cities like New York, Detroit, and
Pittsburgh and toward constituents in prosperous suburbs and the Sunbelt.[89]
His rhetoric of ending "unfairness," restoring the constitutionally mandated
relationship between levels of government, and fixing "broken" service delivery mechanisms obscured the basic assumption underlying his urban policy
prescriptions: that out-of-control residents (and particularly the individual
moral failings of African Americans in inner cities), rather than long-term
structural problems such as racial discrimination and economic inequality,
were the cause of urban social problems.

General revenue sharing proved popular among state and local officials.
"General revenue sharing is the cornerstone of our national strategy and,
as such, must be recognized and built upon," National League of Cities vice
president Allen Pritchard informed his board of directors. "We cannot allow
those who don't understand cities and our problems—as evidenced in their
denunciation of general revenue sharing—to tear apart the coalition of city
governments which triumphed over all odds in this field."[90] Most governors,
too, supported the new funding arrangements, which to them marked the
success of two decades of lobbying for an increased state role in administering and distributing federal funds.[91] Pennsylvania governor Milton J. Shapp,
however, was among the program's most outspoken critics. He broke with the
National Governors' Conference over revenue sharing and attacked Nixon
and his supporters in state houses across the country for implementing a
program that failed to solve the fiscal problems facing heavily industrialized
states like his and manufacturing centers like Pittsburgh in both the short
or long term.[92] But serious critics of revenue sharing were in the minority,
and the program remained popular among governors and mayors because it
allowed them the nearly unrestricted use of federal funds.

Emboldened by the political success of general revenue sharing, Nixon set out to replace the categorical grant system used to administer social programs—the number of which had nearly doubled between 1962 and 1967—with special revenue-sharing "block grants" for particular types of activities, such as community development or public health, without reference to a specific project. Compared to categorical grants, block grants had very few conditions attached, required little federal oversight, and promised to dramatically reduce the number of applications city and state governments needed to file to receive federal aid in any given year. Administrators at all levels of government agreed that the federal grants-in-aid system had become unmanageable.[93] Nixon co-opted bipartisan support for streamlining administrative requirements for his more ideological project of realigning intergovernmental relations and weakening federal agencies that administered liberal social programs.

Gerald Ford signed Community Development Block Grant (CDBG) legislation into law the week after Nixon's resignation. CDBG funds went disproportionately to central cities, and federal officials formulated CDBG as a "hold harmless" program, which ensured that urban areas had access to at least the same level of funding they had received through categorical grants. As a result, the program received fervent support from big city mayors like Pittsburgh's Pete Flaherty.[94] With general revenue sharing and block grants, Nixon chose to sacrifice the fiscal for the ideological: he was far less concerned with transferring the burden of paying for urban development away from the federal government than he was with removing control of federal funds from the hands of Washington bureaucrats. Yet Nixon's success with CDBG was evidence only of a widely perceived need for a streamlined grant application process, not of the emergence of a broad ideological consensus over the appropriate relationship between municipalities and the federal government.

In tandem with his revenue sharing proposals, Nixon decentralized oversight of federal urban development programs away from Washington. Federal housing, highway, and urban renewal programs required a large, centralized bureaucracy to review applications and administer and monitor grants; dismantling that capacity was the final aspect of Nixon's New Federalism. In 1970, Nixon issued an executive order that created Federal Regional Councils (FRCs) charged with improving interaction between federal agencies and the local governments. The FRC system created ten multistate regions, each with a regional office and staff, to coordinate the grant-making activities of federal agencies. Nixon also decentralized HUD to thirty-nine area offices, which had the authority to make final commitments for almost all HUD programs. After expanding the federal bureaucracy in a bid to "streamline" government, Nixon called for drastic federal personnel cuts in the summer of 1971. At HUD, the expansion and almost immediate contraction of staff, combined with a pay freeze, damaged staff morale and capabilities for much longer than the duration of the hiring freeze.[95]

Nixon invoked state and local autonomy to gain support for his attack on centralized planning. Like DREE and MSUA in Canada, general revenue sharing, block grants, and HUD's decentralization fundamentally altered the relationship between the federal, state, and local governments. By minimizing federal "strings" on assistance programs, Nixon hamstrung federal agencies. He ensured that HUD officials "only had carrots and no sticks," as one official complained, and made it difficult for federal agencies to implement a development agenda with a truly national scope. Instead, the federal government could shape national development patterns on a case-by-case basis only, by supporting projects proposed by the private sector or by quasi-public agencies.[96] Under Trudeau and Nixon, Canada and the United States had set out on different paths but arrived at the same destination: greater decentralization of federal authority and an increased reliance on the private sector to carry out urban development. U.S. cities like Pittsburgh had already established institutional mechanisms for public-private partnerships as part of federal urban renewal programs. DREE and MSUA laid the groundwork for Canadian cities like Hamilton to pursue similar arrangements.

In coming decades, the U.S. and Canadian governments would use decentralization and privatization as mechanisms to justify funding reductions in distressed urban areas. Growth coalitions with postindustrial ambitions in Pittsburgh and Hamilton had to work within the parameters of government retrenchment initiated under Nixon and Trudeau. In Hamilton, public officials and civic leaders continued to look to Pittsburgh as a redevelopment model but struggled to form more than an ad hoc public-private partnership. In Pittsburgh, the political coalition that nurtured the city's redevelopment partnership began to lay the foundation for its eventual transition to a growth partnership. But at end of the 1960s Hamilton's postwar urban renewal program remained stalled, Pittsburgh's was completed, and public officials and civic leaders seemed unsure about the future direction of their cities.

CHAPTER TWO

Forging Growth Partnerships

The 1970 census took Pittsburghers by surprise. Mayor Pete Flaherty, who had taken office that January, knew the city had lost residents—nearly 92,000—over the previous decade. But suburban mayors and county officials had not anticipated that the Pittsburgh metropolitan area would be the only one among the country's twenty-five largest to lose population in 1970. The *New York Times* marked the occasion with a feature article that highlighted disparities between the recently completed Golden Triangle and Pittsburgh's declining neighborhoods and mill towns. The *Times* reported that U.S. Steel was about to move into a gleaming new headquarters building downtown and that the Pirates would soon open a playoff series in Pittsburgh's newly completed, state-of-the-art baseball stadium. Outside the Golden Triangle and in working-class neighborhoods near the city's steel mills, however, local businessmen complained that their stores were closing and the city was becoming "a plywood jungle." Flaherty fretted that Pittsburgh needed more taxpayers, telling the *Times* that the biggest problem facing his city was "financial survival—whether we can get through without going broke." For Pittsburgh's corporate leaders, however, slow growth and declining manufacturing jobs were signs of good things to come. In the eyes of local executives, the shift from manufacturing to nonmanufacturing employment heralded "a new era of white-collar stability for Pittsburgh as a service and distribution center." One senior executive who had been "active in community affairs" confidently asserted, "the lack of growth lets you get your arms around the problem."[1]

Pittsburgh's population fell by about 15 percent between 1960 and 1970, but Hamilton's increased by more than 30 percent over the same period, from approximately 385,000 in 1961 to nearly half a million in 1971. That year, city officials said that Hamilton had reached a crossroads between its industrial past and postindustrial future. Canada's steel town, planners reported, "had undertaken ambitious programs to shed this role and develop strong commercial and cultural sectors." They expected publicly funded urban renewal programs and private high-rise construction to revitalize downtown. The expansion of McMaster University, the establishment of Mohawk College, and the construction of a theater-auditorium complex signaled "that the educational and cultural side of Hamilton will be significant forces in shaping the city's future."[2] The city's economic development staff urged Mayor Vic Copps to pursue jobs in commercial and non-industrial sectors. "While manufacturing will always be the foundation of our city's economy," they noted, "in the future the big growth in our jobs will come from the service sector. Already the city's economic base is changing and Hamilton should see its future growth and development spread out into the whole economic unit of which this city is the natural center."[3] Planners' enthusiasm about Hamilton's future was somewhat tempered, however, by their assessment that downtown building conditions remained "generally fair to poor."[4]

Within a few years, public officials' optimism was shattered by upheavals in the federal relationship with cities, made worse for Pittsburgh and Hamilton by the near-simultaneous restructuring of the international steel industry in the wake of the 1973 oil crisis. Between 1973 and the early 1980s recession, the basic steel industry experienced a series of crises of global overproduction.[5] In the United States, integrated steel producers responded to changing competitive conditions by intensifying disinvestment practices already underway and laying off large portions of the workforce, shutting down mills in Pittsburgh, Youngstown, and Chicago. In Canada, the steel industry downsized and automated to remain competitive. On both sides of the U.S.-Canadian border, urban tax bases shrank as industrial and population decentralization accelerated, and local governments could no longer rely on predictable funding streams from higher levels of government.

In Pittsburgh and Hamilton, public officials responded to manufacturing decline and federal retrenchment from urban development by trying to form (in Hamilton) or resuscitate (in Pittsburgh) the public-private partnerships that, from their perspective, successfully remade manufacturing centers after World War II. They did so in a decade in which national policy formulation in the United States and Canada reflected common concerns about intergovernmental relations, the future of industrial cities, and the public versus private role in urban and economic development. In both countries, national policy orientations pointed toward accelerated privatization and decentralization by the end of the decade. The very different public-private partnerships that guided development in Pittsburgh and Hamilton over the course of the 1970s shaped—and were shaped by—national policymakers' ideas about the future of industrial cities and the proper role of the government in urban and economic development.

Pittsburgh's New Partnership

Pennsylvania governor Milton Shapp had been right to be concerned about the effects of Nixon's revenue-sharing programs on the fiscal health of Pennsylvania's cities: the amount of revenue shared was not enough to meet the needs of state or local governments. The Nixon administration had structured general revenue sharing such that booming southern and western states received more federal funds than did cash-strapped northern industrial states.[6] After revenue sharing went into effect, Shapp sought to make up budget shortfalls by raising state taxes. He tried to secure support for tax hikes at the local level by promising mayors that he would increase state funding for cities. Flaherty's response must have come as something of a shock to a New Deal liberal like Shapp: Flaherty told him to keep the money and maintain tax rates.[7] When Flaherty took office in 1970, Pittsburgh's seminal postwar urban renewal program had just wound down. Between 1965 and 1968, Pittsburgh had received over $100 million in federal grants-in-aid, an average of slightly more than $25 million a year. Pittsburgh's debt burden was up in 1970, but city planners predicted that the federal funds they expected to receive, along with anticipated new private investment, ensured a rosy fiscal outlook into 1975.[8] The planners did not account for funding changes under Nixon's revenue-sharing proposals, and, between 1970 and 1977, the year Flaherty left office, the federal government slashed the amount of aid it sent to Pittsburgh by a third.[9] Flaherty took up the challenge of a reduced city budget and greater debt by implementing austerity policies, eliminating public-sector jobs, and reducing some city services.

Unlike his Democratic predecessors, who were beholden to both the Allegheny Conference and the unions, Flaherty demonstrated a concern for the outsized influence of interest group politics that made him more like Jimmy Carter than like Lyndon Johnson. Former city planning director Morton Coleman recalled with some understatement that Flaherty "was not a big government person."[10] He was the first of a new breed of fiscal populists who emerged in the 1970s: liberal Democrats who embraced economic conservatism when faced with tax revolts and urban financial crises.[11] Democratic mayors like Flaherty and, later, Ed Koch in New York City, Diane Feinstein in San Francisco, and William Green in Philadelphia rejected the political legacy of the declining New Deal coalition and promoted instead new modes of governance that they saw as more consistent with their limited resources and emerging middle-class resistance to tax increases. Presaging the centrist New Democrats who seized control of the Democratic National Committee in the mid-1980s, these mayors remained socially liberal even as they attacked the large-scale social programs of their Democratic predecessors. Instead, Flaherty and mayors like him focused on government efficiency—often at the expense of public employees' unions—and sought to placate welfare advocates and African American activists with symbolic but inexpensive programs and appointments of women and minorities to prominent positions.[12]

Pittsburgh's well-oiled Democratic machine had never encountered the likes of Flaherty. Between World War II and 1970, Pittsburgh's mayors (with the exception of Flaherty) were hand-selected by the Democratic Party. After four years on city council and a close relationship with party leaders, Flaherty rejected first an invitation to be Mayor Joseph Barr's handpicked successor, beholden to the party for campaign money, and a subsequent effort by Allegheny Conference members to lure him onto the Republican ticket. He campaigned instead as an unendorsed, independent Democrat and beat the machine candidate in the Democratic primary; in the general election, he ran on the platform that he was "nobody's boy." He financed his campaign through donations, launched innovative billboard and newspaper advertising campaigns, and won handily. Four years later, after alienating the Democratic Party, organized labor, his predecessor, most of the city council, the police, the firefighters, corporate CEOs, African American leaders, and both of the city's major newspapers, Flaherty ran unopposed for a second term, having secured both the Republican and Democratic nominations. The joke around town was that "nobody likes Pete except the voters."[13]

Pittsburgh experienced problems common to North Atlantic manufacturing centers earlier and more acutely than other cities, and Flaherty's focus on government efficiency and the austerity programs he implemented prefigured the more severe policies put in place in the middle of the decade in New York City. Flaherty eliminated a wage tax (which was later reinstated) and cut property taxes three times. He removed 18 percent of the nonuniformed workforce (nearly 2,000 workers) from the city payroll, largely through attrition and departmental reorganization. He fired Democratic Party officials from their longtime patronage positions and replaced them with young department heads tasked with increasing government efficiency. He was openly scornful of city council and saw no reason to respond to interview requests from journalists. He eliminated chauffeurs for city department heads; when Teamsters leader and city councilor Thomas Fagan challenged Flaherty's decision, public opinion was firmly on Flaherty's side.[14] Flaherty improved some city services while allowing Pittsburgh's aging infrastructure to collapse; he infuriated county officials, the Democratic Party, and the business community by blocking an unmanned light rail from downtown to the South Hills; and he severed the carefully nurtured relationship between city hall and the business community. At a time when other cities (New York, Cleveland) faced bankruptcy, Pittsburgh had a budget surplus.

Pittsburgh's political and economic elites interpreted Flaherty's campaign slogan, "nobody's boy," as a rebuke not only to the Democratic machine but also to the Allegheny Conference, its Republican members, and the Mellon family in particular, whom Flaherty believed had too much influence over local politics and urban development. He brought in a new city planning director from Philadelphia, Bob Paternoster, rather than appoint someone from within the existing ranks.[15] He reassigned some Urban Redevelopment Authority (URA) staffers to the City Planning Department and imposed a series of professional indignities, such as mandatory Friday afternoon meetings, on those who remained.[16] Not long after Flaherty took office, he evicted the Allegheny Conference from the URA-owned Civic Building, where city planning and the URA also kept offices. Flaherty cancelled the lease and gave the Allegheny Conference sixty days to clear out; Executive Director Robert Pease described the move as part of Flaherty's strategy, in concert with appointing new heads of planning and the URA, to restrict the Allegheny Conference's influence over public agencies.[17]

The URA, in particular, raised Flaherty's hackles. Established to implement urban renewal programs, the URA from the outset carried out public undertakings (such as seizing property through eminent domain) in support of privately planned renewal schemes, typically at the behest of the Allegheny Conference. By 1970, the URA's loyalties were divided between the Allegheny Conference and the Pennsylvania Department of Transportation. Flaherty saw the funds funneled through the URA as a mechanism for the state to foist the social consequences of highway construction on the city and was suspicious of the continued close relationship between that agency and the Allegheny Conference. "So we had to kind of change the position of the URA and a lot of the people, and change the people in Planning Department," Flaherty recalled.[18]

Flaherty appointed his executive secretary Bruce Campbell head of the URA and replaced the corporate elites who had dominated the URA's board since the agency's inception with what he described as a mix of "downtown, political, and neighborhood people." Jack Robin, long-time Democratic political boss and chairman of the URA first under Mayor David Lawrence and again under Flaherty's successor Richard Caliguiri, accused Flaherty of trying to destroy the agency. In Robin's recollection, Flaherty came to office "thinking that we were all engaged in some terrific conspiracy."[19] Flaherty and Campbell "did their best," Robin charged, "to denigrate, to loot and remove the powers of the Authority." Pease remembered that mayors traditionally attended Allegheny Conference meetings and stopped by to "just talk," but Flaherty delegated that responsibility to Campbell. When Pease asked Campbell to tell Flaherty to let the Allegheny Conference know if he needed anything, Campbell scoffed, "He'll never call you."[20]

The success of Flaherty's attack on the URA and the Allegheny Conference rested in part on residents' widespread dissatisfaction with the redevelopment partnership at the heart of the Pittsburgh Renaissance.[21] While he undoubtedly would have liked to retain the federal-funding largesse of the 1960s, Flaherty's belief that the city's redevelopment partnership had removed too much power from the people aligned with Nixon's devolutionary policies and with public opinion in Pittsburgh. Flaherty wanted to return power to the neighborhoods in much the same way Nixon wanted to restore autonomy to state and local governments. As part of his campaign to weaken the relationship between the city government and corporate elites, Flaherty reoriented the attentions of the URA and planning department toward neighborhood development and away from the Golden Triangle. Through the "more equitable distribution" of URA funds and tax revenue, Flaherty channeled more money and energy into the neighborhoods than any previous administration, "especially the small business areas and so forth," he recalled, "to try to perk them up so they wouldn't have the ghost-like quality of boarded up little neighborhood commercial centers."[22]

Most significantly, Flaherty redirected at least half of the city's federal aid—primarily community development block grant money—into the neighborhoods. Flaherty also implemented a series of neighborhood-based programs: he installed new street lights as a crime reduction measure, provided low-interest home improvement loans in low-income areas, and reduced taxes through a balanced budget and surpluses in the city coffers. "I think the previous mayors had been 'downtown-oriented,'" Flaherty reflected. "Nothing wrong with that, but to be a bit too much 'downtown-oriented' was perhaps a mistake."[23] Pease agreed, saying that, by the time Flaherty took office, the city was "exhausted" by the redevelopment that had taken place over the previous two and a half decades.[24] To ensure that Pittsburgh's planning process focused on residential neighborhoods, Flaherty established a Community Planning Program in the City Planning Department in 1971, which institutionalized a citizen participation process through neighborhood-based advocacy planning.[25] Pease disparaged the community planning boards that developed in response as "pseudo-city planning," and the Allegheny Conference made little effort to cooperate with them.[26]

Flaherty's focus on neighborhood planning did not, however, mean that he ignored large-scale projects, particularly those that would help remake industrial spaces for other kinds of uses. In fact, in the early 1970s, Flaherty's Planning Department proposed many of the redevelopment projects that gained traction under his successor. Most prominently, planners sought ways to encourage the expansion of medical and educational complexes in Oakland and advocated using eminent domain to assemble land for industrial or commercial uses on the South Side, Herr's Island, and in the Strip District, all sites that subsequently became centers of activity for Renaissance II.[27] Flaherty and the city planners had not yet abandoned heavy manufacturing uses within the city limits, but projects already underway pointed to historic preservation as a mechanism for redeveloping remnants of the industrial era for uses compatible with visions for a postindustrial city. By shifting his focus away from Golden Triangle construction projects toward decentralized and neighborhood-based development, Flaherty laid the groundwork for Caliguiri's more ambitious city-wide vision for a second Renaissance. Flaherty's fiscal austerity also created the budget surplus that made it possible for Caliguiri to contemplate such an undertaking. As Flaherty's city treasurer, Joe Cosetti, recalled, "the Caliguiri administration never would have been able to get off a dime had Pete not gotten rid of the load of patronage. If that same payroll was there when Caliguiri became mayor, he would have gone under."[28]

Flaherty softened toward the Allegheny Conference in his second term. By 1976, the last year of Flaherty's tenure, economic conditions in the city had deteriorated to the extent that he could no longer afford to sideline corporate leaders. That year, the Planning Department noted that the city government "in many ways feels helpless to alter the overriding national economic trends that negatively affect the City," prefiguring the mantra of city, county, and state governments in the 1980s that they were impotent in the face of national economic problems and sectoral collapse. The Planning Department identified

sustaining strong links between the city government and the corporate sector, maintaining a favorable tax climate, and supporting continued growth
in the Golden Triangle and Oakland as the city's key economic development
concerns. The planners were likely reacting to recently released population
data that suggested predictions based on the 1970 census had been inaccu-
rate: the four-county region experienced 4 percent employment growth, but
the city lost 9 percent of its jobs between 1960 and 1975, a figure the planners
believed obscured "even more dramatic shifts by sector and geographic area."
In response, Flaherty established the Mayor's Economic Development Committee, an advisory board he described as a coalition between business and
government, to review and coordinate economic development efforts in the
public and private sectors. The Economic Development Committee represented the first step toward reviving the public-private partnership that had
been central to Pittsburgh's postwar urban development.[29]

Flaherty's second-term priorities were very much in line with the pro-
growth agenda articulated under Lawrence and Barr. They heralded the
emergence of policy instruments associated with devolution and privatization that took shape first under Nixon and accelerated as the Carter and
Reagan administrations increasingly withdrew federal resources from the
urban sphere.[30] Pittsburgh's urban development may have provided a model
for Hamilton and other North American industrial centers, but it was Flaherty's austerity policies and neighborhood planning initiatives that piqued
the interest of U.S. officials in the late 1970s. Flaherty had been the first northern mayor to endorse Jimmy Carter in 1976, and he resigned his mayoral post
to become a deputy attorney general in the Carter administration, a reward
for his early and vigorous support. Flaherty's fiscal populism in his years as
mayor presaged Carter's approach to solving the problems facing U.S. cities and pointed the way toward the centrist New Democrat platform that
solidified in the 1980s. Faced with fiscal crises in the early 1970s, Flaherty
and mayors like him across the political spectrum saw neighborhood groups'
demands for community control as an opportunity to shift some of the planning and service-provision functions of cash-strapped local governments to
individuals and nonprofits. Carter drew heavily on these local experiments
to develop and legitimate policies that privileged voluntarism and self-help
over government programs and federal spending, and in the process laid the
institutional foundation for Reagan's neoliberal retrenchment.

With urban constituencies irate over nearly a decade of neglect from
Washington, the formulation of a federal policy to aid socially and fiscally
distressed cities had featured prominently in Carter's campaign promises to

mayors and civil rights groups. In March 1977, Carter convened a cabinet-level working group to review federal urban and regional development programs, consult with state and local government officials, and recommend administrative and legislative reforms.[31] Carter also appointed a National Commission on Neighborhoods (NCN) in 1977 and sponsored a White House Conference on Balanced Growth and Economic Development (WH Conference) in 1978 to make recommendations about urban and economic development policy. Participants in both initiatives—individuals and groups from across the political spectrum and with a diversity of economic interests—pointed toward increased decentralization, privatization, and voluntarism as federal policy responses to urban decline.[32]

In 1978, Carter presented what he described as the nation's first comprehensive urban policy to Congress in a report titled *A New Partnership to Conserve America's Communities*.[33] Carter's much-anticipated national urban policy did not introduce major new federal programs or substantially increase funding levels for existing urban programs.[34] He and his advisors had used the NCN and WH Conference recommendations as political cover to support local-level voluntarism over increased federal funding. The most tangible result of the national urban policy, four executive orders issued in 1978, directed federal agencies to locate facilities in urban areas, emphasize procurement set-asides in areas with high unemployment, consider the impact of programs on urban areas, and establish an interagency council to implement the urban policy.[35] The legislative package attached to *A New Partnership* failed to gain traction because liberal Democrats were unhappy about limits to federal oversight, because of bipartisan political opposition to targeting aid to distressed cities, and because of concern over the financial implications of the proposed programs in a time of stagflation and tax revolts.[36] Most important, with his focus more fully on foreign policy and the economy, Carter did not push Congress to support the proposed legislation.[37]

Carter's distrust of "special interests" and concern for the "forgotten" white middle class led him to step back from expansive federal programs, to oppose increased federal urban spending, and to promote the capacity of the private sector (including both for-profit and nonprofit entities), rather than the government, to address urban problems.[38] Like Nixon, Carter attacked redundant programs and excessive paperwork and passed along as much oversight as possible for urban development to state and local governments. He rejected large-scale job creation programs and housing subsidies in favor of comparatively inexpensive programs such as the National Endowment for the Arts $35 million "Livable Cities" program for local public art and mural projects. In

1977, he introduced Urban Development Action Grants to stimulate private-sector urban redevelopment, and he instituted a countercyclical assistance program as part of an economic stimulus package to provide federal aid to states and localities particularly hard hit by the recession. The Carter administration also shifted a greater share of Community Development Block Grant funds to northeastern and midwestern cities. In general, however, Carter's urban policy was an amplification of Nixon's New Federalism.[39]

For reasons of political expediency—Carter knew he would need to attract both the suburban and southern vote in 1980—the president wanted to emphasize programs that provided "incentives," "leverage," and "catalysts" for private sector activity, which were less of a political liability than increased direct federal expenditures in cities. When it was released, Carter's urban policy unequivocally signaled to big city mayors that the federal government would not provide large federal outlays to reverse urban decline or temper the effects of industrial restructuring. Cities were "more than just simply centers of jobs, communications and commerce," *A New Partnership* reminded its readers. They were also "centers of learning, centers of culture, centers of social services."[40] It was this latter—postindustrial—assemblage of services that the Carter administration wanted to emphasize.

For Pittsburgh's new mayor, Richard Caliguiri, the postindustrialism the Carter administration tacitly promoted was already a familiar paradigm. City council president Caliguiri became acting mayor when Flaherty left for Washington. Flaherty's successor surely would have preferred a national urban policy that included increased federal funding, but his own view of the future of industrial cities hewed closely to that expressed in *A New Partnership*. The son of a milkman from Pittsburgh's working-class, largely Italian Greenfield neighborhood, Caliguiri had followed Flaherty's example and run for City Council as an independent in 1971, beating out the Democratic Party-endorsed candidate. When he ran for mayor in 1977 at the end of Flaherty's term, the Democratic Party refused to support him. He again ran as an independent, backed by a group called "Pittsburghers for Caliguiri" that a suburban newspaper described as "a collection people, Democrats, independents, Republicans, volunteers, city payrollers and others not yet identified."[41] Even with broad support from his constituents, Caliguiri narrowly beat the Democratic candidate, popular Allegheny County commissioner Tom Foerster. When he ran for re-election in 1981 and 1985, he did so on the Democratic Party ticket and won by large margins.

Caliguiri may have taken a page out of his predecessor's playbook when he spurned the local Democratic machine, but his mayoral ambitions for a second Renaissance made him more like David Lawrence than like Flaherty. Where Flaherty sought at the outset of his first term to loosen the bonds between the city government and corporate leaders, Caliguiri set out instead to restore the city's public-private partnership. His desire to do so was seemingly a pragmatic response to national policies that increasingly privileged partnerships for urban and economic development. Renaissance II's success hinged on introducing a wide array of public incentives for private development to induce corporate leaders to undertake large-scale construction projects for downtown office buildings. Caliguiri established the Mayor's Development Council, a more business-friendly version of Flaherty's mayoral advisory committee, to plan Renaissance II; he instructed his department heads to cooperate with developers; and he merged the city's Departments of Housing and Economic Development with the URA to centralize redevelopment activities. One of the new mayor's first official acts was to call a meeting with the Allegheny Conference and ask for help fixing the roads Flaherty had allowed to fall into disrepair. Gulf Oil CEO Jerry McAffee offered to bring in a macadam expert from California and loan him to the city for six months. The following summer, Caliguiri repaved "something like 120 miles of street." That gesture symbolically renewed the close relationship between the Allegheny Conference and the city government, and the Allegheny Conference resumed a leading role in planning urban development.[42]

As soon as he restored the relationship between the city and the Allegheny Conference, Caliguiri launched his second Renaissance "to recover lost ground and to determine a new direction" for the city.[43] He and his Planning Department routinely tried to downplay the devastating effects of industrial restructuring on the urban economy and focused instead on cultural development, high technology, and service sector job creation.[44] "As in any mature city which is undertaking revitalization," the mayor's office announced, "Pittsburgh's efforts are a mix of conserving, maintaining and nurturing its strengths on one hand while introducing new, creative and exciting activities on the other."[45] Caliguiri's staff optimistically pointed out that, while manufacturing work had disappeared, jobs in health, education, and professional and service sectors had increased, which they thought heralded the emergence of "a more diversified and, therefore, healthier" local economy.[46] Faced with difficult decisions about how to save a declining city, Caliguiri and his Planning Department chose to pursue a postindustrial redevelopment strategy without much apparent hand-wringing over its potential impact on low-income and working-class residents.

Caliguiri wanted to redevelop the city in a way that would make it more compatible with the perceived needs of young, white-collar workers. Renaissance II reflected the first Renaissance's focus on downtown construction and improvement projects, but Caliguiri expanded the range of activities to include neighborhood stabilization, economic development, and large-scale projects well outside of the central business district.[47] His ambitious agenda for a second Renaissance benefitted from the Home Rule Charter Pittsburgh's voters had approved in 1974. The charter secured for the city government the authority to carry out any function not expressly precluded by Pennsylvania state law or the U.S. or state constitutions. In this system of local government organization, the mayor was both executive and administrator, while the city council served a legislative function. The mayor independently appointed (and removed) the heads of city departments and members of public authorities and commissions, while the city council created commissions, passed resolutions, and established city ordinances. Under Home Rule, the mayor had veto power over city council decisions, rather than the other way around. Except in cases where Pittsburgh accepted state and federal funds, city officials were free of oversight from other levels of government and not compelled by anything other than political pressure to cooperate with the county government. The Planning Department's land use and economic development decisions were largely autonomous. With few constraints on how he used public funds, Caliguiri issued a six-year, $323 million capital budget for Renaissance II four months after taking office, which he called a "blueprint" for Pittsburgh's revival.[48]

Caliguiri's Renaissance II budget affirmed his commitment to working through what he described as a "city-citizen partnership." When Caliguiri restored the relationship between city agencies and the corporate sector, he incorporated new members into Pittsburgh's public-private partnership. "We believe that the City and the private sector are partners," his office noted. "The City will do its share by providing direct services and projects. But you will have to do your share as well. You, the residents and the businessman, will have to make commitments and investments in your homes, your communities and your businesses."[49] The "civic" partners included neighborhood groups (primarily community development corporations, or CDCs); the University of Pittsburgh and Carnegie Mellon University; and local foundations, especially those of the Mellon, Scaife, Heinz, and Hillman families; and the state government.[50]

Pittsburgh's reconstituted partnership reflected the institutional arrangements of the growth partnerships that took shape in North American and

Western European cities between New York City's 1975 near-bankruptcy and the end of the century. New York's powerbrokers sprang to action when President Gerald Ford told New York City to "Drop Dead," as the *New York Daily News* famously rendered Ford's message to Mayor Abe Beame and Governor Hugh Carey that the federal government would not bail out the insolvent city. New York, like most other major U.S. cities, had worked through a redevelopment partnership to facilitate urban renewal projects in the 1950s and 1960s. New York's partnership differed substantially from those in other cities which undertook large-scale urban renewal programs. In most places, renewal activities were directed by civic organizations modeled after the Allegheny Conference, such as the Greater Milwaukee Committee, the Chicago Central Area Committee, the Greater Baltimore Committee, Central Atlanta Progress, the Cleveland Development Foundation, and St. Louis's Civic Progress. Instead, New York's "master builder," Robert Moses, remade the urban landscape through a series of public authorities. When Manhattan's business elites decided in 1975 to work with the city and state government to solve urban problems, their focus was on the city's looming bankruptcy rather than physical redevelopment through urban renewal.[51] They set out to create a different set of institutions through which to confront a different set of circumstances.

After Ford rejected Beame and Carey's bid for federal aid, Carey turned to the city's corporate leaders for advice. The city's bankers had long warned that Beame needed to cut spending and balance the budget if he hoped to keep New York City credit-worthy. In spring 1975, banks refused to issue new bonds to cover Beame's budget shortfalls, and Carey loaned the city money to remain solvent; by June, New York City could not honor nearly $8 million in maturing securities. Carey asked investment banker Felix Rohatyn, managing director of Lazard Frères, to head an advisory committee composed of financiers, CEOs, and realtors to determine a course of action. Instead of creating a civic organization to work with city and state officials, the committee advised Carey to create a state-chartered independent corporation through which bankers could oversee the bailout. As a result, Carey created the Municipal Assistance Corporation for the City of New York (MAC) in June and appointed Rohatyn as chair of the nine-member board. MAC gained authority through the state legislature to issue bonds and use the money to restore the city to solvency. To support MAC's activities, the state legislature converted New York City's sales and stock transfer taxes into state taxes and used them to secure MAC bonds, mandated that the city balance its budget in three years, and established an Emergency Financial Control

Board to monitor the city's finances and ensure that MAC's directives were met. If Rohatyn and his board thought that city officials were making poor budgeting decisions, MAC could suspend loans to the city and hold back tax revenue. Carey and Rohatyn's efforts were not enough to resolve New York's fiscal crisis; it took more than $2 billion in short-term federal loans and an agreement from public sector unions to buy $2.5 billion in city bonds to stabilize the city's finances.[52]

The financial details of New York's bailout were only part of the story. With MAC, Carey transferred unprecedented control over public finances to private actors, some of whom were the same bankers who refused to extend additional credit to the city. In exchange for bond financing, Rohatyn and MAC demanded that New York City implement austerity measures as part of "best-practice" budgeting. These included tax hikes, wage freezes at levels below inflation, public-sector layoffs, cuts to public services, higher subway fares and, for the first time, tuition at City College. The social costs were immense: day-care centers and firehouses closed down. Six thousand teachers were laid off. Public sector unions lost power as their memberships declined; the same unions found themselves in the uncomfortable position of becoming creditors to their employer, which made strikes a difficult prospect.[53] Compared to many other U.S. cities, in the 1950s and 1960s New York had been a social-democratic stronghold, with an expansive welfare state, strong unions, and a liberal political culture.[54] MAC's austerity measures tore apart the city's social safety net, increased income inequality, and undermined organized labor. These were not, as Rohatyn claimed, unavoidable consequences of MAC's efforts to forestall a bankruptcy that would have been worse for working- and middle-class families.[55] Instead, New York's corporate elites seized leadership in a moment of crisis and pushed through a series of neoliberal reforms to reduce the size and power of what they had for decades considered a bloated welfare state.[56] Their activities marked the emergence of the growth partnerships that would proliferate in North Atlantic cities in coming decades, which had more flexible arrangements between their public and private members than did redevelopment partnerships rooted in federal urban renewal legislation.

The growth partnership that managed New York City's bail-out represented what Timothy Weaver has called "neoliberalism by design"—an example of political and business elites using state power to implement a neoliberal political project—but not all such partnerships reflected the discernible influence of neoliberal ideology. Cities like Pittsburgh and Hamilton (in Weaver's taxonomy) instead turned to "neoliberalism by default." Members of their growth coalitions increasingly abandoned redistributive programs and pursued free-market solutions to urban problems because they did not perceive other politically viable options.[57] Caliguiri, for instance, was undoubtedly influenced by events in New York, but he and his allies in the Allegheny Conference did not set out to use Pittsburgh's revived partnership to break unions, gut pensions, or roll back the welfare state as MAC had. Instead, the city's redevelopment partnership retooled to contend with the changing political and fiscal conditions that accompanied industrial restructuring and federal retrenchment. If New York City and Pittsburgh's growth partnerships' intentions were different, the outcomes were similar. Pittsburgh's postindustrial redevelopment under Renaissance II, like New York's rebirth in the same period, produced hollowed-out manufacturing zones, gentrification of blue-collar neighborhoods, university expansions and new medical complexes, and the perpetual rebuilding of downtown as its role shifted from managing production to managing services and finance.

In Pittsburgh's growth partnership, partners coordinated different aspects of redevelopment that had been centralized through the Allegheny Conference in the first Renaissance, and each shared or adopted Caliguiri's postindustrial vision as a means to further its own institutional interests. "In Renaissance I the government got its ideas from the private sector, and commitment from the private sector was very important," Robin remembered. "In Renaissance II, I think the government had learned how to sell the projects, which it originated, to the private investors. That was a major change."[58] The imprimatur of junior partners in voluntary organizations, universities, and local foundations legitimated particular aspects of the postindustrial transformation envisioned by the primary partnership of local government officials and corporate elites. The growth partnership also reflected the mix of institutions the Carter administration hoped to see engaged with urban development. Yet only the Commonwealth of Pennsylvania, which like most U.S. states became increasingly involved in economic development in the 1970s, achieved a level of influence over development decisions commensurate to the role of the city government and local corporate elites.

Caliguiri's redevelopment plans remained heavily dependent on corporate participation, and the Allegheny Conference, as it had been during the first Renaissance, was the city's most important partner. After R. K. Mellon's 1970 death, Pease shaped both the vision and the programmatic activities of the Allegheny Conference. For much of that period, Pease ran the organization's day-to-day operations from a corner office on the forty-fourth floor of the U.S. Steel Building, a position that hinted at the real power behind the Allegheny Conference. Pease was not a Pennsylvania native; raised in Nebraska, he arrived in Pittsburgh after World War II to attend Carnegie Mellon University (then the Carnegie Institute of Technology). After graduating with a civil engineering degree, Pease initially worked for the university on its postwar physical expansion, and in 1953 he went to work for the URA, where he oversaw a controversial urban renewal program in the city's African American Hill District. Five years later, thirty-three-year-old Pease was named URA executive director, and in 1968 Mellon tapped him to helm the Allegheny Conference.[59]

Until Pease's 1991 retirement, the Allegheny Conference Executive Committee, composed of the city's most powerful corporate and financial leaders, set the organization's agenda based on his recommendations. The organization's structure reflected a dense web of interrelationships between local and regional development organizations and Pittsburgh's corporate elite. "I think that we have one of the finest spirits of cooperation and orientation toward community benefits in the Allegheny Conference that you'd find anywhere," an Executive Committee member said in the mid-1980s. "There is camaraderie among CEOs that, I'm told, is quite lacking in New York, Chicago, Los Angeles or San Francisco. The CEOs of giant corporations in those other cities have no common discourse, they're too busy, they're not interested."[60] In Pittsburgh, to the contrary, between 1968 and 1985, a Mellon Bank or Pittsburgh National Bank executive served as chairman of the Allegheny Conference, and the presidents and CEOs of U.S. Steel, Dravo, Koppers, Gulf, Alcoa, Heinz, and Pittsburgh Plate Glass were executive committee members. In 1977 alone, twenty-one of the twenty-six members of Mellon's board of directors were also Allegheny Conference members, including James Higgins, who was at the time president of both Mellon Bank and the Allegheny Conference. Pittsburgh National Bank chairman Henry Hillman, Dravo CEO Robert Dickey, III, and Pittsburgh Plate Glass CEO L. Stanton Williams all served as Allegheny Conference chairmen or presidents; Higgins's successor at Mellon, J. David Barnes, and U.S. Steel CEO David Roderick were vice presidents.[61]

The CEOs who guided decisions about regional disinvestment and plant closures were also instrumental in determining the urban and economic development agenda of the city's growth partnership. The Allegheny Conference was a "long range kind of organization," according to Pease. "There are no miracles in what we do day by day," he said. "Some people, because of the early myth of what we did—you know, the Conference waved the wand and the smoke blew away—they sort of had the attitude that if the steel mills closed, the Conference would solve that issue." On the eve of his retirement, Pease dismissed the notion that the organization he helmed could have done more than it had. "There is no way that any organization, even government, can solve an economic issue which is the result of global change," he insisted, "and that's what Pittsburgh faced in the mid-1970s and 1980s."[62]

While the Allegheny Conference in the 1970s did not wield the nearly unlimited power to control the physical development of the city that it held in its 1950s heyday, its influence remained significant. The Executive Committee members retained unparalleled access to the city and state governments and to Pittsburgh's corporate decision-making structure. Executive Committee members typically sat on the boards of directors of Pittsburgh-based corporations and community development organizations. Williams, for example, was a board member at Dravo and Mellon Bank, a Carnegie Mellon trustee, and a board member of the Regional Industrial Development Corporation (RIDC) and Penn's Southwest. Carnegie Mellon president Richard Cyert was on the Allegheny Conference Executive Committee, a member of both the RIDC and Penn's Southwest, and on the boards of Heinz, Allegheny International, Koppers, and First Boston.[63]

Representatives of local foundations, tied to corporate elites through board memberships, worked with Pease and the Allegheny Conference staff to achieve the growth partnership's goal of creating new cultural institutions. Caliguiri targeted the development of a cultural district adjacent to the Golden Triangle as a way to attract additional downtown investment, appeal to executives considering locating their companies in Pittsburgh, and create a regional cultural center to capture a share of the money spent on leisure activities by suburbanites. Because cultural development was part of their institutional missions, Pittsburgh-based foundations such as the Carnegie, the Historical Society of Western Pennsylvania, and the Pittsburgh Cultural Trust used their funds to offset the public cost of developing cultural institutions that Caliguiri hoped would attract new residents and tourists.[64]

The participation of CDCs, on the other hand, allowed Caliguiri to claim broad-based public support for the growth partnership's plans. In return, neighborhood-based groups were able to influence and in some cases control development within their neighborhood boundaries.[65] Caliguiri expanded Flaherty's neighborhood planning efforts, in no small part because neighborhood-based organizations were eligible to receive federal community development funds as well as newly available national and local foundation funding. Leaders of the historic preservation and neighborhood organizations that had fought the city's urban renewal plans a decade earlier understood that to secure political support—and public and local foundation funding—for their own agendas, they needed to ensure that their development plans were compatible with the growth coalition's vision for the city. Neighborhood groups legitimated the economic development plans of other organizations but were excluded from making meaningful contributions to the city's physical and economic development agenda.[66] The largely privately funded CDC network channeled citizen participation in such a way that it delegitimized other forms of civic protest, including protests by groups of unemployed workers. The CDCs did not challenge the growth coalition's visions for postindustrial Pittsburgh, and neighborhood groups' activities— historic preservation, commercial district business development, infrastructure improvement, and housing rehabilitation—were largely compatible with the growth partnership's focus on quality of life issues.[67]

Caliguiri's neighborhood stabilization goals became increasingly dependent on the ability of CDCs to acquire funding from philanthropic organizations and from state and federal sources, making neighborhood institutions central to privatization and decentralization on the ground in Pittsburgh in the way Carter had intended in his urban policy. The North Side's Mexican War Streets provided Caliguiri with an especially instructive example of how neighborhood-based organizations might contribute to redevelopment without extensive public expenditures. As urban renewal projects tore apart the North Side's social fabric and residents moved to the suburbs in the early postwar years, the neighborhood's buildings fell into disrepair, and its Victorian homes were subdivided into rental properties. In the mid-1960s, the City Planning Department targeted the neighborhood for demolition. Local residents, the Mexican War Streets Society, and the Pittsburgh History and Landmarks Foundation (Landmarks) worked together to challenge the urban redevelopment plans and ultimately convinced the city to abandon the project. Local residents began to purchase and rehabilitate the homes with financial assistance from Landmarks, and by 1972 philanthropies such as the Heinz Foundation underwrote redevelopment activity in the neighborhood.[68]

The lesson Caliguiri took from the Mexican War Streets was that neighborhood-based redevelopment could occur without extensive financial or institutional commitments from the city government. The reduction of state and federal community development funds in the 1970s, particularly for housing, meant that the nonprofit sector and CDCs would have to play an increasingly important role in planning, developing, and securing financing for neighborhood-based housing, recreation, and commercial district improvement projects. Caliguiri invoked the rhetoric of partnership and self-help that was becoming increasingly prominent in national discourse about cities under the Carter administration when he informed residents that the city's future depended on "the individual" and that "the job is far beyond government alone, it requires a partnership."[69]

Pittsburgh's research universities also played an important role in Renaissance II. The University of Pittsburgh and Carnegie Mellon partnered with the state government and local industry to attract advanced technology enterprises. Such partnerships helped state and local officials realize their desires to establish high-tech industry while advancing the universities' expansion plans and bolstering efforts to improve their national rankings. Entrepreneurial university presidents—Carnegie Mellon president James Cyert and University of Pittsburgh chancellor Wesley Posvar (both longtime Allegheny Conference members)—encouraged their institutions to provide services-for-hire to both the public and private sectors.[70] Under Cyert and Posvar, both universities collaborated with local firms to take advantage of state funding for advanced technology research and to attract federal funds for such undertakings as a robotics institute, software design center, and supercomputing site.[71]

Like the redevelopment partnership forged by Lawrence and the Allegheny Conference in the urban renewal era, Caliguiri's growth partnership became an international model for postindustrial urban regeneration at the end of the twentieth century. In 1988, Pittsburgh hosted a conference on "Remaking Cities," which brought together public officials, developers, and civic leaders from the United States and the UK to share their strategies for confronting industrial restructuring and creating postindustrial cities.[72] In the 1980s, Bilbao's public officials invited experts from Pittsburgh to Spain to discuss their experiences with industrial restructuring. One outcome of the visit was the inauguration of formal and informal exchanges between Pittsburgh, Glasgow, Lille, the Ruhr region, and Bilbao, circuits that were well worn by the 1990s. Policy tourists between the cities participated in workshops with public officials and business leaders, training exchange programs, and study tours.[73] Pease, after his 1991 retirement from the Allegheny Conference, served as a consultant on urban redevelopment projects in Japan, India, Ireland, and the UK.[74] Canadian cities, too, remained interested in Pittsburgh's redevelopment tactics. Despite fundamental differences between the political and institutional frameworks governing public policy, Hamilton, like other declining North Atlantic manufacturing centers, emulated Pittsburgh's postindustrial rebirth and the partnership behind it, with very different results.[75]

Slouching Toward Partnership in Hamilton

When Pete Flaherty took office in 1970, Pittsburgh's first Renaissance and the partnership that facilitated it had just wound down; across the border, however, Vic Copps's redevelopment efforts in Hamilton had finally begun to pick up steam. Copps had already inaugurated an urban renewal program intended to create a new civic square, but federal and provincial wrangling over urban and economic development and the province's subordination of Hamilton's commercial district to Toronto's meant that the project was by no means guaranteed to succeed. Yet, as early as 1972, city officials congratulated themselves for the "ambitious programs" underway "to shed [Hamilton's historic] role and develop strong commercial and cultural sectors." Their plans included establishing a secondary commercial and industrial district on previously undeveloped urban land and a downtown building program tailored to the perceived needs of corporate headquarters and financial institutions. That year, Toronto's *Globe and Mail* ran a feature on Hamilton's downtown facelift, noting that the city's "building plans for the Nineteen Seventies are directed toward reshaping Hamilton as the business and cultural focus for more than a million residents of Southwestern Ontario."[76] Copps aggressively promoted a postindustrial vision of the city, but Hamilton lacked a public-private partnership through which to realize his plans.

Yet the Allegheny Conference remained a popular model for Hamilton in the 1970s. Despite the Chamber of Commerce's declaration in 1970 that "there now appears to be agreement that business must stand up and be counted if it is to offset the all too influential voice of minority groups working so often in their own narrow self interests," Hamilton's Economic Development Commission struggled to get local executives invested in urban development.[77] As Moore had noted after his visit to Pittsburgh four years earlier, Hamilton's executives agreed to participate in community development initiatives but failed to show up at meetings. In 1972, consultants for the city of Hamilton made another pilgrimage to Pittsburgh to meet with John Grove about the Allegheny Conference. Consultant Frank Oxley later wrote to Grove: "If I learned only two things yesterday, my visit would have been worthwhile—(a) that only the most senior local businessmen should work together at the outset towards a common, apolitical, unselfish goal and (b) that not one member of that group should be allowed to delegate his personal attendance." He had also learned, however, "that municipal and State (provincial in our case) help and counsel is essential," a lesson that would vex Hamilton's growth coalition for the next decade. In Ontario, provincial officials' "help and counsel" took the form of industrial development promotion and bore little resemblance to the wide-ranging financial incentives and economic development tools U.S. cities made available to private capital.[78]

Adding an extra layer of complexity to Copps's revitalization efforts, in 1974 Ontario replaced existing counties with a system of regional municipalities, each anchored by an urban center. Local government reorganization emerged from a provincial taxation study, which recommended creating a new form of subprovincial government to alleviate the financial problems facing local governments. Per capita local government expenditures in Canada had begun to exceed spending by the provincial and federal governments in the 1960s, and local revenue was not sufficient to cover municipal spending. Similar territorial reorganization underway in England, Wales, and Scotland influenced Ontario's plans. However, instead of approaching the entire province as a single unit subject to reorganization, as had been the case in the UK, the Ontario government reorganized one local area at a time. Regional municipalities were supposed to create unified service areas in which cities and their hinterlands would become a single political unit.[79]

Provincial officials assumed that local government reorganization would address a number of concerns related to larger provincial development goals. They expected regional governments to combine the planning functions of cities, suburbs, and rural areas in fast-growing regions and replace incompatible municipal growth plans with a single comprehensive regional plan. The new structure was supposed to create economies of scale for service delivery and reduce the costs of municipal services. Officials argued that regional governments would increase equity in taxation and service provision, because all municipalities in a given region would share the wealth of industry and development, and therefore the level of service for all residents would increase to the level of the best-serviced municipality in the region. Provincial officials also believed that the existence of regional governments, in combination with comprehensive regional development plans, would eliminate interurban competition for industry and business.[80]

Efforts to consolidate the city of Hamilton with the surrounding suburban and rural towns in Wentworth County into the Regional Municipality of Hamilton-Wentworth proved controversial, in large part because provincial officials' assumptions about regionalization did not hold true. From the outset, the region's mayors fought over the political structure of the proposed regional municipality because none wanted to lose their existing powers. Hamilton's mayor and councilors advocated for a single municipal unit, which they could dominate. Representatives of the suburban and agricultural communities that comprised Wentworth County demanded a two-tiered system that would allow them to preserve some independence. Hamilton lost the battle, and each municipality retained its local government and supplied representatives to a regional council. Throughout the 1970s, the structure caused significant internal conflict, as Hamilton's mayor and the mayors of the outlying towns—Stoney Creek, Ancaster, Dundas, Flamborough, and Glenbrook—squabbled over who would finance central city cultural and social functions that served residents of the entire region. By the 1980s, inter-municipal tension had largely resolved, but the two-tiered municipal government added another political constraint to Hamilton planners' ability to make land use decisions.[81]

Municipal reorganization did advance the provincial goal of creating regional comprehensive plans, but the regional government structure exacerbated rather than ameliorated local budget constraints. Service expansions proved costly, and it was not economically feasible to extend all the services offered in central cities, such as public transit, to suburbs and rural areas. The reorganization also created new tensions between cities and their hinterlands. In Hamilton-Wentworth, for instance, residents of outlying areas felt that the regional government privileged the interests of the city of Hamilton over those of smaller, less developed areas. The regional government structure failed to eliminate interurban competition because municipalities retained control of limited local means of attracting new investment, primarily by providing serviced land and marketing their comparative advantages. Competition for jobs and resources between the largest cities in Southern Ontario's regional municipalities, including Hamilton and nearby Burlington, increased rather than decreased after regionalization.[82] The Hamilton Chamber, in particular, objected to provincial policies designed to shift urban growth to new, dispersed urban centers throughout the province. Chamber leaders noted the policy's negative implications for the Hamilton region and complained, "the future of the region is a question mark."[83]

Following the creation of the Regional Municipality of Hamilton-Wentworth in 1974, a Regional Planning and Development Department carried out economic development planning on a regional scale, while Hamilton's City Planning Department continued to determine land use within the city limits. In practice, this did not substantially alter the direction of economic development, which always had a regional bent. It did mean, however, that the constituency for economic development expanded to include residents and business owners in Hamilton's suburbs. Tension quickly emerged between the business-focused policies and institutions pursued by the regional Economic Development Commission, the Chamber, and the mayor's office, and the more participatory and redistributionist activities of the City Planning Department and Hamilton's councilors. In one such instance, city councilor (and future mayor) Bob Morrow publicly rebuked Copps for what councilors interpreted as efforts on the part of the mayor's office to subvert local development controls. Copps had sent letters to Southern Ontario developers denouncing zoning controls under consideration in Toronto. He wrote that Hamilton needed "more new hotel, commercial and retail development in our downtown area, and I promise City Council's enthusiastic assistance to the developers who can fill this need." Morrow disavowed Copps's offer, angrily telling a reporter that "we have a planning process here that takes a great deal of time and citizen involvement and we have a process for downtown development."[84]

Growing enmity between local officials was compounded by tensions between the federal and provincial governments over urban and economic development. Before the 1970s, there had not been much serious conflict between provincial and federal officials. Ontario's policymakers generally trusted that the federal government would formulate economic and industrial policy favorable to Ontario, and they saw little reason to interfere in private sector activities. Officials instead focused on rationalizing the province's urban industrial system through Design for Development and regionalization.[85] The provincial government's disinclination to involve itself in economic planning or in the operations of Ontario's businesses helped create an economic culture, shared by government officials and corporate executives, which valued competition between companies more than cooperation through business associations. Because of the province's hands-off approach to business, Ontario's corporate interests did not develop strong advocacy organizations to represent sectoral interests in provincial policy debates.[86]

Ontario's traditional comparative advantages waned in the 1970s. As Canada's growth center shifted from Ontario and Quebec to the western provinces, the provincial government sought an increasingly interventionist role in the economy. By the middle of the decade, provincial officials recognized that the postwar growth boom had ended and that future industrial growth was a tenuous prospect. The quasi-public Ontario Economic Council (OEC), established in 1968 to raise public awareness about economic issues and staffed largely by businessmen and economists, called for "as much decentralization as possible" from the federal and provincial governments to the local level. The OEC also wanted the province to encourage private sector development through "structural changes" that would reduce the power of special interest groups, increase incentives for private investment, improve industrial relations, and introduce changes in the educational system to better match labor skills to employers' needs.[87] In response, Progressive Conservative Premier Bill Davis abandoned comprehensive planning and set out to improve the provincial business climate through strategic planning, a clear shift toward market-based development at the expense of socially inclined regional planning. With what federal officials described as "considerable vigor," the provincial government cut jobs, reduced health and social welfare expenditures, limited grants to municipalities, and reorganized its ministries to eliminate waste. Reduced provincial funding for municipal activities came with an admonishment that, if municipal governments wanted to increase spending, they would have to figure out how to raise the funds themselves.[88] For a city like Hamilton, which already struggled to attract and retain investment and fund its urban development programs, decentralization was an unsettling prospect.

As Ontario turned its focus to market-based economic development, provincial officials undermined the Trudeau administration's forays into policy areas historically and constitutionally considered the purview of the provinces and worked to eliminate DREE and MSUA. Conservatives had controlled Ontario's government since the end of World War II, and, faced with Trudeau's centralized planning initiatives, they had taken the position that urban development and land use planning were "purely a provincial prerogative." The only legitimate federal role in either arena, according to provincial officials, was to determine "basic criteria under which national programs will become available."[89] Progressive Conservative leaders undermined federal initiatives and introduced provincial policies intended to facilitate the decentralization of power back to the provinces and to regional governments, a practice that benefited cosmopolitan Toronto and its industrial suburbs more than it did gritty Hamilton.

MSUA staffers characterized Ontario's government as "rather hostile to Urban Affairs," and cautioned, "new approaches should be taken carefully using all available goodwill."[90] By the mid-1970s, however, provincial opposition had undermined the missions of DREE and MSUA. In 1976, downward revisions of population forecasts meant that an urban crisis no longer loomed. Most importantly, the aftershocks of the oil crisis and its reverberation through the North American economy pushed urban issues to the back burner, and in 1979 the federal government eliminated MSUA as part of its austerity measures under Progressive Conservative Joe Clark, who briefly replaced Trudeau when the Liberals lost control of the government for nine months.[91] DREE's days, too, were numbered. Over time, federal politicians became less enthusiastic about General Development Agreements (GDAs) because provincial governments received the majority of the credit, and the attendant political goodwill, for federally funded programs. Conflict over federal and regional strategies for economic development also played a role: federal officials outside DREE approached economic development from a sectoral perspective, while DREE's structure promoted regional economic development. At the same time that DREE became a political liability in Ottawa, the newly oil-rich western provinces and, to a lesser extent, the Atlantic provinces, gained economic importance and political power. Manufacturing industries in Ontario and Quebec faced harsh adjustments, but DREE's focus on growth centers and its market orientation led officials to direct funding away from troubled manufacturing centers, making DREE unpopular in the heartland.[92] Trudeau eliminated or reassigned DREE's functions to other agencies in 1982. The authorization for GDAs expired in 1983, and the federal government seized the opportunity to terminate provincial delivery of federally funded programs.[93]

When DREE and MSUA shifted course in the mid-1970s to facilitate provincially led development programs and as provincial officials became increasingly concerned with public-private cooperation, Hamilton's Chamber of Commerce began to insinuate itself more fully into local and regional development processes. In 1975, incoming president Bill Cooper expressed an interest in partnering with city officials for urban and economic development. Cooper, the president of an eponymous construction company, argued that businessmen needed a stronger voice in the regional marketplace. He lamented that the Chamber "doesn't really make anybody nervous in this city" and advocated for greater political visibility. "We ought be saying what should happen and what shouldn't have happened," Cooper insisted.[94]

Such was the state of affairs when, in 1976, Copps was forced into early retirement after he suffered a heart attack while running a road race. Copps's predecessor, Lloyd D. Jackson, had served for twelve years and Copps for thirteen; Copps's withdrawal from politics ushered in nearly a decade of political instability, with three mayors taking office between 1976 and 1982. The lack of strong mayoral leadership was compounded by Hamilton's municipal government structure. Hamilton had a Board of Control, a system unique to Ontario that created bifurcated governments for cities with populations greater than 100,000. The system divided Hamilton's municipal council into two sections: the Board of Control, composed of the mayor and four controllers elected on a citywide basis, and the City Council, composed of sixteen aldermen elected by ward. The Board of Control reported to the City Council, and its members' duties included preparing a budget, nominating and dismissing department heads and other appointed officials, awarding contracts, and monitoring the status of municipal projects. The City Council could reverse any decision or action proposed or undertaken by the Board of Control by a two-thirds majority vote. Because higher levels of government had more influence over the local economy than did the local government and because of the rapid turnover of mayors after Copps's retirement, planners noted in the late 1970s that municipal officials' role in directing growth patterns was "somewhat limited."[95]

Institutional impediments to municipal control over land use did not stop local officials from pursuing postindustrial redevelopment or trying to form a public-private partnership. In Hamilton, in contrast to Pittsburgh, public officials disagreed over what a post-steel future should look like. Two industrial studies released in 1977 reported that Hamilton's economy had decisively shifted toward service-oriented activities. The first, prepared by regional planners for the city of Hamilton, cautioned that city officials should not be too eager to divest from manufacturing. "For although the service economy appears the forerunner of the post industrial society," the planners wrote, "it is largely a function of the population it serves, together with certain provincial policies, and is thus dependent on the growth of the population within the city's service area. . . . Industrial activity on the other hand has an established market area beyond that of its service counterpart." In marked contrast to planners in Pittsburgh, Hamilton's regional planners privileged creating jobs for existing residents in a variety of economic sectors. "If we are to assume there is value in a diversity of socio-economic groups being able to use the city as a place of residence and employment," they argued, "then it is essential to provide as wide a range of jobs as is possible." They described the interests of the residential labor force as a primary concern and recommended that "53,350 manufacturing positions must be made available for those persons who wish to reside and work in the City of Hamilton."[96]

In a second report, Toronto-based management consultants Woods, Gordon & Co. offered different recommendations to the regional government. The consultants cautioned that "surveys, analysis and forecasts" did not "bode well for employment opportunities in Hamilton-Wentworth." While they anticipated that Hamilton could remain a major center of steel production for the next fifteen years, the consultants warned regional officials that they could not "look to steel as the generator of substantial new jobs." Instead, they concluded, Hamilton "must look immediately to new manufacturing industries, major retail functions and especially the services sector for the expansion of employment opportunities in the future." As Arthur D. Little and Company had done almost a decade earlier, the consultants urged regional officials to secure "active participation" from the province and the local business community. Public-private cooperation, they suggested, might involve "management training, specially designated downtown redevelopment areas," and "municipal or joint venture industrial parks."[97]

A year after the industrial studies were released, Hamilton's long-desired public-private partnership finally emerged in the form of the Central Area Plan Advisory Committee (CAPAC). CAPAC included representatives from the Chamber, the Real Estate Board, the Downtown Association, the Home Builders Association, the Labor Council, the Social Planning and Research Council, and homeowners' associations, as well as businessmen and ward politicians, who came together at the behest of the City Planning Department to "co-ordinate public and private actions for the growth of downtown Hamilton."[98] Hamilton's weak political leadership, combined with the Chamber's new political advocacy, meant that the latter's influence over local politics had increased substantially by the time CAPAC formed. CAPAC was Hamilton's first formal vehicle for public-private cooperation for urban redevelopment, and the downtown development study undertaken by its members represented the first instance in which Hamilton's growth coalition adopted, at least rhetorically, the model of providing public incentives for private development long institutionalized in U.S. cities. But in contrast to the growth partnerships that had taken shape in New York City and Pittsburgh, CAPAC was an ad hoc partnership with no power to institute the reforms it recommended.

CAPAC urged the city government to find a way to incentivize private redevelopment. "Along with the considerable public investment in the downtown," its members argued, "it would appear that additional incentives are now required to attract a comparable amount of private interest. Private investment cannot be attracted to an area simply by designating lands for the desired use in land use plans."[99] In concert with planners from the Regional Planning and Development Department, CAPAC members produced a plan that echoed the Lunchpail Report's recommendation that the city promote downtown Hamilton as a regional center. CAPAC envisioned downtown as a "multi-use node" with a variety of permitted land uses that emphasized "a unique and attractive environment with a high order of amenity and design" and separated auto and pedestrian traffic. The plan was "based on the understanding that indirect inducements and incentives to private investors and

consumers (and the resulting decisions, investments and consumption patterns) are often far more powerful than providing direct government services." CAPAC's recommendations were impossible to implement at the local
level under the existing structure of intergovernmental relations in Ontario,
suggesting that CAPAC looked to redevelopment models that the group saw
as successful outside of Ontario, and most likely in the United States, without substantial concern for local political constraints.[100] Hamilton had finally
approximated Pittsburgh's public-private partnership, but it operated in an
institutional and legal environment that prevented city officials from implementing recommendations that would make Hamilton more like Pittsburgh.

By the end of the decade, Pittsburgh and Hamilton were in similar circumstances. A widely read 1979 *Washington Post* article classified both cities
as part of North America's distressed "Foundry" region, a vast expanse that
stretched from New York to Milwaukee with the Great Lakes at its center.[101]
The oil crisis and the collapse of the Bretton Woods system had produced
spiraling inflation and high levels of unemployment throughout the North
Atlantic in the 1970s. In the United States, Canada, and much of Western
Europe, stagflation intensified conflicts between labor's demands for full
employment and management's desire for increased profits, conflicts that
were particularly intense in struggling manufacturing centers. Hamilton's
steel producers weathered the storm better than those in the Pittsburgh
region, but, by the 1980s, both local economies struggled more than they had
in the boom times of the 1950s and 1960s.

Relatively prosperous steel centers in privileged regions at the beginning
of the 1970s, on the cusp of the 1980s, Pittsburgh and Hamilton were disadvantaged under U.S. and Canadian federal policies that funneled resources
to the Sunbelt and western provinces. In a November 1980 press conference
that echoed local executives' comments to the *New York Times* nearly ten
years earlier, Caliguiri tried to spin Pittsburgh's population loss—18 percent
over the previous decade and nearly 25 percent over the city's 1960 high—as
a boon to redevelopment plans predicated on attracting middle-class residents. He assured listeners that "we certainly don't need 700,000 residents
in Pittsburgh as we had in 1970." More to the point, he told reporters, he
would "rather have less people with high incomes than more people with
relatively low earning and spending power," a particularly callous expression
of his preference for creating white- over blue-collar jobs.[102] Hamilton's public
officials, too, talked openly about a post-steel era: "We have got to diversify
our economic base, we can't continue to rely on the steel industries," Regional
Economic Development Director John Morand told the *Hamilton Spectator*

in 1980. "We have to become a full regional center." Morand assured Hamiltonians that the regional government was dedicated to changing Hamilton's position in Southern Ontario, stating, "there is a perception now that this community is on the move."[103] Elected officials and civic leaders entered the next decade publicly optimistic in the face of uncertainty. As would become manifestly clear as the economic situations in both cities worsened in the 1980s, Hamilton's policymakers thought more pluralistically than Pittsburgh's about whose interests to serve in a swiftly neoliberalizing environment.

CHAPTER THREE

Postindustrialism and Its Critics

Pittsburgh and Hamilton public officials entered the 1980s full of bravado, boasting about redevelopment projects and hopeful that economic diversification would temper the effects of steel's decline. In Pittsburgh, however, steelworkers doubted that a second Renaissance offered a real solution to the region's problems. In 1981, a group of disaffected labor activists issued a "counter annual report" for the U.S. Steel Corporation. In it, they urged Pittsburgh-area workers not to believe corporate press releases designed to convince them their employers were upgrading plants and equipment. "The facts are that production is contracting, jobs are shrinking and some of the great steel mills of the Mon Valley are nearing the same fate visited last year on Youngstown and fifteen other cities across America," the activists contended. "The press releases are intended to help the company avoid the moral questions about the human tragedy its policies are compounding." The group hoped to jolt rank-and-file steelworkers out of complacency and shake workers' confidence in the increasingly accommodationist United Steelworkers. Citing Department of Labor predictions that new positions created in the 1980s would "predominantly employ secretaries, stenographers, retail sales clerks, building custodians, cashiers, and bookkeepers," activists warned Pittsburgh's manufacturing workers that new service-sector jobs would "pay half as much as the old factory jobs now disappearing." A toddler holding a lunch pail peered forlornly from the cover of the "counter" annual report. "Will he have a future in the Mon Valley?" activists asked.[1] By January 1983, the answer was a resounding "no": that month, 212,000 of the region's workers were unemployed.[2]

Between 1979 and 1988, the Pittsburgh region lost 44 percent of its manufacturing jobs.[3] Beginning in 1973 and peaking (in North America) in 1982, the basic steel industry experienced a series of crises of global overproduction.[4]

The U.S. government's unwillingness to introduce new import restrictions or to enforce existing ones, combined with domestic producers' disinvestment in their older facilities and diversification into non-productive lines, led to a functional collapse of integrated steel production. Major producers permanently shuttered mills in traditional steel-making regions, such as Pittsburgh, Youngstown, and Chicago. U.S. Steel, the Pittsburgh region's single largest employer, cut its labor force by 42.5 percent nationally and by 66 percent in the region between 1979 and 1983. Internationally, United Steelworkers membership fell from 1.35 million in 1979 to 750,000 in 1983, with half those losses in 1982 alone.[5]

In Canada, government import restrictions, workforce reductions, and capital investment allowed the steel industry to weather the sectoral crisis. As labor activists in Pittsburgh became increasingly frustrated by United Steelworkers concessions and rank-and-file apathy in the 1980s, workers in Hamilton walked off the job. Stelco employees won 50 percent wage and benefit increases after a bitter 125-day 1981 strike. The Canadian steel industry largely avoided the cycles of over-production and under-consumption endemic to global steel production, and to the U.S. steel industry in particular, between the end of World War II and the 1981 recession. In Canada more than that in the United States, companies produced steel for domestic consumption, which, combined with high tariffs, created a secure market. Canadian steel producers were the first in North America to introduce basic oxygen furnaces and continuous casters, the two most important technological innovations in steel production in the second half of the twentieth century. As Pittsburgh producers shuttered mills, Hamilton-based steelmakers Stelco and Dofasco actually increased employment between 1974 and 1980. Despite Canadian government intervention through import regulation, the effects of the steel crisis finally hit Hamilton between 1983 and 1986, when domestic demand was not high enough to offset losses from sluggish exports.[6] In response to the 1981 strike and what Canadian workers derisively called the "Reagan recession," Stelco slashed its workforce by nearly half over the course of the decade, all while producing records levels of steel.[7]

The local manifestations of the international steel crisis made Pittsburgh and Hamilton's growth coalitions even more determined to hasten a postindustrial transition—to diversify their local economies, attract more white-collar jobs, and remake urban space for new uses. They did so with less financial support from their respective federal governments than had been on offer in the 1970s. Decentralization strategies initiated under the Nixon, Carter, and Trudeau administrations had been harbingers of national government retrenchment to come throughout the North Atlantic. In European nations with strong centralized states, particularly France, Italy, Spain, and Belgium, decentralization was intended to reduce social and economic tensions within metropolitan areas. Decentralization became a major political issue in the UK and Canada, as Scotland, Wales, and Quebec demanded greater autonomy from their central states. In France, among the most centralized states in the world, François Mitterrand dramatically expanded the authority of subnational governments in one of his earliest pieces of legislation.[8]

As neoliberal ideology gained influence among a new generation of conservative and centrist political leaders, public policies that had decentralized and privatized urban development in the 1970s were folded into an ascendant neoliberal political project on both sides of the Atlantic. In the United States and Canada, national debates about the relationship between different levels of government became tangled up with a decisive shift to devolutionary, free-market urban development tactics. To various degrees in different cities and diverse national contexts, once-prosperous manufacturing centers were politically and economically marginalized.[9] In the North American manufacturing belt, unemployment rates soared in the 1980s. Factory jobs were no longer a likely route to the middle class for most Americans, and it appeared increasingly improbable that jobs in heavy industry would continue to provide social mobility for Canadians. As the decade wore on, the fate of the Great Lakes region was echoed in European industrial areas, such as the English Midlands, the German Ruhr, and northeast France. The opening paragraph of a 1983 *New York Times* article about French steel town Longwy might have described Southwestern Pennsylvania or the Ruhrgebeit: "In the valley, the carcass of an abandoned steel mill. On the slopes above, row houses, the color of mud," began the elegy to thirty miles of "rusting" factories in Lorraine along the Belgian border.[10]

At the national and metropolitan scale, postindustrialism became inextricably bound up with urban citizenship. Urban growth coalitions recognized that, in the emerging Rust Belt, physical redevelopment was linked to the fortunes of basic industry. In manufacturing centers in the throes of a postindustrial rebirth, like Pittsburgh and Hamilton, growth coalitions made hard choices about whose interests they intended to serve. They did so with little apparent anguish over the social costs to those neighborhoods and populations that did not receive increasingly scarce resources. In Pittsburgh, the city's growth partnership was desperate to attract middle-class residents and white-collar jobs. Caliguiri and his private-sector partners overcame resistance to redevelopment plans from labor activists and cooperatively undertook large-scale projects designed to meet the needs of new, rather than existing, residents. In Hamilton, elected officials struggled in their persistent efforts to form a durable partnership with local business leaders. Rifts within Hamilton's growth coalition meant that, far more than in Pittsburgh, public officials continued to treat all residents as citizens with a right to a voice in the future of the city.

Federal Retrenchment

In the 1980s, postindustrialism became a guiding tenet of national urban policy on both sides of the Atlantic. In the United States and Canada, the last days of the Carter and Trudeau administrations pointed the way. Carter and Trudeau appointed independent commissions to advise them on public policy challenges for the decade ahead. The final reports of both commissions endorsed market orthodoxy, increased decentralization, and privatization. The reports provided political cover for neoliberal policies instituted by Carter's and Trudeau's successors as part of an emerging North Atlantic political project, which had dire consequences for declining manufacturing centers. As Ronald Reagan and Brian Mulroney, to different degrees, eliminated or devolved social programs and put their faith in the "natural" operations of the market, entrepreneurial public-private partnerships in cities like Pittsburgh reconfigured urban space for the white-collar workers they hoped to attract. In places like Hamilton, where social democratic impulses still held sway, postindustrial redevelopment plans stalled as city officials tried to balance the competing demands of business and residents.

Carter convened his Presidential Commission for a National Agenda for the Eighties in October 1979. Chaired by Bronx-born former Columbia University president William McGill, who had recently retired to California, the Agenda for the Eighties on the whole proved profoundly anti-urban and encouraged sectarian divides in the name of a healthy national economy. McGill established nine thematic panels, including one on "policies and prospects for metropolitan and non-metropolitan America." Agricultural economist Charles Bishop chaired the subcommittee created to study "Urban America in the Eighties," a panel that also included League of Women Voters president Ruth J. Hinerfeld; CEOs Frank Pace, Jr., and Robert S. Benson; and University of Chicago urban policy professor Pastora San Juan Cafferty. All the commissioners except Cafferty held MBAs and had long corporate resumes.[11]

The panel's report, *Urban America in the Eighties: Perspectives and Prospects*, drew on Daniel Bell's research to welcome the coming of postindustrialism and toll the death knell of the industrial North. The United States, Bishop's urban panel determined, was "on a trajectory toward an increasingly consumer-oriented, post-industrial society where employment growth rates in service sectors are higher than those in the manufacturing sectors." The urban future lay not in old industrial centers, ravaged by decades of systematic plant closures and disinvestment, the report stated, but in the "new" cities of the South and Southwest. The "industrial heartland"—Pittsburgh and cities like it—had reached maturity in the early twentieth century and, in 1981, represented nothing more than "bricks-and-mortar snapshots of a bygone era." Northeastern and midwestern manufacturing centers had been damaged beyond repair by industrial restructuring, racial violence, and fiscal crises, the panelists determined, and the only practical course of action was to make labor as mobile as capital and encourage workers to follow industry as it relocated to more "geographically desirable" areas. The urban panel urged the federal government to create programs that encouraged rather than resisted the "transformation" of the national economy from manufacturing to service- and finance-sector employment.[12]

Given Bishop's background, it was no surprise that the panel he directed recommended increasing federal subsidies to the South and Southwest while reducing infrastructure and public services in distressed northern and midwestern cities. When McGill appointed him in 1979, Bishop was at the end of his tenure as president of the University of Arkansas. By 1981, when McGill presented the commission's findings to Carter, Bishop had taken over as chancellor of the University of Houston. Born in rural South Carolina, he attended college in rural Kentucky and earned a master's degree at the University of Kentucky. In 1952, he received his doctorate in economics at the University of Chicago, where he completed a dissertation on agricultural labor in the southeastern United States. Bishop had a long history of serving on federal advisory committees, though previous stints, including executive director of Lyndon Johnson's National Advisory Commission on Rural Poverty and Richard Nixon's Food Advisory Council and White House Task Force on Rural Development, bore some relationship to his area of academic experience. Bishop had also served on Carter's Advisory Commission for the White House Conference on Balanced Growth and Economic Development, which influenced the direction of Carter's national urban policy, a position that might have made McGill and Carter think an expert on rural agriculture was suited to the task of heading an investigative panel on urban issues.[13]

The urban panel's focus on moving people to jobs in booming regions and out of manufacturing centers like Pittsburgh, Detroit, and Newark found some support in the Carter administration, but academics and state and local officials in the Northeast and Midwest lambasted the report and its authors. A representative for the more than two-hundred-member, bipartisan Northeast-Midwest Congressional Coalition charged that federal policies already unduly privileged Sunbelt states. New York deputy mayor Nathan Leventhal told the *New York Times* that Mayor Ed Koch's reaction to the report was "unprintable." Leventhal, more measured than Koch, called the report's recommendations "dumb" and destructive. "It all reminds me of the last scene of 'Fiddler on the Roof,'" he joked. "Perhaps the McGill Commission expects us all to get together, pack our goods, and get out of town in three days."[14] Carter, all but out of office by the time McGill delivered the final report on December 31, 1980, immediately tried to distance himself from the recommendations of the commission he had appointed two years earlier. He thanked the commissioners for their service but chided, "We cannot abandon our older urban areas."[15]

Due to the report's timing and the Reagan administration's subsequent embrace of the spirit, if not the letter, of the McGill Commission's recommendations, Reagan has been credited with (or blamed for) much of the policy that explicitly or implicitly developed out of the report. Nixon and Carter had pragmatically reoriented national urban policy toward privatization and devolution. In doing so, they created a foundation for Reagan's more ideologically driven version of New Federalism, which contracted the welfare state, changed federal tax policy to favor large corporations over small businesses and the more affluent over the disadvantaged, further decentralized federal programs, and reduced federal regulation of business. Reagan also mounted an attack on federal urban programs as part of his devolutionary agenda.

Reagan appointed New York City attorney Samuel Pierce as secretary of housing and urban development. Pierce, the only African American member of Reagan's cabinet, was so peripheral to the administration that Reagan failed to recognize him at a 1981 luncheon for the U.S. Conference of Mayors. Reagan marginalized the agency along with its director. He parked his least-favored political appointees at HUD, where they plundered low- and moderate-income housing programs. The agency budget dropped from more than $30 billion in 1980 to around $10 billion in 1988, HUD eliminated staff and programs, and its leadership became embroiled in scandals.[16]

Sidelining HUD was only one step in Reagan's attack on federal urban development programs. As expediently as possible, Reagan eliminated

Nixon's popular general revenue sharing program and Carter's Urban Development Action Grants. Block grants, on the other hand, were of paramount significance for the Reagan administration. Reagan's Omnibus Budget Reconciliation Act of 1981 eased federal restrictions on education and urban programs and established or revised nine block grants for public health, social services, education, and community development. Under Reagan, block grant funds were allocated to state governments with virtually no federal oversight. Unlike Nixon, Reagan did not buy support for block grants by making them hold harmless. Instead, he cut the budget for programs consolidated under the Budget Act by an average of 25 percent. State government officials, who had long lobbied for a more central role in the federal aid system, were tentative in their support because their increased autonomy came with reduced funding. New regulations for community development block grants shifted funds away from the neediest communities. Local governments were decidedly unenthusiastic, fearing that state, rather than municipal, governments would control the limited federal funds that remained.[17] Between 1980 and 1985, aid to cities like Pittsburgh, which the federal government classified as "distressed," fell by 18 percent, while aid increased by 23 percent in "healthy" areas.[18]

The Reagan administration also threw its support behind legislation for Enterprise Zones, modeled after a similar program Margaret Thatcher had introduced in Britain in 1979. Enterprise Zones required no federal appropriations, and Reagan described them as "the direct opposite" of liberal social programs like Model Cities, which relied heavily on federal subsidies to distressed cities. "The Enterprise Zone concept is based on utilizing the market to solve urban problems, relying primarily on private sector institutions," Reagan noted in a message to Congress. "The idea is to create a productive, free market environment in economically depressed areas by reducing taxes, regulations and other government burdens on economic activity."[19] The proposal Reagan supported never made it out of committee, but, by 1985, at least forty states had implemented enterprise zone legislation—Pennsylvania enacted one in 1983—in anticipation that Reagan would succeed in pushing through a federal version. In the wake of the Enterprise Zone failure, Reagan pursued no new federal urban or economic development programs for the remainder of his presidency. Reagan's de facto urban policy became economic development through public subsidies for private investment.[20] For most cities in the emerging Rust Belt, the shift was disastrous. Pittsburgh, like its regional neighbors, suffered from funding reductions, but its growth coalition had already established the institutional capacity for entrepreneurial urban development and was well positioned to respond to the new federal environment.

When Reagan's sweeping Budget Act made it through Congress, Trudeau was a year into his second round as prime minister. The political climate in Canada had shifted since the heady early days of his first term, in part in response to the elections of Reagan and Thatcher. Trudeau's attempts at centralization in the 1970s had strained the relationship between federal and provincial officials; by the early 1980s, his goals for national economic planning made Keynesian tactics (and Trudeau's leadership) seem untenable to Canada's business leaders. The Canadian government, in contrast to the U.S. government, had expanded its political autonomy from business interests in the 1960s and 1970s. While business associations' views were given special weight in formulating macroeconomic policy, federal and provincial officials otherwise treated business as one among many competing interests.[21] In the United States, national business associations and conservative think tanks such as the Chamber of Commerce, the National Association of Manufacturers, the National Bankers' Association, and the Business Roundtable, had mounted a sustained attack against Keynesian policies by the early 1970s.[22] Compared to their counterparts in the United States, Canadian business interests more readily accepted the mixed economy of the postwar period and, from the 1950s to the mid-1980s only sporadically resisted federal officials' efforts to regulate business activities.[23] Small business owners were more politically powerful in Canada than in the United States because small business associations often had a disproportionate influence on local and provincial elections. And while Canadian chambers of commerce could be quite conservative, their constituent members were far more politically and economically heterogeneous than the corporate elite who most directly influenced U.S. public policy in the second half of the twentieth century.[24]

By the early 1980s, however, Canadian corporations had established themselves as multinational firms, Canadian direct investment abroad was far more significant than it had been in previous decades, and Canadian manufacturers began to increase exports to the United States and elsewhere. Trudeau's interventionist strategies had encouraged the formation of the Business Council on National Issues (BCNI) in 1975. The BCNI, modeled after the Business Roundtable in the United States, promoted pro-business, pro-free trade policies. Faced with a sluggish economy, the Canadian Manufacturing Association endorsed free trade and trade liberalization (a reversal of its position in earlier decades), and the BCNI more assertively promoted laissez-faire economic policies.[25] Canadian business leaders accused federal officials of overregulation, incompetence, and insensitivity to the competitive pressures facing Canadian business in the 1980s. In turn, many public officials saw corporate concerns about the size and scope of government as out of sync with public sentiment and Canada's liberal political culture.[26]

Under these circumstances, midway through his short second tenure, Trudeau in 1982 established a Royal Commission on the Economic Union and Development Prospects for Canada, popularly known as the Macdonald Commission after its chair, Donald Macdonald. Macdonald's appointment was likely intended to help mend Trudeau's troubled relationship with Canadian and U.S. business interests. Macdonald, as a young Liberal MP from Toronto, had joined Trudeau's cabinet in 1968 as a policy advisor and subsequently served as minister of national defense, minister of energy, and minister of finance, where he introduced interventionist economic development policies. Macdonald left Trudeau's government to resume his law practice in 1977, returning to public service when Trudeau tapped him to chair the Royal Commission in 1982. In the intervening years, Macdonald came to believe that Trudeau's interventionist policies had failed to grow the Canadian economy. By the time Macdonald assumed the chairmanship, he had sat on the boards of several of Canada's most powerful domestic and U.S.-owned corporations, including the Alberta Energy Corporation, Dupont Canada, and McDonnell Douglass Canada. He was also a member of the C. D. Howe Institute, a Toronto-based think tank that, by the 1970s, aggressively promoted free markets, free trade, and reduced federal intervention in the economy. As chairman of the Royal Commission, Macdonald advocated for policies that advanced free trade, opened markets, and ended government subsidies for industry.[27]

Trudeau appointed to the Royal Commission twelve members from business, labor, the cooperative movement, public servants, all three national political parties, and the legal and academic professions. The commissioners were chosen to represent ideological, sectional, and linguistic differences. Their public hearings and briefs solicited the ideas of a diverse group of Canadians, but the commission's final recommendations reflected Macdonald's own conservative and corporatist views. Over its three years of activity, the Macdonald Commission held two rounds of public hearings across Canada and undertook extensive policy research, ultimately producing a three-volume final report with seventy-two volumes of supporting materials. The exercise exposed growing polarization in Canadian society between state-centered nationalism, supported by "social interests"—organized labor, churches, women's groups, social service agencies, Native peoples, farmers and advocacy organizations—and continentalism, supported by "economic interests" represented by a substantial but not unanimous portion of the business community. Yet in stark contrast to the assault on the welfare state from business in the United States, few Canadian business leaders wanted to dismantle Canada's safety net, and those who took that position were poorly organized. Representatives of the corporate sector were themselves divided over issues of welfare provision and federal intervention in economic development.[28]

In Canada, as in the United States, geographic mobility became a flash-point for the conflict between regional interests and sectoral concerns. Business representatives from central and western Canada argued that people should be "encouraged to go where there is productive and efficient work for them" and that education, job retraining, and pension reform should be directed toward encouraging mobility rather than toward shoring up troubled regions. Representatives from single-industry towns, particularly in the depressed Atlantic provinces, rejected the notion that people should be forced from their homes and communities to secure employment. Supporters of local development for local residents allied themselves with union leaders to demand corporate responsibility to cities and regions, espousing everything from a vague notion that business should be held accountable to communities to the more specific proposal by the United Steelworkers that corporations should shoulder the cost of retraining laid-off employees.[29] Far more than was the case in similar U.S. policy debates, Canadians treated workers as citizens with rights to employment who should be able to remain where they lived if they so chose. In Hamilton, public officials followed suit, seeking to balance the needs of all residents, rather than narrowly construe which groups mattered in urban and economic development plans.

Despite substantial popular support for social democratic programs, the Macdonald Commission recommended a reversal of what had been, decades earlier, the foundational assumption at the center of both the welfare state and the Canadian planning profession: that government oversight of and intervention in the market served the public interest. Taken together with the abolishment of DREE and MSUA and with the larger implications of the Macdonald Commission report (in particular, free trade with the United States), the commissioners' conclusion that urban and economic development were best conducted at the local level, with individual initiative and a greater reliance on market forces as an equalizing mechanism, was a regional variation on the broad shift from state-centered, interventionist Keynesian economic policies to business-friendly, deregulationist policies underway in

North Atlantic nations. For troubled manufacturing centers, the recommendations were not good news.

When Progressive Conservative Brian Mulroney replaced Trudeau in 1984, he used the popular consensus implied by the Macdonald Commission's recommendations to legitimate his endorsement of sectoral free trade, to initiate trade negotiations with the United States, to cap federal transfer payments to provincial governments, and to begin financial liberalization.[30] Mulroney, like Trudeau, hailed from Quebec. The child of Irish immigrants and a lawyer by training, Mulroney stepped down as president of the Canadian Iron Ore Corporation to become prime minister of a nation still struggling to recover from a recession and facing a fiscal crisis caused by increased national debt.[31] Mulroney came to power promising an end to federal intrusions into provincial jurisdictions and a renewed commitment to decentralization; a reduced role for the state in the Canadian economy through fiscal restraint, spending cuts, and public services reductions; and limited privatization and deregulation.[32] While the general contours of Mulroney's agenda reflected Reagan's and Thatcher's influence, Mulroney did not share their determination to roll back the welfare state, which he described as a "sacred trust" that he would not violate.[33] Mulroney did share Reagan's and Thatcher's views on the relationship between business and the state. With U.S. executives in mind, Mulroney pronounced Canada "open for business" in 1984. He told nearly 1,500 U.S. businessmen at the Economic Club of New York that the role of his government was to "assist and not to harass the private sector in creating new wealth and the new jobs that Canada needs."[34]

As had been the case with U.S. state governments a decade earlier, decentralization under Mulroney came as a response to provincial discontent more than to fealty to neoliberal economic ideas. Provincial officials pressed for more control over certain policy areas, such as economic development, without anticipating or desiring the eventual outcome—federal funding cuts and the devolution of social services to the provinces. In Ontario, the Chamber of Commerce successfully lobbied the provincial government for regulatory reforms and praised provincial officials for "on-going efforts to ensure the lessening of regulatory burdens."[35] Pressure from the Chamber and other business organizations led the provincial government to pursue an increasingly market-oriented approach to urban and economic policy. Mulroney initially tried to insulate the provinces from the effects of the federal government's deficit-reduction schemes. After 1988, however, he restrained equalization payments and reduced the federal contribution toward social welfare programs in the wealthier provinces.[36]

Mulroney's policy shift reflected the economic and political realities of the late 1980s and early 1990s—recession, debt crisis, and devolution. Liberal provincial officials unsuccessfully attacked Mulroney's trade and monetary policies, as well as proposed changes to the intergovernmental financing of social programs.[37] By the end of the decade, Canada's political culture and public policies had become more like those in the United States. Canadian cities, too, became more entrepreneurial in the 1980s. Without the kind of public-private cooperation that allowed Pittsburgh to compete successfully for jobs and residents, Hamilton, with a growing population and declining manufacturing jobs, struggled to achieve its postindustrial ambitions in Canada's shifting political climate. On the ground in Pittsburgh and Hamilton, federal retrenchment created very different circumstances for workers, activists, and the growth coalitions who struggled for control of each city's future.

"Choices for Pennsylvanians"

Record unemployment rates in the Mon Valley, combined with deep cuts to federal funding for urban development and social services, made Ronald Reagan's April 1983 visit to Pittsburgh an uncomfortable affair. Testing the waters for his reelection campaign, Reagan went to Pittsburgh to attend a conference on displaced workers. More than 4,000 protestors waited to greet him in pouring rain outside the downtown Hilton. The protestors were mostly white and working class, but newspapers reported that an "unusually large and vocal" number of African Americans and women had turned out.[38] Mel Packer, an organizer with the Mon Valley Unemployed Committee, the group that coordinated the rally, attacked Reagan and the corporate leaders attending the conference inside the Hilton. "They're in there eating their steak and lobster, talking about us when they should be talking to us," he roared. "We're the displaced workers." Even the United Steelworkers, originally set to sponsor the conference Reagan had come to attend, withdrew its support and sent its representatives to the protest instead. The increasingly accomodationist steelworkers' union had just negotiated $29 billion in contract concessions with the major steel producers, and its leaders were furious that Reagan planned to buy imported steel from Britain. Reagan's advisors quickly determined that they would not send the president into another economically distressed manufacturing center until unemployment rates improved.[39]

The disastrous trip was Reagan's first to Pittsburgh since his 1979 campaign. By the time Reagan took office in January 1981, the writing was on the wall for Pittsburgh's steel industry. U.S. Steel chairman David Roderick proclaimed that his company, once the largest steel producer in the world, "was not in the business of making steel. It was in the business of making profits."[40] Between 1976 and 1979, U.S. Steel's non-steel assets grew by 80 percent. In 1979, the year of the first round of major layoffs in Pittsburgh, the company's realty division opened a joint-venture mall in the Pittsburgh suburbs and signed a letter of intent to build a chemical facility in Houston.[41] Shortly after successfully lobbying Congress for changes to the Clean Air Act and the federal tax code, Roderick announced in November 1981 that U.S. Steel had acquired Marathon Oil for $6 billion. A year later, he determined his company would only invest in projects with an annual profit rate of 20 percent or better; the steel industry had averaged below 7 percent annually in the 1970s. By 1984, steel production represented only one-third of U.S. Steel assets.[42] "Of course when I was Chairman, we got ready," Roderick recalled. "We took all the capital money we had and directed it to our most efficient mills. The mills that were very, very old; both in product and technology, we starved them in capital. . . . Because you knew they were never going to be competitive." He had undercapitalized Pittsburgh's steel mills in an effort to protect U.S. Steel's other assets, because he "knew the day was coming, big time!! And it did. It did. It did come big time."[43]

As U.S. Steel and other domestic producers diversified their assets, Pittsburgh's major banks moved their money out of the U.S. steel industry and invested instead in steel production abroad.[44] The region's labor activists castigated Mellon Bank, in particular, for overseas investment practices dating to the 1960s that directly and indirectly subsidized foreign steel producers. "While U.S. Steel Chairman David M. Roderick was publicly complaining that he could not get the capital to modernize Mon Valley mills because bank interest rates were too exorbitant," charged union officials from the Homestead United Steelworkers local, "Mellon Bank was investing $50 million in Kobe Steel of Japan and $50 million more in China Steel of Taiwan."[45] Mellon CEO J. David Barnes defended as sound business practice decisions that undercut the region's steel industry, such as purchasing one of Homestead-based Mesta Machine's Japanese competitors, which then underbid Mesta on a lucrative contract to supply a continuous caster to U.S. Steel.[46]

Executives like Roderick and Barnes may have anticipated what was in store for Pittsburgh's steel industry, but, for former Pittsburgh city planning director Morton Coleman and city officials like him throughout North Atlantic manufacturing centers, the decline of basic industry was simultaneously long awaited and unimaginable. "There were other forces at work, that none of us really did much about, and that was we knew that steel was on its way out," Coleman remembered. "We knew that a long time ago, and nobody really did much about it." Two decades after Pittsburgh's mills shut down, Coleman lamented, "you pretty well know when U.S. Steel buys an oil company that they're thinking about doing stuff, and you know, David Roderick was somebody that was close to the political processes of the city. But you may not have been able to do anything. I don't know. . . . At least we wouldn't have had the shock. We could have had some preparation for it."[47]

But of course political and civic leaders had tried to prepare, though perhaps not in the way Coleman, in hindsight, might have chosen. As elected officials in Pittsburgh and their allies in the state government and the private sector faced the coming industrial crisis, the city's growth partnership chose to encourage rather than resist a transition from industrial to postindustrial society in an effort to save the city. When Pittsburgh Republican Richard Thornburgh beat popular Democratic nominee Pete Flaherty to become governor of Pennsylvania in 1979, he faced many of the same problems on a state level that Caliguiri inherited from Flaherty locally. Pennsylvania had lost nearly 200,000 manufacturing jobs between 1969 and 1979, and Thornburgh came to office deeply worried about short- and long-term revenue generation.[48] The Thornburgh administration premised its response to the state's economic problems on the assumption that national and international "economic forces and conditions" beyond the governor's control guided the state's economy. Like Reagan, Thornburgh held that private sector decisions to invest, expand, or relocate—rather than government intervention—would ultimately determine whether Pennsylvania experienced economic growth.[49]

Thornburgh's victory over Flaherty in a heavily Democratic state was something of an upset. He had beaten prominent Philadelphian Arlen Specter in the Republican primary and campaigned on a platform of clean government and fiscal austerity. In much the same way that Flaherty's activities as mayor of Pittsburgh prefigured Carter's political strategies, Thornburgh's decision to court the state's disaffected Democrats—particularly African Americans and union members—anticipated Reagan's 1980 campaign strategy. Thornburgh also came to office with an undergraduate degree in engineering from Yale and predilection for "knowledge economies" that suggested more than passing familiarity with Bell's post-industrial society thesis.[50]

In his eight years in office, Thornburgh reoriented Pennsylvania's job creation strategy away from "smokestack chasing," a term his advisors invoked derisively to describe interstate competition for heavy industry, toward small businesses and "entrepreneurial" economic development focused on

advanced technology.[51] His initiatives built on local economic diversification strategies long underway in the state's two largest cities, Philadelphia
and Pittsburgh. Thornburgh changed the corporate tax structure to make
the state more appealing to new and existing businesses, established regional
seed capital funds and business incubators, and leveraged the public employees' pension fund for venture capital.[52] His administration opened offices
abroad in an effort to attract foreign investment to Pennsylvania and revised
state banking laws to allow the state's banks to expand beyond their existing
regions.[53] Thornburgh created a Small Business Action Center and quadru-
pled funding for the Pennsylvania Industrial Development Authority with
the goal of attracting new employers. He also developed a largely unsuccessful job training program, unveiled a tourism initiative, and earmarked $20
billion for infrastructure improvements.[54]

In 1981, the Thornburgh administration released its strategic plan for economic recovery, "Choices for Pennsylvanians." "Choices" formed the foundation of a statewide strategy to improve the business climate, modernize heavy
industry, attract advanced technology, provide job training, make infrastructure improvements, and promote Pennsylvania's "quality of life" to attract new
residents and businesses. Employing the same rhetoric as national urban and
economic development policy, "Choices" promoted decentralization, greater
private-sector involvement in areas traditionally considered the purview of
the federal or local governments, and an increased state role in economic
development.[55] Pittsburgh's growth coalition was particularly receptive to
Thornburgh's strategic planning framework because the city already had a
host of institutions in place to capitalize on the redirection of state and federal funds to public-private partnerships, universities, and community development organizations.

Like their counterparts in many financially strapped states with declining basic industry, Pennsylvania's economic development officials sought
to recreate the perceived conditions for the success of advanced technology
industries in Silicon Valley, Route 128 outside Boston, and North Carolina's
Research Triangle. In 1982, Thornburgh created the Ben Franklin Partnership
(BFP), which brought together state agencies, private industry, and Pennsylvania's research universities to leverage public funds for advanced technology research and development.[56] The BFP established four regional advanced
technology centers through consortiums of research universities, corporations, and economic development organizations, including one in Pittsburgh. The University of Pittsburgh and Carnegie Mellon jointly operated
the Western Pennsylvania Advanced Technology Center, which engaged in

research and technology transfers and nurtured the expansion of advanced technology throughout the region. The BFP cannily differentiated between advanced technology and high technology, interpreting the latter as developing new technological products, while the former included research on how to apply new technology to older production processes. By defining the activities the BFP supported as advanced rather than high technology, the Thornburgh administration spun the new initiative as a solution to the problems facing Pennsylvania's manufacturing sector.[57] When Thornburgh left office, he claimed credit for 500,000 new jobs statewide, most in services and technology.[58]

Thornburgh's investment in advanced technology aligned well with Caliguiri's vision for postindustrial Pittsburgh. In 1969, city planners had described Pittsburgh as "a city of projects in search of plan."[59] By the time Thornburgh issued "Choices," that was no longer the case. During Renaissance II, Caliguiri expanded the postindustrial redevelopment projects begun in a more piecemeal fashion under Flaherty. He worked through the city's growth partnership to establish new cultural institutions and redevelop former sites of heavy industry along the waterfront for technology centers, business incubators, medical complexes, and tourism and leisure activities. He funded streetscape and facade improvements in neighborhood commercial districts. And with the aid of the Allegheny Conference and Penn's Southwest, he marketed Pittsburgh as a "twenty-four hour city" suited to the professional and leisure pursuits of young, well-educated workers—the residents the growth coalition hoped to attract, rather than those already living in Pittsburgh.

The region's unemployed manufacturing workers were less enthusiastic than Caliguiri and his corporate partners about the postindustrialism embedded in "Choices" and Renaissance II. In the early 1980s, two labor-ecumenical coalitions, the Tri-State Conference on Steel (Tri-State) and the Denominational Ministry Strategy (DMS), formed to protest what they viewed as an unholy alliance between the city government and Pittsburgh's executives. Tri-State and DMS mounted a rank-and-file response to shutdowns unsanctioned by the international leadership of Pittsburgh's unions. Theirs was an alternative vision of progress in which regional revitalization and national economic health required the restoration of large-scale manufacturing. The activists sought to establish worker-owned mills in the Mon Valley, a proposition that threatened to undermine Caliguiri's Renaissance II commitment to expanding service-sector jobs and downplaying industry. Tri-State and DMS also advanced an alternative vision of urban citizenship, in which the workers who had built the region's industrial might, rather than the corporate executives who grew wealthy from their labor, had the right to determine Pittsburgh's future.[60]

Both groups organized against layoffs and shutdowns, but Tri-State and DMS had different political agendas, different tactics, and, often, an oppositional relationship. Despite their differences, the organizations' attacks against Renaissance II and the growth partnership behind it were fundamentally similar. Their members protested what they perceived to be an inappropriate use of public resources for the benefit of private interests. They held that Pittsburgh's growth partnership commandeered city, state, and federal funds—the tax dollars of citizens like themselves—for a cultural district intended to attract tourists and enhance the region's new image. At the same time, the mill town activists charged, the growth coalition dismissed workers' pleas for disaster aid and steel subsidies as impossible requests in a market-based economy.[61]

Tri-State, influenced by Youngstown activist Staughton Lynd, argued that community rights to industrial property outweighed those of the corporations that owned the means of production. Tri-State's members came mostly from steel and steel-related industries, and the group worked closely with Lynd and Pittsburgh's labor priest Monsignor Charles Owen Rice. Organizers set out to create a public authority with the legal capacity to seize shuttered factories through eminent domain and reindustrialize the Mon Valley, preferably through worker-owned cooperatives.[62] To do so, they turned to the Municipal Authorities Act, a state law originally proposed by the Allegheny Conference in 1945 to support Renaissance I development plans. The act facilitated the formation of local public authorities endowed with the power of eminent domain, which included taking industrial properties for public good.

Like Tri-State, DMS members believed that corporations had a moral responsibility to their workers and the communities in which their plants were located. DMS drew its support from the mill towns, where workers teamed with Lutheran and Episcopal clergy who had become increasingly radical in their efforts to address the economic problems of their parishioners. The organization commonly known as DMS was in fact composed of two distinct groups: the Denominational Ministry Strategy, a group of Protestant church pastors originally organized to make the church more relevant to urban parishioners, and the Network to Save the Mon/Ohio Valley, a coalition of labor activists, including the leaders of several Mon Valley locals, who sought a way to influence corporate actions beyond international unions' narrow focus on wages.[63]

While Tri-State pursued worker-owned cooperatives, DMS called the corporations who threatened to close plants "evil" and enjoined Pittsburgh's CEOs to reinvest in the Mon Valley. Activists exposed investment patterns that funneled funds to foreign steel companies, demanded meetings with executives to discuss local employment protection, and insisted that corporations needed to be responsible to communities as well as to stockholders. Led by Charles Honeywell, a community organizer trained in confrontational tactics at Saul Alinsky's Industrial Areas Foundation, DMS engaged in direct action against U.S. Steel and Mellon Bank at bank branches, corporate headquarters, and business leaders' places of worship in the city and its affluent suburbs.[64]

Elected officials offered some support when Tri-State and DMS advocated for laws that would regulate when and how employers could close plants. In 1983, the Pittsburgh City Council proposed an ordinance that required three to nine months notice in advance of any plant closing, relocation, or layoff of more than 15 percent of the workforce of a company located inside the city limits. Philadelphia had ratified such a requirement over mayoral veto the previous year; Wisconsin and Maine had passed similar legislation in 1975. Pittsburgh's corporate leaders mounted a swift and well-coordinated attack against the proposed ordinance. City Council president Tom Flaherty (former mayor Pete Flaherty's brother) received a pile of angry letters from top executives who wrote at the encouragement of the Allegheny Conference and the RIDC. A. W. Calder, president and CEO of Joy Manufacturing, charged that the ordinance would "destroy the Renaissance image" and scare away new industries, a sentiment echoed in missives from IBM, Sears Roebuck, and Heinz.[65] Francis B. O'Neil, Pittsburgh Plate Glass vice president of corporate development, took a gentler tack, assuring Flaherty that his company supported City Council's efforts to attract new business. "We are convinced that the proposed ordinance would frustrate those efforts," O'Neil wrote. "We can only believe that incentives will work better than regulations in accomplishing the goal of making Pittsburgh a better place to live and work."[66] Robert Dickey, III, a former Allegheny Conference chairman and the recently retired president and CEO of Dravo, scoffed of the ordinance: "while in a superficial sense it has great voter appeal, like apple pie and motherhood, it will do nothing but worsen our economic vitality."[67] Dickey had laid off nearly 1,500 shipbuilders the previous year.

Letters from Alcoa president and CEO Charles W. Parry and Thomas F. Fought, Dickey's successor at Dravo, struck an injured tone. Parry reminded Flaherty how much his company paid in taxes, pointing out that "nobody had to shackle us to Pittsburgh to make that commitment."[68] He predicted that a plant closing ordinance would make Pittsburgh a "pool of stagnation," stunt growth, and cause the city's tax base to deteriorate. The "layoff problem" City Council sought to address, Fought wrote, was "caused by economic conditions and not by capricious management action."[69] The executive vice president of the Smaller Manufacturers Council bypassed Flaherty and wrote directly to the editor of the *Pittsburgh Post-Gazette*. "You can't put a barbed-wire fence around the city of Pittsburgh to keep all the existing businesses in without shutting out those other businesses who might be willing to locate their jobs here," he complained.[70]

Pittsburgh's industrialists led the charge against the ordinance, but executives from finance and services were also worried about advance notification requirements. John W. McGonigle, vice president of financial services firm Federated Investors, noted that, while the city had a storied past as an industrial center, "it is now becoming clear that Pittsburgh is also an important center for the service sector of the economy." McGonigle's letter tied his concerns about the plant closing ordinance to Caliguiri's postindustrial vision for the city. "Renaissance II in large measure is predicated on the continuing development of the service industry in Pittsburgh, and it is likely that Pittsburgh's continued economic growth will depend on Pittsburgh's ability to attract and keep firms who operate in that sector of the economy," McGonigle warned. "Firms in the service sector of the economy can be extremely mobile; they are not generally tied down by geography or by immovable capital resources." Any restrictions on corporate decision-making, he suggested, would dissuade the postindustrial jobs that Renaissance II was designed to attract.[71]

City Council was unmoved by executives' objections to the plant closing ordinance and passed it over Caliguiri's veto in July 1983. Like McGonigle, Caliguiri saw the ordinance as a threat to Renaissance II. In his veto letter, Caliguiri accused "irresponsible populist politicians"—presumably a reference to Tom Flaherty—of attempting "to profit from the pain and suffering of others by advancing measures which, on the surface, appear to be desirable but in fact make more difficult our primary task of attracting new industry and increasing employment in this area." The ordinance was illegal under Home Rule, Caliguiri contended, and "it does not even serve the legitimate needs of our citizens. Above all, what our citizens need is not illusory gestures but jobs."[72] The City Council's victory over Caliguiri was short-lived; six weeks later, he secured a court ruling that the advance notification ordinance violated the Home Rule charter.[73]

Caliguiri's invocation of jobs for Pittsburgh's citizens must have been particularly galling for the mill town activists, who saw Renaissance II as part of a strategy to destroy union jobs in traditional manufacturing and replace them with low-paid, non-union, service sector positions. Tri-State, in particular, condemned public subsidies for high-tech jobs, culture industries, and service-sector employment that constituted "economic development" in Pittsburgh's postindustrial redevelopment strategy. "Communities can not survive without jobs," Tri-State organizers told laid-off workers. "Young people can not expect to build a decent life for themselves if they can not find work."[74] To garner support for their reindustrialization plans, Tri-State members presented a slide show in mill towns throughout the valley critiquing Renaissance II projects. At screenings, activists informed their audiences, "The steel companies have judged the mills, workers, and mill communities to be expendable." They pointed out that workers were told that there were no public funds available to the mill towns for disaster relief, but there was plenty of money available to subsidize new corporate headquarters for the very companies that had laid them off. "Our tax dollars have been used to finance these corporate headquarters. Billions of dollars in our tax dollars have been used to promote the Renaissance," Tri-State activists exhorted. "Our tax dollars built the Golden Triangle while our own neighborhoods were neglected. Our work in the mills, and our tax dollars have financed our destruction. . . . Our tax dollars and the profits made from our labor must be put back in our neighborhoods and our mills."[75]

As Tri-State worked to build local support for reindustrialization, DMS activists launched a direct action campaign against corporate disinvestment that also undermined Caliguiri's campaign to sell Pittsburgh as a city with a good business climate. DMS's earliest protests targeted Mellon Bank branch offices. Activists devised elaborate schemes to disrupt service, such as depositing dead fish in safe deposit boxes and spraying skunk oil in bank lobbies. The "Smellin' Mellon" campaign forced Mellon to close branches, sometimes for days, while bank staffers and professional cleaners located and eradicated the source of the odor, but it had no discernible impact on the bank's investment decisions. In June 1983, DMS activists from labor and the clergy withdrew an estimated $100,000 from Mellon's Homestead branch to protest Mellon's overseas investments, which totaled 20 percent of the bank's total assets. They encouraged workers throughout the Mon Valley to boycott the bank.[76] The Washington Post reported that the Homestead protest was "a public relations headache" for bank officials.[77] Financial analyst James McDermott told the paper that activists' campaign against Mellon was not likely to hurt the bank's bottom line but that DMS was damaging Mellon's image at a time when the bank was rapidly expanding its holdings and seeking to establish itself as a nationally, rather than regionally, important financial institution. "Mellon is a worldwide institution," McDermott said, "but on its own home turf it wants the best possible relations." Mellon, the *Wall Street Journal* reported, was working hard to repair its public image through charitable donations to cultural programs and a new slogan, "A neighbor you can count on."[78] The irony was not lost on the mill town activists: one quipped, "Their slogan should be, 'A neighbor you can't count on.'"[79]

When their actions failed to provoke much reaction from Mellon or U.S. Steel, whose executives refused to meet with activists, DMS members took their protest from bank lobbies to the church pews and front lawns of U.S. Steel executives. Skunk oil became the group's signature: they also released it at a Lutheran convention to protest the Lutheran Synod's sanctions against ministers involved with DMS and in three downtown department stores in a Christmas demonstration against Pittsburgh's executives.[80] Declaring that executives would not be allowed "to sit up in the comfort of their homes and ignore the suffering their decisions have caused," DMS began to stage actions during Sunday and holiday services at Shadyside Presbyterian church, where many high-ranking executives worshipped.[81] They charged that CEOs and public officials had produced plans for Pittsburgh's future "which call for the elimination of the Mon Valley steel mills, the development of small industrial parks which will hire people at wages significantly below union scale, and the development of river front condominiums and water recreation facilities for the 'new residents' of corporate Pittsburgh."[82]

If there was doubt about the validity of activists' analysis of Renaissance II, it was quashed by the middle of the decade. In 1985, Democratic state senator (and future Pittsburgh mayor) Tom Murphy and Allegheny county commissioner Tom Foerster asked Allegheny Conference executive director Robert Pease to oversee a regional planning process through which the city, county, and universities cooperated, rather than competed, in their applications for dwindling state and federal grant money. Murphy had observed that the Philadelphia region had successfully coordinated state and federal aid requests and set out to do the same in Pittsburgh. The son of a steelworker, Murphy earned a master's degree in urban studies at Hunter College and served in the Peace Corps before returning to Pittsburgh as a North Side neighborhood organizer. Like others who had worked in the burgeoning neighborhood movement in the 1970s, Murphy was skeptical of big business and big government, but he was also pragmatic and well versed in national urban development trends. From Harrisburg, he worked closely with Caliguiri and Foerster to advocate for the region's interests in the state house.[83]

Both the Allegheny Conference and the University of Pittsburgh had a laundry list of projects ready to propose. Pease and Chancellor Wesley Posvar quickly assembled Strategy 21, a strategic plan to secure state and federal aid to complete unfunded Renaissance II projects and extend Pittsburgh's postindustrial rebirth beyond the city limits. The Allegheny Conference had formed an Economic Development Committee four years earlier and convened a task force on the problems facing the region. In 1983, the University of Pittsburgh sponsored a conference to solicit ideas about regional economic development and recovery strategies from over two hundred community members—primarily academics and business leaders—and the Allegheny Conference issued a set of recommendations based on these activities in 1984.[84] When they developed Strategy 21, Allegheny Conference staffers drew on the 1984 recommendations, folded in existing underfunded projects that Caliguiri and Pease hoped to see completed, and secured Caliguiri's endorsement for the "post-steel" economic development strategy contained in the final document.[85]

Allegheny County, the City of Pittsburgh, the University of Pittsburgh, and Carnegie Mellon jointly submitted Strategy 21 to the commonwealth in June 1985, asking for roughly $430 million in state funding to support projects that the Allegheny Conference anticipated would cost $1.9 billion. Even more than Renaissance II projects already completed downtown and in the cultural district, Strategy 21 reflected the growth coalition's commitment to postindustrialism and to the public-private partnership that made it a viable development model. The city, county, and universities pitched Strategy 21 to the state as a "joint/public private partnership designed to transform the economy of the greater Pittsburgh region as it enters the 21st Century, in order to take maximum advantage of emerging economic trends toward advanced technology, international marketing and communications systems." Funding for a new midfield terminal at the regional airport took top billing; high technology funds were second on the list, largely for a host of University of Pittsburgh and Carnegie Mellon University projects.[86]

The coalition also sought funds for industrial redevelopment for light or high tech industry on former mill sites in Allegheny County. In the city limits, they asked for money to redevelop formerly industrial Herr's Island, a project that had been underway since the 1970s, and to convert Jones & Laughlin's Second Avenue mill site into the Pittsburgh Technology Center. Funds for recreational facilities near Three Rivers Stadium on the North Side and money to complete stalled mixed-use projects in the Strip District also made the list. Highway projects and funding for a county-wide metals retention study ostensibly to determine which facilities had potential "for becoming competitive in the international market and which facilities have no long-term viability" rounded out the proposal.[87]

Strategy 21 extended Caliguiri's Renaissance vision throughout the region. Tri-State and DMS, the most vocal opposition to the growth coalition's postindustrial plans, were unable to mount a meaningful challenge to Strategy 21. Increasingly negative popular opinion and purges of DMS leadership by the Lutheran synod and the United Steelworkers crippled DMS's membership by the middle of the decade. By the time Strategy 21 was on the horizon, Tri-State had narrowly focused its efforts on creating a public authority for regional reindustrialization. In 1986, Tri-State finally succeeded with the establishment of the Steel Valley Authority (SVA), chartered under the Municipal Authorities Act and sponsored by the cities of Pittsburgh and McKeesport and the boroughs of Homestead, Munhall, Rankin, East Pittsburgh, Turtle Creek, Swissvale, and Glassport. On its face, the SVA's reindustrialization mission appeared to be almost entirely at odds with the growth coalition's plans for Pittsburgh and the region as it was embodied in Strategy 21. The SVA's institutional structure, however, neutralized the political threat Tri-State posed by bringing its members into the growth coalition's decision-making process in much the same way that neighborhood organizations were incorporated in the 1960s.

Tri-State organizers described the SVA as a workers' victory in the fight against plant closures, but the SVA's charter protected the interests of the sponsoring city governments by ensuring that they were not financially beholden to the new authority, which severely circumscribed the SVA's powers to influence redevelopment plans. The SVA was also subject to restrictions that did not extend to Pittsburgh's other public authorities: it could not levy taxes or assessments and was not eligible for tax exemptions for the property it acquired. The SVA could only raise money through grants, bond sales, and sale or use fees on properties it acquired. Furthermore, the SVA could not use eminent domain to take a property without prior approval from the municipality in which the property was located, as well as the consent of all nine chartering municipalities. By virtue of its restrictive charter, the SVA could not pursue any action within the city limits without permission from the city government or in the Mon Valley without the support of all chartering members, including the City of Pittsburgh. The charter effectively afforded Caliguiri veto power over any reindustrialization attempts. In exchange for these constraints, Caliguiri contributed $50,000 to the SVA's start-up costs.[88]

Planner Morton Coleman later dismissed regional reindustrialization as a nonsensical proposition, but, at the time, "political leaders had to look like they were doing something," he recalled. Elected officials, he said, had been "impotent" in their response to plant closures. "I mean, this was like a huge cancer. I mean, the impact of losing 100,000 jobs; losing the industrial base of your community, losing middle-class, high paying jobs; changing the nature of the culture of the community," he remembered. "That was, except for a war, about as devastating a blow as a community can face. So the elected officials are sitting there, and they see all this pain going on, and there's not much they can do about it, so, you know they get engaged in something to try to at least, maybe for themselves or for political reasons, look like they're trying to face the situation. But it was hard. You know, it's like a doctor facing a massive hemorrhage. You don't [know] where you can put the gauze, or whatever, to stop the bleeding."[89] The SVA, for the region's elected officials, was the gauze. Caliguiri died shortly after the SVA received its charter, and a *New York Times* obituary praised him for "steering the city through the death of big steel to the birth of a diversified economy"—a posthumous triumph for the fallen mayor and an unwitting epitaph for the mill town radicals.[90]

By 1990, the SVA's reindustrialization bid had failed. When the Strategy 21 coalition submitted an updated funding request that year, its authors entirely eliminated basic industry from regional strategic planning. The growth coalition requested funds to support the Andy Warhol Museum on the North Side, to expand the downtown cultural district and the convention center, and to build a regional history center and a downtown library center. The only aid on offer for the mill towns was to create industrial parks on the sites of former steel mills in Duquesne and McKeesport and at an old Westinghouse plant in Turtle Creek. Between 1970 and 1990, the city shed nearly 30 percent of its population; the region lost 289,000 workers and 158,000 manufacturing jobs.[91] Gulf Oil, Koppers, Rockwell International, Union Electric Steel, Pittsburgh Brewing, Fisher Scientific, and Brockway Glass had all moved or closed. Gulf alone took 1,600 jobs with it when it left the region. In 1984, Nippon, a Japanese steel producer, purchased National Steel. Wheeling-Pittsburgh Steel went bankrupt in 1985. In 1986, Allegheny International filed for bankruptcy, Volkswagen closed its Westmoreland County plant, and Westinghouse closed its East Pittsburgh plant.[92] In the wake of economic devastation, with little hope of aid from the Reagan administration, the region's disorganized and demoralized labor activists mounted little protest to the continued expansion of the postindustrial agenda institutionalized during Renaissance II.

Hamilton's "Pittsburgh Solution"

In Hamilton, on the other hand, basic industry continued to thrive in the early 1980s. Hamilton-Wentworth Regional Economic Development director John Morand confidently described Hamilton as a "city on the move" in 1980, but city planners were more cautious in their assessment of the postindustrial future. Manufacturing employment had declined by around 5 percent between 1961 and 1971. Planners complained that they found "little evidence to suggest that counter-measures were taken to avert the exodus of many Hamilton based firms to locations outside of the City limits," particularly Burlington and Stoney Creek. They wrote that the harbor industrial area was "undergoing a natural succession as the private market runs its course" and reported that Texaco, Ontario Hydro, and Canadian Industries Limited had already moved to the suburbs. "Hamilton's economic base, then, while still resting heavily on manufacturing, and notably the steel industries, is fast becoming more diversified," the planners determined. "Hamilton will likely be dominated by a service economy by the [1981] census, entering a new era of development."[93] They were right: between 1971 and 1981, jobs increased in the finance, insurance, and real estate sector by 69 percent, commercial business and personal services by 64.4 percent, agriculture by 51.9 percent, transportation/communications by 49.9 percent, and trade by 47.4 percent. Manufacturing jobs increased, too, but at the significantly lower rate of 26.3 percent.[94]

Planners predicted a coming postindustrial transition that would be characterized by "a high per capita income; a high proportion of employment in the service sector, especially quaternary activities (services for their own sake, such as recreation, education, the arts, information services, and certain government services); and in increase in time available for certain leisure activities." To assist, rather than resist, that transition, they mandated that "manufacturing interests must be re-assessed on functional merit rather than a historical basis."[95] Hamilton's 1980 plan reflected a shift in provincial policies, which sought to regionally rationalize and spatially contain industrial development while increasing service sector employment. To attract new enterprises to Ontario and keep the businesses already located there from leaving, provincial officials vowed "to free up resources for the private sector" by reducing social spending, restraining public sector wages, and determining which provincial services could feasibly be privatized or converted to fee-for-service. Like their counterparts on the U.S. side of the Great Lakes region, Ontario's provincial officials saw no alternative but to compete for jobs on terms set by Sunbelt states, a competition in which Ontario's cities lacked the tools to participate effectively because the provincial government precluded municipalities from offering capital subsidies to private corporations.[96]

As Southern Ontario's economic situation worsened in the late 1970s and into the 1980s, the provincial government increasingly sought to bolster the region's troubled manufacturing sector. In 1980, the provincial treasurer announced that Ontario's fiscal policy would center on "reducing the size of government to lessen inflationary pressures on the economy and free up resources for productive private sector investment" by maintaining a stable and competitive "profit and taxation" environment.[97] To facilitate investment, Premier Bill Davis announced a $1.5 billion economic development initiative, the Board of Industrial Leadership (BILD). Ontario would supply half of the $1.5 billion for BILD, and Davis expected the remainder to materialize from some combination of federal, municipal, and private sector contributions.[98]

In his fourteen-year tenure, Davis marshaled the rhetoric of private enterprise and traditional values to gain support from rural precincts while largely governing as a centrist.[99] BILD reflected Davis's desire to satisfy conservative voters without alienating Liberals and supporters in Southern Ontario. The program provided financial support on a discretionary basis for industrial restructuring, job creation, and, like the BFP in Pennsylvania, the construction of advanced technology centers.[100] To ensure that Ontario's labor force had "the skills, mobility and productivity to maximize the province's growth potential," provincial officials allocated $200 million of BILD funds over five years to retrain workers. BILD became the centerpiece of the province's economic development strategy, complemented by an industrial promotion program introduced in the late 1970s. Like Pennsylvania governor Thornburgh, Davis envisioned a transition to an economy increasingly based on research and development and high technology—in Ontario, centered around electrical power and nuclear technology—and sought to nurture these industries through BILD and a $50 million Ontario Development Corporation-financed start-up fund for Canadian-owned high technology enterprises.[101]

Davis used BILD and his advanced technology initiatives to commit his government to free market solutions to the economic problems facing Ontario. To reinforce his pro-business orientation, he referred to Ontario's residents as "our shareholders."[102] By 1981, Davis was self-congratulatory about his efforts to reduce government regulation and promote entrepreneurial activities in a way that anticipated Mulroney's later retrenchment. "Our commitment to strengthen the private sector and to ease up on government interference was not a gamble but a proven success," he said. "Indeed, our new economic development program [BILD] will work with our entrepreneurs and risk-takers because creative forces are alive and well in the private sector." Davis promoted his administration's successes in establishing research and development and high technology industries in Ontario—very little of it in the Hamilton region—noting that BILD allowed the province to "envision a high technology industrial society, eager to make the choices necessary to sustain both economic prosperity and social progress."[103]

Hamilton's officials remained hamstrung by provincial industrial development policies that made it difficult to take up Davis's call for partnership and diversification. Regional Economic Development Department officials complained about the "seeming inconsistencies of Federal and Provincial government industrial strategies."[104] Local officials' difficulty navigating federal and provincial economic development initiatives was compounded by their troubled relationship with Hamilton's business community. The Central Area Plan Committee disbanded shortly after it released its final report in 1981, and no similar organization had emerged to take its place. Chamber members had long blamed the local, provincial, and federal governments for the region's declining industry, jobs, and population, while municipal officials accused the Chamber of complaining without offering any real solutions. In an attempt to diffuse tension between public officials and the Chamber, Economic Development Department staffers began to visit local businessmen "to exchange views on development opportunities, to become acquainted with their problems, expansion needs or plans and to assist with resolving any development impediments."[105]

Most of the conflict over Hamilton's redevelopment came from within the growth coalition in the 1980s; Hamilton's residents and labor activists exhibited little concern over civic and political leaders' broad vision for a postindustrial future. While Pittsburgh-area labor activists moved beyond bread-and-butter issues to fight against deindustrialization and downtown redevelopment in the early 1980s, Canadian steelworkers remained narrowly focused on negotiating strong contracts. Instead of mounting a challenge to the postindustrial ambitions of civic and political leaders, Hamilton's steelworkers contemplated severing ties with the United Steelworkers and forming a domestic union inspired, in part, by the Canadian Auto Workers' separation from the United Auto Workers international.[106] When the United Steelworkers international assumed an increasingly concessionary position in the 1980s, Stelco Local 1005, the largest and most powerful steelworkers' local in Canada, balked. In 1981, Stelco workers struck for 125 days, and in 1982 they refused to reopen their contract to provide givebacks when Stelco started to feel the effects of the recession. The powerful president of the

Canadian Postal Workers union rallied United Steelworkers members to resist pressure for concessions as Canadian autoworkers had with Chrysler in 1980, saying that Canadian workers needed to send the message that they would not compete with each other for wages.[107] Focused on their fight for jobs and wages and preoccupied by conflict among union leaders, Hamilton's labor activists took little interest in urban redevelopment plans.

In 1981, the incoming Chamber of Commerce president, Stelco executive James McMurrich, told the *Hamilton Spectator* that he hoped to establish good working relationships with local politicians. "We've opposed them from time to time and there has been some misunderstanding of our position and of our reasons for opposing some of the ideas," he said, and "downtown redevelopment is an issue that we have just recently started to look very seriously at." McMurrich was also worried that the "balkanization" of the business community through new business groups such as a Jackson Square retail association and a downtown merchants association would diminish the power of the Chamber.[108] Despite McMurrich's conciliatory words and the Chamber's strong statement of interest in downtown development, by the time the effects of the recession hit the city, Hamilton still lacked a civic organization that could coordinate public and private redevelopment activities as the Allegheny Conference did in Pittsburgh.

The Chamber sponsored a second group modeled after the Allegheny Conference, the Task Force for Economic Recovery, under the direction of new Chamber president Maurice Carter in 1982. The task force styled itself as a "businessmen's campaign to promote Hamilton" and announced that it would undertake a $150,000 promotional campaign.[109] Regional councilor Bill McCulloch praised the Chamber for taking an important step toward bridging the divide between Hamilton's elected officials and its business community. McCulloch, himself a restaurateur, saw the task force as evidence that the local business community was finally accepting its share of responsibility for economic conditions in the city. He assured the task force that the regional government would cooperate with the campaign. Harry Greenwood, the president of the Hamilton and District Labor Council, also endorsed the task force, saying "labor is as interested in getting the city of Hamilton working as the business people are." McCulloch and Greenwood had travelled (separately) to Pittsburgh earlier that year, and both returned full of praise for Caliguiri's second Renaissance. Greenwood described Hamilton as a "ghost town" next to Pittsburgh. McCulloch unfavorably compared Hamilton's businessmen to Pittsburgh's, pointing out a "marked contrast" between the efforts of the Allegheny Conference and the "negative comments" from Hamilton's Chamber of Commerce.[110] The formation of the task force, as far as McCulloch and Greenwood were concerned, meant Hamilton was a step closer to becoming like Pittsburgh.

McCulloch's hopes that government cooperation with the task force might temper the Chamber's criticism of the regional government were soon dashed. A month after the Chamber established the task force, Dofasco announced plans to lay off 2,100 workers, and Carter attacked the municipal and federal government for creating an economic environment hostile to business. He pulled out the Chamber's old saws and claimed that there was not enough serviced industrial land in the region, that companies were relocating to suburban Burlington and Stoney Creek, that not enough had been done to attract light industry, that the federal government was not moving quickly enough on the airport expansion, and that the regional planning department was useless.[111]

The tension between Chamber leaders and city and regional officials spilled into the local newspaper that fall, when the *Spectator* ran a feature on "the Pittsburgh Solution" to urban decline. The article cited "determined cooperation between political and business leaders" as the primary difference between Hamilton and Pittsburgh. *Spectator* writer Paul Mitchell pointed out that Pittsburgh, with a higher unemployment rate and a greater crisis of its regional economy, had more revitalization projects underway than Hamilton. Mitchell laid out the components of Pittsburgh's "solution" to urban and industrial decline, which he suggested Hamilton might emulate. Hamilton, he wrote, needed to recruit "big business tycoons, with staggering financial clout" to lead redevelopment efforts; pursue high-tech jobs; aggressively seek government aid; and provide incentives to companies willing to relocate to the region. Mitchell's "Pittsburgh Solution" echoed the recommendations in the Lunchpail Report nearly fifteen years earlier and reflected a similar unfamiliarity with political and institutional differences between Pittsburgh and Hamilton. Hamilton simply did not have "big business tycoons" of national or international prominence like those in Pittsburgh, and provincial regulations prohibited Hamilton's public officials from offering tax incentives and other financial inducements for private redevelopment that were the foundation of Caliguiri's Renaissance II.

The article fueled the flames between local elected officials and the Chamber. It appeared four months after the task force announced its planned $150,000 ad campaign and reported that the group had raised only $40,000 toward the project. "I've never seen such a dynamic gung-ho community in my life as I did in Pittsburgh and I just think how much we could learn from them," McCulloch told Mitchell. "In Pittsburgh, they prefer to do it privately and put their money where their mouth is. That is something we have to do here. We have to get the private sector to be out for boosterism." Task Force member Alec Murray, head of Hamilton's largest real estate company, blasted back that "the failure of the public sector to provide the necessary economic infrastructure to stimulate growth" hurt businessmen. Chamber executive director and task force treasurer Reg Whynott defensively said that the organization needed a "Mellon who would give us a couple of million dollars." The primary difference between Pittsburgh and Hamilton was that "we don't have a benefactor like they do," Whynott pointed out.[112] Of the public and private officials pointing to Pittsburgh as a model, only Morand seemed to grasp the differences between Pittsburgh and Hamilton's abilities to offer public subsidies for private redevelopment. Like McCulloch and Greenwood, Morand had recently returned from a fact-finding trip to Pittsburgh. "They give away buckets of money in Pittsburgh from sources that aren't available here," he told Mitchell. "We don't have any industrial revenue bonds or tax-free incentives. Under the Ontario Municipal Act, municipalities here can do zero."[113]

"The Pittsburgh Solution" ran in September 1982; by December, the region's unemployment rate had soared to nearly 17 percent.[114] In the Hamilton-Wentworth and Halton regions, 191 businesses went bankrupt in 1981, 239 in 1982, and another 124 in the first six months of 1983. Hamilton's steel producers laid off workers and weathered the recession, but other large companies, including Arrow, Consolidated-Bathurst, and Allen Industries, had closed their doors by the end of 1983. Morand blamed high taxes and the lack of land on which to expand for the closures. "At a time when people were expanding in the late 1960s, the early 70s, we missed the boat," he said. "We didn't have the land. We didn't have the overall integrated economic development because there was no region." To compensate, the region increased its available serviced industrial land from 114 acres in 1978 to over 2,000 acres in 1983, most of it outside the city limits. Morand noted that a factory assessed at $500,000 in Hamilton would pay $130,000 in property taxes, but less than $110,000 in Kitchener and less than $95,000 in Brantford, two of Hamilton's regional competitors for new industry. He complained bitterly about executives who located their facilities in nearby Burlington, knowing that their employees would still have convenient access to Hamilton's cultural institutions. By 1983, Morand and Murray, who had become Chamber vice president, agreed on one thing: there was no regional industrial strategy in place that had the full support of both government and industry.[115]

As economic conditions worsened, the task force quietly disappeared. The failure of the "businessmen's campaign," however, did not diminish Hamiltonians' desire to replicate Pittsburgh's partnership. Unemployment rates dropped to 8.6 percent at the end of 1983, well below the national average. As Hamilton's economy appeared poised for recovery, civic groups resumed their efforts to bring together key actors from the public and private sectors and create a durable partnership.[116] The years 1983 and 1984 brought the formation of the Hamilton Jobs Committee, the McMaster University Advisory Committee, the Hamilton Union of the Unemployed, the Hamilton Image Group, and the Economic Advisory Conference, all announced with great fanfare. Participants in a 1984 corporate-sponsored regional economic development conference recommended that CEOs of local corporations, senior government officials, McMaster University and Mohawk College faculty, and labor leaders establish a Bay Area Council on Community Development modeled after the Allegheny Conference.[117] The council "kind of dissipated" after a handful of meetings, according to cochair Peter George, a McMaster economics professor. Corporate leaders had "their own problems to deal with" in the mid-1980s, he said. Echoing Jack Moore's 1968 complaint, George noted that they had agreed to participate but failed to show up for meetings.[118]

None of CAPAC's presumptive successors managed to produce so much as a single set of recommendations (only the Bay Area Council appears to have held more than one meeting). By the middle of the decade, it was clear that Hamilton would not be able to sustain a growth partnership modeled after the Allegheny Conference. It was also clear that not all businessmen wanted to. Bob Martin, the director of Hamilton's Downtown Business Improvement Area, and other area businessmen rejected Mayor Bob Morrow's contention that the "whole community has to pull together" to spur development. An anonymous businessman voiced a common complaint about civic and political leaders' efforts to convince representatives from Hamilton's major corporations to engage in community development activities: "the meetings go on and on."[119] Murray, by then Chamber president, took Hamilton's corporate and business community to task in 1984 for not showing the same leadership as their counterparts in Pittsburgh. With the local economy largely recovered, his rebuke seemed to carry little influence.[120]

Two years later, the *Spectator* ran a five-part series on "The New Hamilton" and declared that the city was "Back From the Edge and Flying High," as it learned to be "less and less reliant on the two major steel-makers." In 1986, small businesses were opening and expanding at twice the provincial average, and small business loans had increased by 24 percent over the previous year, a rate 10 percent higher than in Ontario as a whole. South Central Ontario Better Business Bureau president Bob Irvine said he was "pleasantly surprised" to find that Hamilton was "not as it is depicted nationally." Instead, Irvine found, "There is still a lot of entrepreneurial spirit." Local executives, too, praised residents' entrepreneurialism. Ray McCormick, a retired Westinghouse executive who headed the regional Economic Development Department's Business Advisory Centre, said, "We're shedding the cloak of being a steel town. We're more than a steel town today." Stelco vice president Frederick Telmer held that the steel companies "can't really support the city like we used to. We're just not as big as we used to be." Stelco, Telmer noted, wanted to "see the city diversify." Shopping mall developer Jim Bullock thought that the city's economic diversification made it a good investment. "You don't like to go into a one-industry town," he told the *Spectator*. "While Hamilton's still dependent on the steel industry, there are other major employers."[121]

Unlike their counterparts in Pittsburgh, members of Hamilton's growth coalition did not have to contend with substantial public resistance to their postindustrial visions. Without a mechanism for public-private partnership in place, however, they were left unprepared to handle the provincial retrenchment that accompanied the federal government's withdrawal from urban and economic development. In 1985, the Progressive Conservatives were ousted from Queen's Park, but the election of Liberal premier David Peterson codified rather than halted the shift to neoliberalizing planning strategies. Peterson's administration pitched the new economic development agenda as an adjustment policy intended to move Ontario into a postindustrial "information society."[122] In a 1986 speech, Peterson adopted neoliberal rhetoric to describe his economic recovery plan, saying, "The role of government is to assist business and labor in adjusting to changing economic circumstances."[123] Peterson asserted that his "government believes, as a matter of principle, that the private sector is the primary source of economic growth. We must not attempt to substitute bureaucratic decisions or fiats for the sound business judgments of enterprises throughout the economy." Peterson indicated that he hoped to construct a "permanent mechanism for cooperation and consultation" with the private sector to set provincial economic priorities.[124]

Despite more than twenty years of efforts by local political and civic leaders, Hamilton lacked the institutional capacity to respond to provincial privatization and devolution. The city's growth coalition, however, pursued the markers of postindustrialism—downtown revitalization, mill neighborhood

redevelopment, and urban branding—just as doggedly as their better-orga-
nized and funded counterparts in Pittsburgh. By the end of the decade, even
as U.S. and Canadian political cultures became more alike, and both regional
economies began to diversify, Pittsburgh and Hamilton's postindustrial paths
had clearly diverged. Because Pittsburgh's leaders worked through a powerful
growth partnership and within an entrepreneurial public policy framework
and Hamilton's did not, Pittsburgh was more able and Hamilton less able to
adopt tactics such as capital subsidies, supply-side intervention, central-city
makeovers, and branding campaigns common to postindustrial redevelopment schemes throughout the North Atlantic. On the ground in Pittsburgh
and Hamilton, contradictions between stabilizing cities in ways that encouraged new investment and ensuring socially just outcomes for urban residents
came into sharp relief.

CHAPTER FOUR

The New Geography of Downtown

In 1984, Robert McLean, III, a senior vice president at Cushman & Wakefield and a director of the Greater Pittsburgh Chamber of Commerce, published *Countdown to Renaissance II: The New Way Corporate America Builds*. He dedicated the book to "corporate America and the communities it serves." McLean had worked with the City of Philadelphia on its bicentennial make-over and with the City of Pittsburgh on eight downtown construction proj-ects. In *Countdown*, he chronicled how Pittsburgh's CEOs and city officials had worked together to meet corporate construction needs and to market the second Renaissance. Westinghouse's senior executive vice president E. V. Clarke, Jr., provided a blurb for *Countdown*, praising McLean for link-ing corporate strategic planning to urban revitalization and place promotion. McLean's book, Clarke enthused, laid out a blueprint for "how the corporate marketing discipline, a hallmark of the free-enterprise system" could be tied to downtown redevelopment to promote cities locally and nationally.[1]

The book also included a foreword by prominent conservative ideologue William F. Buckley, Jr. Buckley was more interested in the "new" Pittsburgh as a symbol of an ascendant conservatism than he was in urban revitalization. He described Renaissance II as proof positive that the liberal steel belt, with its entrenched unions and Democratic machines, was in the throes of a polit-ical as well as economic rebirth. For Buckley, the corporate welfare packages the city supplied under Renaissance II were evidence that "the central insight of supply-side economics is now getting acceptance everywhere: wealth has to be created before it can be consumed." He praised "a school of 'neoliberal' politicians and thinkers"—centrist forerunners of the New Democrat coali-tion like Gary Hart and Paul Tsongas—who recognized that that the "whole redistributionist strategy is radically self-defeating." The Democratic Party, Buckley observed, showed signs of "yearning for rapprochement" with the business community that it had treated like "a beast of burden" since the New Deal. "Mayors of our large cities still like federal money," he noted archly, "but they are increasingly trying to attract capitalists too." Pittsburgh, in his estimation, was one of the cities that had "seen the light." Buckley credited elected officials with "inviting and fostering corporate building downtown" and described Caliguiri's Renaissance II building program as "leading the way in achieving the only kind of revitalization that can really take hold"— the kind predicated on market fundamentalism rather than on liberal social programs.[2] McLean, Clarke, and Buckley looked at entrepreneurial, market-oriented downtown redevelopment and saw "free enterprise" at work. Pittsburgh's growth coalition, in their estimation, wisely used scarce resources to make the city safe for private investment.

Countdown's focus on corporate construction projects unwittingly obscured a shift in how planners and developers thought about what constituted "downtown." Historian Carl Abbott has described downtown as a "contested concept" with no firmly fixed meaning in the postwar period.[3] For planners, policymakers, academics, and the public, downtown was the undisputed center of the American metropolis in the decade after World War II. By the mid-1950s, the same observers understood "downtown" to be a place in crisis. Rapidly failing real estate markets in central cities in the Northeast and Midwest required federal intervention to save central business districts (CBDs) through large-scale urban renewal programs. Backlash against urban renewal, the emergence of community development corporations, and new environmental and historic preservation regulations led planners from the middle of the 1960s to the middle of the 1970s to think of "downtown" as a set of multiple, intertwined centers of activity. Downtown districts, they came to realize, had varied social and economic geographies, and housed different kinds of activities for different kinds of users, most of whom were residents.[4]

When elected officials and civic leaders in North Atlantic manufacturing centers set out to make postindustrial cities, their activities followed the same general pattern. They typically focused earliest and most intensively on CBD redevelopment projects designed to meet the physical needs of the corporations and commercial services on which their economic visions were dependent, with some attention to neighborhood planning as urban renewal fell out of favor.[5] In the 1970s and 1980s, city officials and civic leaders drew new mental maps of downtown, expanding it to include culture-leisure-entertainment districts that could support development in the CBD. Planners and researchers began to think of downtown as a site for individual leisure activities, rather than as a set of interrelated spaces for social reproduction.[6]

In Pittsburgh, for instance, Richard Caliguiri's strategy for a second Renaissance hinged not only on commercial construction and CBD improvements but also on developing cultural, recreational, and leisure opportunities in the adjacent Strip District, South Side, and North Shore for young professionals and "city users"—transitory tourists, suburbanites, and students who did not permanently reside in, and did not always work in, the city but consumed its public and private resources through their use of service, recreational, and cultural spaces.[7] Other cities followed similar paths. In the UK, urban renewal cleared away "blight" in Manchester in the 1960s, which made way for a shopping mall and new housing near the historic city center in the 1970s and 1980s. The industrial buildings in the city's Northern Quarter, historically home to a wholesale food market, were converted to lofts in the 1990s. After shipbuilding declined in Belfast in the 1970s and 1980s, city officials worked with private developers to turn shipyards on the River Lagan into an entertainment district with hotels, restaurants, and nightclubs.[8]

Hamilton's leaders, too, sought to make over the Ambitious City's downtrodden downtown, but they undertook far fewer projects with much less private sector involvement than did their counterparts in Pittsburgh.[9] In Hamilton, downtown redevelopment pivoted on a single, large-scale, federally and provincially funded urban renewal project. Despite comparatively less robust redevelopment, public and private activity significantly reshaped the downtown core in the 1970s and 1980s. Pittsburgh's growth coalition wanted to replace services that catered primarily to existing residents with services directed toward imagined new residents and a regional (and in the case of financial services national or international) clientele. Hamilton's public officials, by contrast, sought to balance the commercial and service needs of local and national business elites with those of the existing residential working class, while simultaneously trying to develop services for imagined new residents. In Hamilton, manufacturing companies maintained their factories but moved their head offices, while in Pittsburgh manufacturers closed their factories and invested in new corporate headquarters downtown. This made Pittsburgh's growth coalition's vision of a city spatially reoriented to emphasize office towers rather than smokestacks infinitely more attainable than a similar imagination of Hamilton's future.

In both Pittsburgh and Hamilton, consultants, public officials, and civic leaders indeed shared the same idea of what a postindustrial downtown might look like, regardless of existing local conditions: office towers, rather than smokestacks, should dominate the skyline; culture and leisure activities should cater to city users rather than residents; and commercial services should reflect the perceived needs of the white-collar residents that growth coalitions hoped to attract. Even though growth coalitions' imaginations of what constituted a postindustrial downtown were conceptually very similar, projects were implemented very differently in the two cities. In Pittsburgh, city officials and civic leaders sought to replace factories with urban forms suited to service-sector functions, such as malls and high technology parks. Their downtown redevelopment plans foremost served the interests of locally headquartered corporations, particularly U.S. Steel, Mellon Bank, Dravo, and Pittsburgh Plate Glass, and secondarily addressed the executives whom they imagined might relocate their companies and white-collar jobs to Pittsburgh. Meeting the needs of existing residents ran a distant third. In Hamilton, the mayor's office instead worked to decentralize industry away from the CBD, distract the eye from the manufacturing still taking place on the harbor, and attract white-collar workers, all while remaining attentive to the interests of diverse groups of residents.

Pittsburgh's Second Renaissance

Buckley had reason to be impressed by downtown Pittsburgh in 1984. Major construction projects over the previous ten years included a convention center; commercial and retail space at Liberty Square, One Oxford Centre, Two Chatham Centre, and the Firstside complex, which incorporated the existing National Steel headquarters; the Allegheny International headquarters building; Pittsburgh Plate Glass's PPG Place; One Mellon Center, which housed Mellon Bank's headquarters; and a hotel. Together with earlier headquarters buildings for Westinghouse at the Gateway Center (1969) and U.S. Steel at Grant and Seventh Streets (1970), the new construction ensured that skyscrapers, rather than smokestacks, dominated Pittsburgh's skyline and projected an urban form associated with a headquarters city rather than with a steel town. Less than a decade earlier, those buildings were only a glimmer in executives' eyes. At a 1977 gala dinner, Allegheny Conference chairman Robert Dickey, III, president and CEO of Dravo, announced that a dramatic spatial transformation was on the horizon for Pittsburgh. On the city's South Side, the redevelopment of a historic train station into a festival marketplace marked the "beginning of a renaissance," he declared. Commercial and residential development on the North Shore promised to make that neighborhood "Pittsburgh's North Bank, sparkling with apartments, gardens, and marinas."[10] Dickey's focus on projects located outside, but in close proximity to, Pittsburgh's CBD exposed a shift in the growth coalition's understanding of what constituted downtown.

Dickey's speech opened a decade of major downtown development projects in Pittsburgh, only a fraction of which were in the Golden Triangle. City officials focused most intensively on leveraging corporate-sponsored projects in the CBD, Allegheny Conference executive director Robert Pease turned his organization's attention to creating a downtown cultural district adjacent to the Golden Triangle, and nonprofit and neighborhood groups remade nearby residential neighborhoods and their commercial districts. The Pittsburgh History and Landmarks Foundation (Landmarks) developed a festival marketplace on the South Side at Station Square; shops and restaurants emerged piecemeal in the Strip, the city's wholesale district, with little (positive) intervention from the Planning Department; and a mixture of public and private development, large and small, reshaped the North Side. Between 1976 and 1984, two billion dollars in public and private investment reshaped Pittsburgh in the way Dickey had predicted.[11]

Successfully rebranding Pittsburgh as a headquarters city rather than a steel town became a measure of success for Renaissance II. To public officials, headquarters buildings represented corporate investment, service-sector jobs, and increased tax revenue. Despite Dickey's predictions and Caliguiri's careful attention to his corporate partners, however, by the end of the 1970s there was scant evidence of a downtown revival. The amount of office space had increased in and around the Gateway Center—the 1.5 million square foot office complex that had been the centerpiece of the first Renaissance—and in the five blocks between Liberty and Fifth Avenues. Two decades of renovations and conversions had provided a net increase of nearly two million square feet of office space concentrated in peripheral areas, often displacing existing retail uses that served low- and middle-income residents. But, city planners noted, in 1979 over half a million square feet of office space remained vacant in buildings in two areas of the CBD targeted for redevelopment.[12]

By the time the recession hit in the early 1980s, however, many corporations had built or begun work on expensive real estate development projects downtown, and their CEOs remained active participants in the Allegheny Conference. They had already heavily invested in real estate for front office functions when CEOs began to lay off manufacturing workers and shutter plants. It is not entirely clear why the CEOs of Pittsburgh's largest

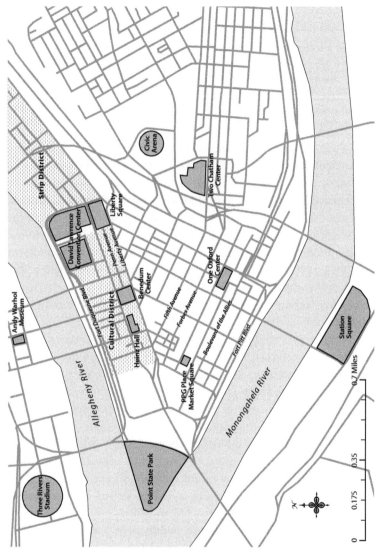

Figure 6. Major Renaissance II projects in Pittsburgh's "new" downtown.

corporations—U.S. Steel, Heinz, Mellon Bank, Pittsburgh National Bank, Dravo, Westinghouse, and Pittsburgh Plate Glass—decided to invest in downtown through the construction of new headquarters buildings and through corporate contributions to a cultural district rather than relocate their headquarters as their manufacturing interests in the region declined. One executive said that he thought it was "part of the culture of a company that makes it build corporate headquarters like this." His corporation, he recalled, "had considerable discussion about it and debate as to what we should do as a company. In terms of economics, there was a great case to be made to move elsewhere; we would have saved a lot of money. . . . But that's a short-sighted view." A core principle of his company, he reported, was "being a good citizen." "We just felt that it was an obligation that a company like ours should take on," he said. "If we were going to have a headquarters building, it should be in the city that helped us grow to the size we are, whose people have supported us, and so forth. Our building has helped create a new environment in downtown Pittsburgh."[13] The Allegheny Conference, too, described its members as community leaders committed to "the region's long-term future, through decisions, for instance, to retain their headquarters here."[14]

Executives' sense of civic duty was fortified by public subsidies. The city and state governments offered substantial corporate welfare packages to induce corporations to build or expand office complexes in the city, regardless of whether those corporations intended to close some or all of their regional manufacturing interests. There is no evidence that other municipalities were trying to lure away the corporate headquarters of floundering manufacturing firms. CEOs had no compelling reason to relocate out of the region, and their participation in Renaissance II, as had been the case in the first Renaissance, was likely intended to protect the value of their real estate holdings.

Caliguiri's vision for a second, postindustrial, downtown Renaissance finally found traction when Pittsburgh Plate Glass (PPG) constructed a Philip Johnson-designed headquarters building and redeveloped the adjacent mixed-use Market Square. PPG Place was exemplary of the types of projects the growth coalition pursued, promoted, and funded through a combination of public and private activity. PPG first proposed building a new headquarters in 1976, and over the course of two years winnowed nine potential sites downtown and on the North and South Sides down to three.[15] Two of these sites were of paramount interest to the mayor's office: Market Square and a parcel on Grant Street adjacent to the U.S. Steel headquarters shorthanded as "Grant Street East." While the city was initially eager to move PPG to the Grant Street East site and promised extensive subsidies to facilitate that project, CEO Stanton Williams and PPG's board ultimately decided to keep the company near Market Square, where the city had already begun to develop an outdoor space for shoppers, tourists, and office workers to congregate.[16]

Even though Williams declined to relocate to city officials' preferred site, he expected to receive public subsidies for PPG's headquarters building. The Caliguiri administration, for its part, was unwilling to risk losing a large-scale development project that signaled ongoing private investment in the city. PPG's consultants unofficially approached the Mayor's Development Council (MDC), the City Planning Department, and the Urban Redevelopment Authority (URA) about designating a parcel adjacent to Market Square as an unassisted urban renewal site. Unassisted urban renewal, in policy parlance, meant that that the project would not involve a direct public subsidy for land acquisition. Instead, the city would use its powers of eminent domain to take properties in a designated area and sell them to a developer for the same amount the city paid. PPG's consultants warned the MDC that, unless the URA worked more aggressively to acquire a site that would accommodate PPG's space requirements, the company would abandon its construction plans.[17] The city's development process, for decades predicated on corporate welfare and capital subsidies, was particularly responsive to this type of corporate blackmail.

Caliguiri's advisors on the MDC initially expressed alarm over some of Williams's financial and aesthetic requirements but eventually acceded to most of PPG's stipulations to ensure the project went through. URA officials agreed to acquire the properties in the redevelopment area (with the exception of a church) and sell them to PPG. To do so, the URA invoked its powers of eminent domain but also found new office space for several existing businesses and subsidized their relocation costs in an effort to avoid backlash. The city's Parking Authority assumed the costs of providing adequate parking for Market Square and PPG Place, and the mayor's office earmarked $1 million for landscaping and facade improvements near the project.[18] The city government also exempted the project area from real estate taxes for nearly three years, until construction was finished. When the neo-Gothic building was completed in 1984, it provided the growth coalition with the kind of iconic architecture its members hoped would signal Pittsburgh's postindustrial transformation.

The MDC lost a promising developer for Grant Street East when PPG selected Market Square for its headquarters, but planners remained intent on redeveloping the site. Flaherty's planning staff had first identified Grant

Figure 7. Pittsburgh's skyline after Renaissance II. Philip Johnson's neo-gothic PPG Place is center-right; the U.S. Steel Tower (more recently occupied by the University of Pittsburgh Medical Center) is on the left. Photograph by Brian Donovan.

Street East as a "market for potential development" in 1976.[19] Two years later, the Allegheny Conference released the results of a study it commissioned on how to "transform Grant Street from a chaos of trolley tracks and wires, traffic signs and signals, decaying concrete and disunified paving styles into a stately 'Grand Boulevard' that could serve as a model for other downtown street improvements."[20] Caliguiri, too, was eager to find a developer for the series of parcels owned by the URA, the city, and U.S. Steel. His planners envisioned the construction of a 400-room luxury hotel, 600,000 square feet of office space, 100,000 square feet of commercial space, 900 housing units, 2,800 parking spots, a subway station, street realignment, and a park. City officials estimated the private-sector share of the massive project at $143 million and city costs at $17 million and asked U.S. Steel to function as the primary developer. The corporation had ventured into real estate development a few years earlier, when its real estate division began construction on Century III mall on a slag pile in suburban West Mifflin. At the MDC's behest, U.S. Steel agreed to expand its real estate development activities to include the

Grant Street site. In this way, the Caliguiri administration encouraged U.S. Steel's shift into non-productive activities.[21]

By 1980, development was underway. Allegheny Conference staffers described the Grant Street redevelopment project as evidence of a return to the "traditional pattern of cooperation" between corporate leaders and the city government under Caliguiri. Caliguiri's planners congratulated themselves on establishing what they described as a "receptive process sensitive to the changing realities of the business community" and a development environment that "encourages investment, guides the nature of specific proposals to maximize public benefit, and analyzes responsible public investments which may be necessary to make the projects a reality."[22] Dickey committed to constructing a headquarters building for Dravo on the Grant Street East site, but his successor sold the 54-story building to Mellon Bank before construction was complete; Mellon renamed the building, Pittsburgh's second-tallest, One Mellon Plaza.[23] U.S. Steel built a $150 million office and hotel complex, state and federal funds subsidized a $30 million midtown subway terminal, and the city financed a streetscape makeover between the courthouse and the U.S. Steel Building.[24] Pease and city officials praised the Grant Street redevelopment as evidence of the corporate sector's renewed commitment to Pittsburgh. Planners described it as "a demonstration of the kind of public-private cooperation, which has been visualized in the Renaissance II idea."[25]

Increased tax revenues, newly created service-sector jobs, and an office construction boom heralded Pittsburgh's transition from a site of production to a headquarters for the international management of capital. The PPG and Grant Street East projects projected an image of investor confidence in Pittsburgh, and city officials expected the six major new office buildings and two new hotel complexes to generate around $5 million a year in taxes and create 36,800 new permanent jobs downtown.[26] As production became increasingly internationalized, corporate headquarters became potent symbols of Pittsburgh's shift away from manufacturing and toward services and finance.[27] However, not all observers of the downtown redevelopment process were enthusiastic about the public expenditures required to create what planners called a "positive business environment."[28]

DMS activists attacked Mellon Bank, Dravo, and U.S. Steel executives, in particular, for their simultaneous disinvestment in regional manufacturing and expansion of front office operations in the Golden Triangle. "Dravo, U.S.S. and Mellon level our workplaces by demolition with real bombs," DMS charged in 1985. To expose the link between corporate disinvestment in productive capacity and the expansion of service and professional industries, as well as repudiate CEOs' claims that they had no money to invest in steel mills even as they undertook multi-million-dollar headquarters projects, DMS members (unsuccessfully) applied for an explosives permit "to blow up the corporate leaders work place as they are blowing up our work places in the valleys."[29] Despite largely symbolic protests from unemployed steelworkers, downtown redevelopment plans proceeded without much serious impediment.

Headquarters buildings were not the only projects that the city leveraged. For Caliguiri and Pittsburgh's civic leaders, establishing a cultural district and building a new convention center and stadium were essential components of their strategy to attract businesses and tourist dollars to the city. In 1982, the Planning Department announced that it had earmarked $67 million of public funds for a host of projects intended to the bolster the CBD. The department expected the city's investment to attract more than $2 billion in private development that would help realize Caliguiri's expansive vision for a postindustrial downtown. Planners anticipated the funds would support the construction of five million square feet of new office space, half-a-million square feet of commercial and retail space, historic restorations of two train stations, and a host of transportation and infrastructure improvements.[30] In addition to retail, restaurants, and other services designed to appeal to the imagined future downtown workforce, the mayor's office and the Allegheny Conference aggressively pursued economic development through culture industries. "Culture," to city and Allegheny Conference officials, primarily meant high culture—museums, the symphony, ballet, and theater. Prior to 1969, Pittsburgh was home to two major museums, the Carnegie Museum of Art (1895) and the Carnegie Museum of Natural History (1896), both located near the University of Pittsburgh in Oakland, and to the Buhl Planetarium (1939) on the North Side. Forbes Field, the city's sports stadium, was also in Oakland. There were some performing arts venues and movie theaters downtown, most located between Liberty Avenue and the Allegheny River, but Pittsburgh lacked a unified theater district.

The openings of the Frick Museum of Art in Point Breeze in 1969, Three Rivers Stadium on the North Side in 1970, and Heinz Hall (a conversion of an old Loews theater into a symphony hall) on Penn Avenue in 1971 were the first indications that the cultural center of Pittsburgh was shifting away from the University of Pittsburgh campus, both to sites dispersed throughout the city and to a new cultural complex downtown. Heinz Hall foreshadowed the Allegheny Conference's focus on economic development through a cultural district in the 1980s. The Mattress Factory, a contemporary art museum in an

old Stearns & Foster factory that opened on the North Side in 1977, proved
equally important. Heinz Hall had been a labor of love for Senator John Heinz
and largely funded through his family's charitable trust, but a local sculptor
developed the Mattress Factory for contemporary art installations without the
benefit of significant foundation or government funding.[31] Heinz Hall provided
an anchor for a downtown cultural district, while the success of the Mattress
Factory proved that culture could flourish elsewhere in the city and in venues
not sanctioned by the mayor's office or Allegheny Conference officials.

The growth coalition quickly moved to incorporate independent arts
development into a cultural strategy for the city. The Allegheny Conference
set up an ad hoc steering committee to raise funds from private sources to pay
for a redevelopment study of Pittsburgh's red light district, the Penn-Liberty
corridor, after Executive Committee member H. J. Heinz, II, took a "special
interest" in Pittsburgh's cultural development. Penn-Liberty was a booster's
nightmare: retail and restaurant activity was in decline, movie theaters had
closed, and the streets had been ripped up for a stalled one-station subway
expansion. In December 1979, the Allegheny Conference's design consultants
met with Caliguiri and the Executive Committee to present their plan to
redevelop the area as a historical and cultural district with housing and retail
development, a "riverfront promenade" along the Allegheny River between
the Seventh and Ninth Street bridges, and facade and street improvements on
Penn and Liberty Avenues.[32]

The Penn-Liberty study became the "primary guide" for the cultural district that took shape over the course of the next decade.[33] Under Pease's direction, the Allegheny Conference promoted the fledgling cultural district as "a
positive selling point for attracting and retaining businesses for the region"
that held "the potential for sparking a new arts/entertainment industry that
could create jobs and add dollars to the regional economy."[34] Inspired by the
redevelopment of Boston's infamous "combat zone" into an entertainment
district that attracted suburban visitors, Caliguiri's office threw its political
and financial support behind the Allegheny Conference's plans in the hope
that the cultural district would supplant the prostitution, porn palaces, and
adult bookstores that dominated Liberty Avenue.[35] In 1984, the Allegheny
Conference incorporated the Pittsburgh Trust for Cultural Resources (Cultural Trust) to coordinate the district's development and programming.
Funded with Heinz Foundation money and chaired by Dickey, who had
retired from both Dravo and the Allegheny Conference, the Cultural Trust's
mission was to stimulate economic development through the creation of a
cultural district in the Penn-Liberty corridor.[36]

The cultural district that took shape over the next decade comprised a fourteen-block section of downtown bounded by Fort Duquesne Boulevard, Liberty Avenue, Stanwix Street, and Tenth Street, anchored at the west end by Heinz Hall and at the east end by the Convention Center.[37] In its first three years, in cooperation with Allegheny International, the Cultural Trust converted the Stanley Theatre to the Benedum Center for Performing Arts, which housed the opera and ballet, and constructed an adjacent office building, CNG Tower, as an income-generating property.[38] Through the URA, Pittsburgh secured a $17 million federal Urban Development Action Grant, the Benedum Foundation and the Heinz Foundation donated $5 million and $2.5 million respectively, and the city and county shared the costs of a $7.5 million public bond issue.[39] Pease praised the Benedum Center project as "one more example of what can result from public and private cooperation." Dickey congratulated city, county, and federal representatives for securing supplementary funds to create the theater. He called city and county officials "amazing in their support of the project," and thanked elected officials in Washington for securing funding for the project.[40]

The cultural district provided another target for the mill town activists' assault on public funding directed toward a corporate-driven redevelopment agenda instead of for mill town recovery. While it would surely be incorrect to suggest that the cultural district did not appeal to Pittsburgh's existing residents, or meet their needs for a richer cultural life (museums are, after all, public projects), city officials supported the cultural district primarily because they thought it would appeal to tourists and suburbanites and help attract wealthier residents. DMS, less impressed than Pease and Dickey with the public-private cooperation that had produced the Benedum, marshaled an attack against public officials for funding the project. The jobs created in the cultural district, they noted, were primarily low-paying, non-unionized service-sector positions. Activists distributed fliers that condemned federal aid for a cultural district when the mill towns were repeatedly told that there was no money available to fix their crumbling infrastructure or help unemployed workers. "What would Clairton be like if Clairton would have gotten the $17 million in Federal Aid that Senator Heinz obtained for the Stanley Theatre renovations," DMS asked. "It seems there is plenty of federal money for the new Renaissance in Pittsburgh but no money for the valley or the people of Clairton."[41] As had been the case with DMS's efforts to end public subsidies for corporate headquarters buildings, the mill town activists simply did not have the organizational strength to meaningfully disrupt plans for the fledgling cultural district.

The Cultural Trust quickly expanded its mission beyond site development to include broad support for the city's existing and proposed cultural
institutions and a commitment to develop downtown nightlife. As one local
executive noted, "The cultural climate of this community is quite important
to attracting industry, attracting people to the community and it isn't a frill
at all."[42] At the end of 1985, Caliguiri appointed an Entertainment Task Force,
which identified Station Square on the South Side, the Strip District, and
the stadium area on the North Side as ripe for tourism and leisure-related
developments.[43] The Entertainment Task Force's recommendations codified a
series of ad hoc efforts long underway. The North Side's North Shore neighborhood—the area Dickey described as downtown's "North Bank" in 1977—
had long represented an area of mutual concern for the city government and
the Allegheny Conference. Allegheny Conference staffers described the area
between the stadium, the Allegheny River, and Allegheny Center as "100
acres of urban wasteland." Caliguiri and his planners saw the North Shore
as an engine for economic development, "a prime development site and one
which can stimulate private development and provide further job opportunities."[44] Pease and the Allegheny Conference envisioned a revitalized North
Shore populated by the downtown white-collar workforce they hoped to
lure into the city from the suburbs. The staffers echoed Dickey's declaration
that, because of its proximity to the Golden Triangle, the area could become
Pittsburgh's "spectacular 'Left Bank.'" North Shore redevelopment, they predicted, would link the rest of the North Side to the downtown and "knit the
lower North Shore into a coherent, functional whole."[45] In this way, the North
Shore, historically composed of tight-knit working-class communities and,
in the 1960s and early 1970s, a front line in neighborhood resistance against
urban renewal, became an extension of the downtown core in the minds of
Pittsburgh's growth coalition.

Federal officials certified the North Side for urban renewal in the 1960s,
and the city government had already used federal funds for site acquisition
before the Flaherty administration halted the planned renewal project under
pressure from the community and historic preservation groups. The dedica-
tion of Three Rivers Stadium in 1970 as the "keystone" in an eighty-four-acre
North Shore redevelopment project represented a continuation of the planners' long-term urban renewal focus on that part of the city.[46] The Alcoa-
developed Allegheny Center, with its complex of office buildings, high-rise
apartments (including affordable housing), together with the city-owned
North Shore Riverfront Park and Roberto Clemente Memorial Park, served
as catalysts for North Side redevelopment in the 1970s. By 1980, the *Pittsburgh*

Post-Gazette reported "serious developer interest" in the North Shore, signaling to Caliguiri that he had spent the city's money well.[47] A decade later, the Carnegie Corporation developed two new museums on the North Shore: the Science Center (which incorporated the existing Buhl Planetarium) opened in 1991, and the Andy Warhol Museum, funded in part by the Dia Foundation, opened in 1994. As the city and the Allegheny Conference co-opted these independent projects, they wove neighborhood-based initiatives into the narrative of Renaissance II.

The Allegheny Conference and city planners focused their attentions on remaking the North Shore for a new type of resident but showed little interest in the South Side, the neighborhood across the Monongahela River from the CBD. Instead, Landmarks spearheaded a major redevelopment project at the west end of Carson Street, the neighborhood's central artery. With $350,000 in seed money from R. K. Mellon's nephew, Richard Mellon Scaife, Landmarks converted the abandoned Pittsburgh and Lake Erie railroad into Station Square, a festival marketplace inspired by the Rouse Corporation's projects at Faneuil Hall in Boston and Baltimore's Inner Harbor. Landmarks president Arthur Ziegler had been searching for a demonstration project to show how private sector-driven historic preservation could be a potent economic development tool.[48] Scaife, a philanthropist and the publisher of a conservative daily, the *Pittsburgh Tribune-Review*, had previously funded Landmarks's activities on the North Side. By the mid-1970s, he was interested in using his Allegheny Foundation to support a project like San Francisco's Ghirardelli Square. Station Square, situated at the foot of Mount Washington at the west end of Carson Street, was easily accessible to residents of the working- and middle-class South Side and Mount Washington and Pittsburgh's prosperous southern suburbs. Scaife's backing—the Allegheny Foundation eventually contributed $12 million to the project—enabled Landmarks to purchase a forty-one-acre site and break ground for the construction of restaurants, shops, hotels, and office space on the site in 1976.[49]

City officials initially viewed Station Square as competition for city-funded North Shore projects. Caliguiri's office publicly praised the group's efforts to preserve the railroad station and lauded the success of the mixed-use development, but Ziegler recalled that the mayor originally opposed Station Square and that the city planning department tried to quash the project in an effort to preserve city officials' control over development.[50] Eventually, the Caliguiri administration co-opted the project as part of Renaissance II. In the same way that planners incorporated the North Side's independent arts venues and community activists into the Renaissance II plan, the Caliguiri administration sought credit for Station Square as it siphoned off restaurant and retail traffic from the CBD. Like the North Shore, Station Square had been absorbed into Caliguiri's downtown strategy by the early 1980s.

Perhaps with the missed opportunity to control the development of Station Square in mind, as early as 1978, city planners identified the Strip District as the industrial area that warranted the most immediate public attention. A half square mile bordered by the Golden Triangle to the west and the more residential Lawrenceville neighborhood to the east, the Strip had in the nineteenth century housed facilities for U.S. Steel, Westinghouse, Alcoa, and H.J. Heinz Co. In the early twentieth century, produce, poultry, and meat wholesalers moved in as industry moved out. By the 1970s, much of the Strip's land, factories, and stores were vacant, dilapidated, or underused. Planners announced an expansive, if unfocused, interest in the "creation of new development sites, accommodation of growing industries and firms, retention of existing firms, improvement of transportation access and movement, identification of port development potential, consolidation of the wholesale food industry, expansion of retail trade and reuse of significant buildings."[51] Planners' goals for the Strip District remained vague in 1980, when the Planning Department again indicated that it wanted to pursue city-led projects in the neighborhood. The *Post-Gazette* reported that "some planners consider it the 'hottest' single area for potential development in the city," in no small part because they were looking at the successful redevelopment of Boston and Baltimore's wholesale markets, but Renaissance II projects already underway strained the city's limited budget and no formal plan emerged. Planning director Robert Lurcott said his department was looking for ways to package Strip District projects for federal aid.[52] Instead, over the next two decades, small businesses moved into the neighborhood without sanction or subsidies from the growth partnership. As had been the case with Station Square, the eventual redevelopment of the Strip into an arts and entertainment district occurred largely outside the purview of the City Planning Department and the Allegheny Conference. Unlike Station Square, developed by a nonprofit with a master plan for the site, the retail, restaurant, and residential spaces created in the Strip emerged piecemeal and coexisted with the neighborhood's historic wholesale food market.

As the growth coalition reimagined the boundaries of downtown to include the cultural district, the Strip District, and portions of the North and South Sides, planners praised themselves for creating distinct retail markets and entertainment zones that served "both low and high income buyers, city residents, workers in the CBD and suburbanites."[53] Planners may have believed that downtown land uses served the needs of city residents and provided retail and services geared to different income levels, but members of at least one of Caliguiri's downtown task forces recognized that the proposed commercial development was not intended to continue a diversity of uses, nor was its goal to attract full-time residents to the Golden Triangle. Instead, task force members pointed out that developers sought to meet the perceived needs of daytime office workers who would return to the suburbs in the evening.[54] McLean, too, described the downtown development process as one from which city residents and even office workers were almost completely absent. Competitive market forces, local and national developers, the design community, city agencies and, most important, the "increase of strategic planning by corporations in their development and selection of long-range real estate alternatives," he wrote, were the chief determinants of the nature of downtown development.[55]

In 1984, a Harrisburg newspaper reported of Pittsburgh, "battle lines have been drawn in this city caught in a choice between smokestacks and skyscrapers." The world of unionized, well-paid American steelworkers was being replaced by "a shining city of corporate headquarters, cultural amenities and white-collar professionals who know and care little about steel," the article noted. City officials told the reporter that they hoped to attract 100,000 new executives to Pittsburgh over the next decade, and that they were targeting workers in finance, health care, engineering and high technology fields. "If we want these folks to live here, the white-collar folks," said one city planner, "we have to give them something to do to keep them here." The "something to do" was to shop in Station Square, attend sporting events, and visit museums. The reporter noted that "the question facing Pittsburgh might be, Who gains here and who will be left behind?"[56]

Members of DMS and Tri-State contended that the city government and local corporations were leaving workers behind in their focus on economic development through headquarters construction and high-culture amenities. Tri-State agitator Charles McCollester, in a letter to the editor of the *Pittsburgh Catholic*, lambasted the growth coalition's plans for remaking the region in a way that pushed manufacturing workers to the margin of civic life. "Instead of steel mills, we have office buildings. Instead of supermarkets and hardware stores, we have Station Squares and boutiques for the rich," he wrote. "The shot and a beer taverns of forty years ago are massage parlors and porno shops. The poor pay the highest bus fares in the county to get to work or the unemployment line, so the wealthy will be able to ride a subway from the US Steel building to Hornes [Department Store]."[57]

Caliguiri and the Allegheny Conference's leaders were unmoved by activists' complaints about the costs of downtown redevelopment for the region's manufacturing workers. Their downtown development strategy remained focused on attracting new corporate citizens at the expense of the working- and middle-class residents already living in the city. The growth partnership continued to funnel public funds toward projects like PPG Place, Grant Street East, and the cultural district, which were designed to serve the professional and leisure interests of white-collar workers. Redevelopment in the Strip District, at Station Square, and on the North Shore began outside the growth coalition's purview and initially resisted the displacement of existing residents and sought to provide neighborhood, as well as regional, services. But Caliguiri co-opted those projects as well, incorporating groups that might otherwise have resisted his postindustrial plans for the city into the growth coalition that facilitated Renaissance II. Former URA chairman Jack Robin, whose involvement in Pittsburgh's redevelopment schemes spanned four mayoral administrations, recalled shortly before his death in 2000 that the growth partnership had "changed the urban geography of Pittsburgh . . . crossing the Allegheny and cross[ing] the Mon in the North Side and the South Side." Renaissance II, he noted with pride, had made "a different central city than we've ever known."[58] Robin was referring to the physical geography of downtown. But the social and economic characteristics of the areas newly incorporated into downtown had changed as well, from neighborhood commercial districts serving working-class residents to culture, leisure, and shopping districts built for and marketed to tourists and suburbanites.

Hamilton's Civic Square

Pittsburgh's perpetual downtown redevelopment between the 1950s and the 1980s served as a model for similar plans undertaken by Hamilton's public officials. During his 1961 mayoral campaign, Vic Copps vowed to revitalize Hamilton's aging downtown. He wryly observed that "while other cities have skyscrapers going up in the downtown area, Hamilton has 147 parking lots," and his desire to create a new central city filled with tall buildings and cultural amenities occupied his mayoral tenure.[59] Copps set out to realize plans for a civic square first proposed in 1947, when E. G. Faludi created a master plan for the city. Faludi recognized that Hamilton would increasingly find itself in competition with nearby Toronto, London, Brantford, and Kitchener, and urged the city government to pursue industrial development to remain competitive. He also advised city officials to undertake a comprehensive downtown redevelopment program that would expand the public market, move city hall and replace it with commercial buildings, and redevelop "blighted" portions of the CBD and adjacent residential areas.[60] The Planning Department completed its first downtown renewal study in accordance with Faludi's recommendations in 1958, but at the time the arrangements of the federal-provincial cost-sharing program for urban renewal programs did not include commercial district redevelopment.

A few years after Copps was elected, the Hamilton Downtown Association (HDA), a civic organization composed of local business owners, submitted an ambitious proposal for a downtown "cultural-athletic center" that would showcase Hamilton's "Space Age achievements" and scientific and technological advances. The proposal echoed Faludi's 1947 recommendations. HDA urged Hamilton to "answer the growing need for the cultural development and physical improvement of its people in their leisure hours" and to counter the "Pied Pipers of other cities and countries," which, members lamented, had "lured too many of our young people from our midst." The businessmen identified a "cultural void" in downtown Hamilton and proposed to fill it with a two-block cultural and athletic complex near the center of the city. The cultural complex, they thought, would stimulate a wholesale physical redevelopment of downtown, foster a cultural renaissance that would allow Hamilton to compete with other cities for young residents, and create a regional attraction to draw people into the city. HDA members proposed that Copps carry out their plan through a foundation sponsored by City Council. The institutional arrangements of the proposed foundation reflected the kind of public-private cooperation at the heart of Pittsburgh's redevelopment partnership: HDA wanted City Council to appoint a board of trustees that would include representatives from the council, manufacturing enterprises, local businesses, labor, and cultural and athletic organizations. The board would "plan, arrange finances, construct and operate" a cultural and athletic complex, jointly funded by public and private "grants and subscriptions." The HDA pointedly noted that the City Council required the "continuing support of the Hamilton Downtown Association and other civic-minded organizations" to carry out projects of the magnitude that Copps desired.[61] The HDA president cited Pittsburgh's Golden Triangle as a model for what Hamilton might become if the public and private sectors worked together, and he invited the developer in charge of one Pittsburgh's urban renewal projects to town to talk to civic leaders about Pittsburgh's redevelopment.[62]

Hamilton's local businessmen and corporate leaders joined city officials to lobby the federal and provincial governments to expand urban renewal programs beyond housing construction to finance downtown redevelopment. In 1964, the federal government amended the National Housing Act to fund commercial district projects. The Copps administration made plans to use federal urban renewal funds to replace the existing, declining downtown core with modern, architecturally innovative, retail, office, and residential buildings, which city officials anticipated would inspire further private redevelopment downtown. Four years after the federal government extended urban renewal to commercial districts, Hamilton had dedicated nearly 7 percent of its capital budget to downtown urban renewal.[63]

Despite provincial efforts to forestall interurban competition, between 1968 and 1981 Hamilton's city officials chanelled their downtown development resources into the civic square project, called Jackson Square after Copps's predecessor, in the hope of challenging Toronto's preeminence as a service and finance center. In the late 1960s, Hamilton's downtown commercial development was concentrated along King, Main, James, and John streets. City planners complained in 1968 that the CBD was supposed to be a vital hub of urban life, but downtown Hamilton was instead "threatened by obsolescence, decay and congestion." Downtown, they contended, "should not be allowed to decline through neglect."[64] It was only after receiving Arthur D. Little's Lunchpail Report, however, that city officials and civic leaders actively renewed their interest in competing with Toronto for head offices and business services.

In the report, consultants cited Hamilton's proximity to Toronto, the declining physical condition of the downtown shopping district, and its steel town image as the primary causes of the city's "lag" in commercial activity compared to nearby London and Toronto and to the province and Canada as a whole.[65] The consultants found "retail sales deficiencies" in several areas, including business services, recreation, and tourism, and they determined that suburban residents were more likely to go to Toronto than to Hamilton to acquire luxury goods and amenities. They judged Hamilton deficient in per capita sales in "those lines of retailing activity that offer the amenities of life," but similar to Toronto in terms of "day-to-day types" of commercial activity. They suggested that city officials should work to attract corporate headquarters and business services such as advertising, accounting, legal services, printing, and publishing.[66] The consultants had visited Cleveland, Pittsburgh, and Bridgeport and, based on their studies of those cities, informed Hamilton's city officials that successful downtown redevelopment required significant support from the mayor and "prominent private citizens" through economic, social, and cultural organizations.[67] Their recommendations were impossible to implement within Hamilton's (and Ontario's) existing political institutions because provincial growth policy precluded the entrepreneurial interurban competition the consultants promoted based on their studies of more autonomous U.S. cities.

Consultants praised city officials' efforts to create a civic square and cast off Hamilton's lunch bucket image. They wrote that it was "obvious" that attracting headquarters and business services would create demand for new office space and could think of "few more worthwhile" long-term goals than the development of modern office space.[68] They thought that Jackson Square, then in the planning stages, promised new "high standards of appearance" for downtown and urged city officials to take "beautification steps" to improve the areas adjacent to the project. When the city unveiled the construction plans in 1968, the *Hamilton Spectator* heralded Jackson Square as "more than a facelift for an area that has become run down at its heels." A few months before his Pittsburgh trip, Jack Moore confirmed, "we're going to make a determined drive to attract other head offices here—especially those of non-industrial companies." Economic diversification, he intimated, would necessarily lead to urban revitalization: "I think you can see what this will do for the downtown," he said. The *Spectator* predicted Jackson Square would "not only make Hamilton the industrial center but the commercial heart of the area as well."[69]

In the midst of this ambitious, if implausible, reimagining of Hamilton as a headquarters city, Stelco caused a furor when it revealed, via a 1968 quarterly report, that the company planned to move its head office functions to Toronto. The announcement came on the heels of Stelco's purchase of a large site at Nanticoke on Lake Erie in anticipation of expanding its steel-making capacity outside Hamilton. "For absolute rudeness and crudity Stelco's departure announcement was without parallel," the *Spectator*'s editorial board complained. "No one in Hamilton, be he cabinet minister, mayor, business associate was given the courtesy of prior glimpse."[70] Hamilton East MP John Munro lambasted Stelco for its expansion and relocation plans, saying, "Hamilton is apparently good enough to sweat for Stelco but not good enough for anything else."[71] A Hamilton alderman focused his outrage on Stelco's abrogation of its "strong obligation to the community," whose workers created the company's wealth. The *Spectator*'s editorial board urged city officials to seek out desperately needed alternative revenue sources once Stelco left. "With the brass here," the editorial noted, "Hamilton always tended to treat Stelco with kid gloves on the theory that it might somehow, sometime, perform some civic service uniquely related to the city's steel relationship." The move, suggested the *Spectator*, might finally convince the city government of what most residents already knew: that Stelco and Hamilton did not have the same material interests and that the city's largely unsuccessful efforts to convince Stelco to serve as the city's patron led the mayor to act like "a kid begging for handouts on Hallowe'en."[72]

Copps was more forgiving of Stelco's decision; he expressed disappointment but tried to redirect public attention toward the company's agreement with the city to relocate its general office staff to a building in Jackson Square.[73] Stelco's defection nonetheless dealt a harsh blow to the Economic Development Department's plan to promote Hamilton as a good place for companies to locate their head offices.[74] Stelco's agreement to relocate back-office functions to Jackson Square had, however, saved the renewal project, which was fraught with problems from the outset. The city began to expropriate and clear the downtown lots required for the project in 1966, before securing a site developer. By the time Stelco announced it was pulling up stakes, the city had evicted merchants of existing stores and demolished forty-three acres of buildings, and the project had stalled with no developer in sight.[75] The area sat vacant for nearly a decade as officials scrambled to assemble corporate and commercial prospects for the site. A prominent local lawyer brokered a deal with Standard Life and Montreal-based developers Yale Properties, Ltd., to assume control of the project in 1969, but it took eight months to convince city officials to sign off on a redesign of the original project that would emphasize commercial rather than public space. After Stelco announced its commitment to Jackson Square, banks and department stores signed leases, and construction finally began in 1970. "Once this thing takes off, there should be no looking back," enthused Moore. He reported that several developers had waited to see if "Hamilton could get Civic Square off the ground. If we couldn't," he said, "they felt this wasn't the kind of city they wanted to invest in." Chamber of Commerce president Burnie Gillespie optimistically predicted that the civic square, along with McMaster University's planned expansion, a new regional airport, and the proposed regional government, would allow Hamilton to "rival or surpass Toronto."[76]

The Jackson Square development undeniably altered Hamilton's social and economic geography along with downtown's physical orientation. Gillespie described the development as a "springboard to a complete transformation of the city." Downtown "will change dramatically, even outside the 12-block Civic Square itself," he said. "It will turn our entire face away from the east and make our main entrance the south-west, towards Lake Erie." A local realtor predicted that the new complex would "encourage a better class of development both inside and outside the Square." Building owners, he said, "are going to have to remodel or rebuild if they want to keep their tenants." City councilor Jack MacDonald admitted, "certainly, some people will be hurt. But if we didn't go ahead with a project like this, the whole downtown area would have decayed."[77]

The initial plan for the civic square, drafted by Toronto's Murray Jones and Associates, included ample green space, room for air circulation, and pedestrian-friendly streets. It also featured a planetarium, gardens, wading pools, a skating rink, and a public auditorium. Jackson Square as it was ultimately constructed bore little relation to its original design, which Hamilton historian John Weaver described as an "overly-optimistic sketch" followed by "a disillusioning series of revisions that did not measure up to promised benefits."[78] The construction drawings for the $300 million, forty-two-acre project replaced Hamilton's Victorian commercial district with two sets of concrete modernist superblocks, designed to facilitate auto rather than pedestrian traffic.[79]

Two groups emerged to protest the altered design. Sheila Zack, the wife of a downtown businessman, founded the first, Save Our Square. Save Our Square's members were primarily middle-class residents concerned with preserving open space and historic architecture in the downtown core; the group's resistance to the civic square project was in response to the altered design, not to the urban renewal plan generally or to the emerging postindustrial vision for the city. The second, composed of five prominent businessmen led by lawyer Herman Turkstra, wanted the city to privilege pedestrian-friendly development that would attract shift workers and people living in nearby apartments into the city center. Turksta's group proposed a town hall-style design review to solicit community input; Zack's organization instead appealed the land use plan to the Ontario Municipal Board.[80] In the end, provincial rather than local officials served to mitigate the threat posed to development plans through civic protest because the urban renewal project served the provincial government's emerging interest in establishing Hamilton as a regional center.[81]

As it was constructed, the civic square included services for existing residents, hoped-for residents, suburbanites, and tourists. The growth coalition expected the new leisure and cultural facilities, including a theater/auditorium (Hamilton Place), the Art Gallery of Hamilton, the Canadian Football Hall of Fame, Copps Coliseum (a hockey rink), and the Hamilton Convention

Figure 8. Aerial view of downtown Hamilton looking west toward the harbor and its industry, ca. 1950. Courtesy of Local History & Archives, Hamilton Public Library.

Center, to draw tourists away from Toronto. City officials expected a shopping center anchored by Eaton's department store to lure urban residents as well as suburban shoppers away from suburban malls. A new public library and relocated public market would largely serve Hamilton residents. Three new office buildings—the twenty-six-story Stelco Tower, the Robert Thomson Building, and the Standard Life Center—signaled Hamilton's importance as a commercial center.

Gillespie anticipated that the owners of older buildings downtown would lose tenants because they would not be able to afford to modernize their properties. Those who remained, he suggested, might lose clients to new businesses.[82] Gillespie was right: Jackson Square recentered the city's downtown core and established a new central business district a few blocks west of the existing commercial district. The project created tension between new businesses in Jackson Square and older businesses that remained, and struggled, on the east end of King Street, no longer part of the commercial core. In 1968, Chamber president A. R. Prack noted, "many of our members and many of our citizens have been caught in the path of progress, in the

Figure 9. Aerial view of downtown Hamilton after urban renewal and
construction of Jackson Square, ca. 1980. Courtesy of Local History
& Archives, Hamilton Public Library.

exciting redevelopment of our city." He recognized that "to some it will be
a burden with varying degrees of sacrifice," but he believed that "the long
awaited rejuvenation of Hamilton will more than repay them for their sacrifice and they will be proud of their contribution."[83] A year later, his successor,
H. K. Embree, acknowledged members' concerns about continually shifting
plans for downtown. "Change is disturbing and perhaps nowhere more so
than in the field of the small and medium business," Embree wrote. "The
businessman is feeling pressures never before imagined and this will maintain and increase if he is to survive in our economy."[84] By 1970, the Chamber
congratulated itself for "directly" assisting in the "successful negotiations"
that allowed the civic square project to break ground.[85]

Hamilton's public officials and civic leaders began to think in different
terms about what constituted downtown once Jackson Square was underway. When Faludi referred to "downtown" Hamilton in 1947, he meant the
central business district narrowly bounded by Main Street to the south, York
Boulevard to the north, Wellington Street to the east, and Queen Street to
the west. By the late 1970s, Hamilton's planners began to use the more expansive designation "Central Area"—bounded by the Niagara escarpment ("the
Mountain," in local parlance) to the south, the harbor to the north, Victoria

Avenue to the east, and Queen Street to the west—to describe the CBD and the commercial and residential areas adjacent to it. Rather than simultaneously redevelop the CBD and the ancillary areas that planners began to think of as part of downtown, as had occurred in Pittsburgh, Hamilton's planners first carried out the renewal project and, only as it neared completion, turned their attention to the rest of the Central Area. They struggled to spatially delineate the new downtown, ultimately declaring that its "amoebic nature" required them to define it based on activities instead of topography. For planners, downtown had become a set of intertwined spaces for different types of activities, "that area of the city which has a high concentration of a variety of commercial activity, high service employment, cultural roots, entertainment and generally speaking provides the stage for unprecedented human interaction on all scales." Through their focus on services, entertainment, and culture, planners imagined the Central Area as a series of postindustrial land uses and sought to divest from the light manufacturing that was still present in the mid-1970s.[86]

CAPAC members lamented the failure of the Jackson Square project to spur additional large-scale redevelopment. The 1981 Central Area Plan, produced in concert with the Regional Planning and Development Department, represented the culmination of the efforts of Hamilton's first formal (albeit short-lived) public-private partnership. The plan's authors noted that Jackson Square had "provided key image-boosting attractions" as well as new commercial space, yet failed to stimulate private commercial development. CAPAC members blamed the national economic climate and the city government's inability to provide incentives to the private sector for the continued lack of private investment in the downtown core. They noted that rezoning efforts had created plenty of opportunities for office functions to locate in downtown Hamilton, but only 7 percent of the commercially zoned space in downtown was occupied. New public and private actions would be necessary to resuscitate "the city's image and material well-being," they contended. To foster private investment and improve Hamilton's image, they mandated that the city and regional governments should work to increase the downtown resident population, direct all new development toward King Street East and to commercial nodes at Catharine and Wellington Streets, divert through traffic away from downtown, encourage mixed-use development north of Main Street, and focus on "human-scale" land use.[87]

The Central Area plan largely conformed with existing land uses and with the regional plan's broad mandates. Provincial growth plans had consigned Hamilton to the status of a regional center, which meant that its social and

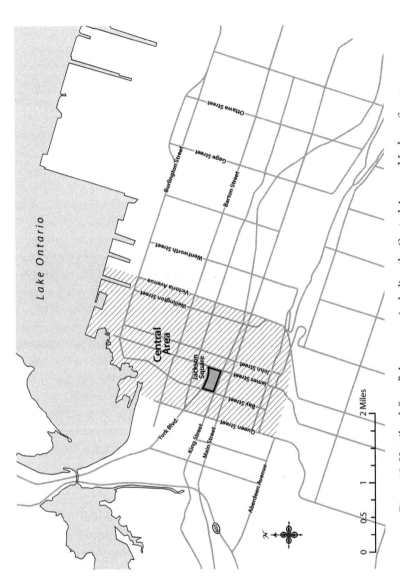

Figure 10. Hamilton's "new" downtown, including the Central Area and Jackson Square.

economic geography were expected to support the rapidly expanding Toronto region. In this context, CAPAC members and regional planners sought to encourage "a wide range of retail outlets," such as department stores, specialty stores, and small groceries to locate in and near Jackson Square. They believed that new retail development would attract consumers from the Southern Ontario region.[88] At the same time, CAPAC members and Hamilton's planners sought to spatially segregate the uses that they expected to serve the residential population from those that they imagined would appeal to tourists. Dating back to the Lunchpail Report, consultants had urged Hamilton's leaders to establish a block of ethnic shops and restaurants adjacent to the civic square, writing that "diversity in national origin is a democratic virtue and when properly used it stimulates the quality of civic life."[89]

The recommendations issued by CAPAC's provisional partnership, like those in the earlier Lunchpail Report, were premised on entrepreneurial economic development strategies used by U.S. cities that were untenable in Canada's regulatory environment. But even as Hamilton's city officials sought to establish a partnership with businessmen, planners continued to work within the redistributive framework of federally funded urban renewal to develop the long-planned civic square. In 1968, local officials saw promoting ethnic diversity as a goal with questionable value, but, by the early 1980s, just such a district had emerged without inducements from the city government. CAPAC members expected "local, ethnic or specialized clientele" to patronize establishments along James Street North and sought to direct the spending power of tourists and "other particular clientele" toward Hess Village's boutiques and restaurants. Planners duly designated James Street South's shops and services "local," while they classified King Street East and Jackson Square, with restaurants, specialty shops, a farmer's market, library, and other services, as regional attractions.[90]

Flouting provincial mandates, CAPAC members proved unwilling to abandon plans to attract headquarters buildings to downtown Hamilton. Ontario's regional planning documents stipulated that corporate headquarters should be directed toward Toronto, but the authors of the Central Area Plan employed a tricky turn of phrase to signal noncompliance, writing that "the Plan promotes the location of head offices and large branch offices of finance, insurance and real estate firms serving Region-wide or specialized interested in downtown Hamilton."[91] In other words, even though city planners and CAPAC members seemed to understand by 1981 that provincial development plans constrained their abilities to use entrepreneurial tactics to compete with Toronto, the Central Area Plan contained recommendations that willfully ignored that fact, and CAPAC urged city and regional officials to court headquarters operations on a more limited basis.

The public subsidies for private development recommended first in the Lunchpail Report and again in the Central Area Plan were prohibited by provincial law, placing public officials and civic leaders in a bind. City and regional officials and Chamber of Commerce members certainly wanted to implement many of CAPAC's recommendations, but they could not adopt the economic development tactics that consultants and CAPAC members recommended. In the end, Hamilton lost rather than gained corporate head-quarters in the last quarter of the twentieth century. The relative lack of new commercial and hotel space downtown only served as a reminder of Toron-to's preeminence as both a tourist destination and as the region's commercial and financial center.

The nature of downtown redevelopment in Pittsburgh and Hamilton was typical of North Atlantic industrial cities seeking to position themselves as centers of the emerging knowledge economy. Growth coalitions remade city centers to emphasize commerce, culture, and leisure rather than production. Revealing a dearth of ideas about how to address perceived urban decline in the 1970s and 1980s, consultants, planners, and government and private sec-tor officials increasingly turned to a "best practices" model for urban rede-velopment that privileged public subsidies for private sector development, regardless of whether the development met public purposes. In Britain, cities like Manchester built urban malls. The Basque government pinned its hopes on a cultural strategy and in 1981 invited the Guggenheim to build a new museum in Bilbao's aging port district. Following the advice of consultants from U.S.-based McKinsey & Company, who had recommended using pub-lic-private partnerships based on those in U.S. cities, Glasgow subsidized the private redevelopment of industrial buildings in a historic wholesale district for middle-class housing targeted to young professionals.[92]

Civic leaders and public officials in declining manufacturing centers shared common visions for postindustrial downtown development, but Pitts-burgh's and Hamilton's growth coalitions had disparate capacities to realize similar goals due to differences in the two cities' institutional frameworks, positions in their regional economies, participation of local business elites in planning processes, and approaches to meeting the needs of existing residents. Pittsburgh's growth coalition, which functioned in a federal, state, and local policy environment that promoted corporate welfare and fostered mayoral entrepreneurialism, increasingly understood local corporations as its most important constituency. Public officials and civic leaders replaced services that catered to existing residents with services for imagined new residents or a regional (and, in the case of financial services, national or international) clientele. Hamilton's leaders, too, imagined their steel town remade as a headquarters city, dominated by service- and finance-sector activities, but they were impeded by provincial policies that prevented the city government from providing the sort of corporate financial inducements that were essential to Pittsburgh's postwar downtown redevelopment. They were also constrained by provincial planning guidelines that consigned Hamilton to the position of a regional center in which commercial activity was supposed to support, rather than compete with, Toronto's role as Southern Ontario's finance and corporate center. And in contrast to Pittsburgh, Hamilton's growth coalition continued to accommodate the needs of the city's residential working class, even as it worked to create services that might attract new residents and suburban and regional clients. While downtown redevelopment in the two cities exposed a different range of ideas about for whom cities should be remade, plans for the mill neighborhood laid bare the renegotiations of urban citizenship that were part and parcel of postindustrialism.

CHAPTER FIVE

Spaces of Production and Spaces of Consumption

Downtown redevelopment may have occupied most of public officials' and civic leaders' attention, but uneven development within and between the neighborhoods that housed each city's steel mills—Pittsburgh's South Side and Hazelwood, and Hamilton's North End and the residential enclaves in its harbor industrial area—posed the greatest threat to their postindustrial plans. In Hamilton, downtown and mill neighborhood redevelopment went hand in hand. Vic Copps had targeted Hamilton's North End, a working-class residential neighborhood next to the harbor industrial area, for urban renewal in 1964. Planners set out to restore the North End's once-grand Victorian homes to their former splendor, plotting out new housing, parks, community centers, and schools. The civic square project, said urban renewal commissioner Lloyd Berryman, would be a "catalyst" for new residential redevelopment in the North End. "As it progresses," he predicted, "you'll find more and more people will want to move back downtown from the suburbs." Pointing to back-to-the-city movements in Toronto and U.S. cities, Berryman said he was confident that the North End, with its proximity to downtown and the waterfront, would once again attract middle-class homeowners. "Give people a shopping centre, cultural and institutional uses in the centre of the city, and they'll move back in," he assured Hamiltonians.[1]

By 1977, North End residents and city officials had judged urban renewal a failure. The *Hamilton Spectator* ran an article on the "North End Nightmare," which charged, "After $10 million spent over 16 years, residents, bureaucrats, businessmen and some politicians say the city's landmark redevelopment scheme has been largely bungled." Residents held the city culpable; Hamilton community development commissioner Ed Kowalski and his predecessor Reg Monaghan blamed the federal government's retreat from urban renewal, the province's poor planning of low-income housing, and private developers' resistance to building up the neighborhood. "The North End would have been improved considerably if the federal government hadn't pulled out," Kowalski insisted.[2] By 1985, city officials' focus on how to make the North End a middle-class rather than working-class neighborhood gave way to concern over providing space for industry to expand. Residential enclaves in Hamilton's harbor industrial area had become a nuisance to city officials who were required by provincial mandate to make more land available for manufacturing.[3]

Pittsburgh's mill neighborhoods, on the other hand, did not fall into decline until the 1970s. By the middle of the next decade, they were, like downtown, in the throes of postindustrial rebirth. "While downtown Pittsburgh basks in the splendor of its new skyscrapers and emerging white-collar image," began a 1984 *Pittsburgh Business Times* article about the city's South Side, "a more subtle renaissance is gaining momentum across the Monongahela River." Jones & Laughlin's (J&L) South Side works sat idle at the east end of the neighborhood, and East Carson Street, three decades earlier the commercial hub of a vibrant blue-collar neighborhood, was getting a facelift. Led by the South Side Chamber of Commerce, business owners and arts organizations remade the South Side as a regional destination for shopping, dining, and nightlife. In only eighteen months, the *Business Times* reported, more than $4 million in public and private investment had flowed into the neighborhood's commercial district. "We have activity on the streets at night, and it's not all arsonists," joked Donald Carlson, president of the neighborhood's community development corporation. Carlson assured his interviewer that there was a "good rapport" between longtime residents and newcomers.[4] Across the river in Hazelwood, on the site of J&L's other urban steel mill, city and state officials laid the cornerstone for a high technology center. Hazelwood's commercial district, however, remained boarded up. No one bragged to business reporters about the activities on its streets at night.

When the mills remained in service, Pittsburgh's growth coalition largely ignored the neighborhoods around them; when the mills shut down, city officials set out to erase evidence of the industrial past from the urban landscape. The South Side's mill eventually became a mall, the East Carson Street commercial district became a regional shopping and dining destination, and the young professionals city officials and civic leaders so desperately sought to attract flocked to the neighborhood for its historic character. The historical relationship between Hazelwood's mill site and its residential and commercial districts, by contrast, was severed with the construction of a high technology center designed to signal Pittsburgh's postindustrial rebirth. In Hamilton, city officials and civic leaders remained committed to the steel industry in its reduced form and to the workers who remained. The North End, unlike the South Side, did not gentrify in the 1980s and 1990s. Yet even as city officials expanded serviced land for industrial growth and abandoned their urban renewal era plan to reinvent the North End as a middle-class enclave, Hamilton's growth coalition worked to make manufacturing less visible to potential tourists and imagined new white-collar residents. In both cities, the mill neighborhoods became sites of struggle between residents, elected officials, and business leaders over access to urban space, whose interests the city government would serve, and the future of the industrial city.

Pittsburgh's Urban Steel Centers

After World War II, the only steel produced within Pittsburgh's city limits rolled out of J&L's Pittsburgh Works. The Pittsburgh Works occupied both sides of the Monongahela River and historically had employed many of the residents of the South Side and Hazelwood neighborhoods. Hazelwood is on the north side of the Monongahela River, next to Oakland and near the downtown business district. The South Side, located about a mile from the Golden Triangle and Oakland, is on the opposite bank. In the late nineteenth and early twentieth centuries, the residential populations and urban landscapes of the two neighborhoods closely resembled those of the region's mill towns. Between 1880 and 1920, the Pittsburgh Works attracted an influx of immigrants from Ireland, Italy, Hungary, and Poland, and the South Side and Hazelwood saw continuous industrial growth in steel and metals from the end of the nineteenth century through World War II.[5] In the 1960s, however, the populations and physical development of Hazelwood and the South Side began to diverge. Both neighborhoods suffered greater population losses than the city as a whole between 1960 and 1990, first because of suburbanization and later because of regional plant closures.[6] The South Side remained overwhelmingly white and working class, while Hazelwood's white population and income levels declined.[7]

Dallas-based conglomerate LTV acquired a controlling interest in J&L in 1968; from that point forward, the Pittsburgh Works was fraught with financial problems. By 1974, LTV wholly owned J&L and had laid off a quarter of its employees, reducing the company's Pittsburgh-based workforce to six thousand. In 1980, LTV announced that it would close its continuous strip and sheet department, leaving only 2,500 workers at the Pittsburgh Works. Six

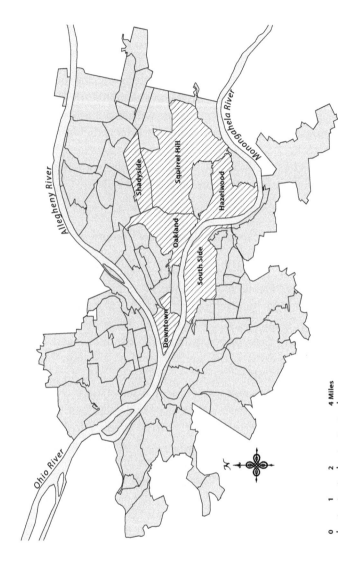

Figure 11. Pittsburgh's mill neighborhoods, the South Side and the Hazelwood, were in close proximity to downtown, the universities in Oakland, and elite Shadyside and Squirrel Hill.

years later, LTV filed for bankruptcy and shuttered everything except Hazelwood's coke works, reducing the workforce to 875.[8] While this process on
the whole reflected general patterns of regional steel industry restructuring,
LTV retained control of the Hazelwood site and operated its coke plant with
a reduced staff until 1998. By comparison, the South Side Works had only a
skeleton staff after 1981 and ceased operation completely after the bankruptcy
filing. By 1996, no buildings or structures remained on the South Side site.[9]
With the fortunes of the neighborhoods linked to the status of the mills, the
South Side slowly gentrified, and Hazelwood declined precipitously.

City officials, preoccupied with projects in and near downtown, showed
little serious interest in the South Side, which they judged a stable, if declining, neighborhood, until the early 1990s.[10] Before LTV shut down the South
Side Works, in fact, the strongest programmatic statement about the South
Side from the mayor's office or the City Planning Department was planners'
tepid assessment that the East Carson Street commercial district required
"some level" of revitalization.[11] What emerged from the city's benign neglect
was a neighborhood-based planning process driven by social service organizations, historic preservationists, community development corporations
(CDCs), and small business owners. The key actors in the South Side's redevelopment between the late 1960s and early 1980s were members of the
South Side Chamber of Commerce, active since the 1950s; the Pittsburgh
History & Landmarks Foundation (Landmarks); the Sarah Scaife Foundation, a Mellon family philanthropic trust; and the South Side Local Development Corporation (SSLDC), a CDC created by the South Side Chamber of
Commerce in 1982.

With the city government and the corporate sector disengaged and multiple civic groups involved, planning on the South Side initially resembled
the ad hoc, resident-focused efforts more characteristic of Hamilton's partnerships. In 1968, members of the South Side Chamber of Commerce and
Landmarks initiated a neighborhood-based economic development process
based on historic preservation. Landmarks, with an eye to displacement and
demolition in the Hill District and East Liberty neighborhoods during urban
renewal, wanted to keep the Urban Redevelopment Authority's (URA) bull-
dozers away from the South Side's Victorian commercial district. Landmarks
collaborated with the Chamber and the South Side Community Council to
establish a commercial district facade restoration program. Proclaiming that
"the South Side's Future Is in Its Past," Landmarks emphasized redevelopment that would restore existing buildings and retain residents. Under the
auspices of the Birmingham Self-Help Community Restoration Program (the

South Side was originally known as "Old Birmingham"), Landmarks provided technical assistance for property owners willing to undertake historically sensitive building improvements.[12]

Because its residents' income levels made the South Side eligible for programs funded by Richard Nixon's Community Development Block Grants (CDBG), South Side civic organizations benefited from the turn toward neighborhood-based community development during Pete Flaherty's mayoral tenure. After Nixon froze federal urban development funds and terminated urban renewal nationwide, the mayor's office announced that Pittsburgh would use its CDBG money to support neighborhood-driven projects, rather than previously planned renewal programs.[13] Flaherty established the Neighborhood Commercial Improvement Program (NCIP) in 1975 as the centerpiece of his neighborhood-stabilization efforts. South Side business owners took advantage of NCIP's low-interest loans for building improvements, grants for storefront design, and public space improvement funds to renovate existing businesses that served the neighborhood's working-class residents.[14]

Flaherty's neighborhood planning agenda reflected national trends toward community-based planning and laid the groundwork for a politics of neighborhood development that was, as historian Suleiman Osman has suggested, neither Left nor Right. In Pittsburgh, as in other U.S. cities, neighborhood-based activism around urban development came as a response to urban renewal programs in the 1950s. Pittsburgh's public support for neighborhood planning dated back to 1961, when the City Planning Department, under Mayor Joseph Barr, divided the city into five planning districts to better manage the department's participation in the federally mandated Community Renewal Program. By 1963, Pittsburgh had at least twenty-seven neighborhood-based civic or business organizations. Nationally, neighborhood activism accelerated after 1964 when, as part of the Equal Opportunity Act, Lyndon Johnson created Community Action Programs to empower the poor through their "maximum feasible participation" in determining how local governments spent federal funds allocated through the War on Poverty and the Great Society. Subsidies from the Ford Foundation and federal antipoverty programs hastened the creation of neighborhood organizations capable of assuming physical and economic development functions that were previously the purview of local governments. Several neighborhood-based groups formed a citywide umbrella organization, Community Organizations of Pittsburgh, in 1964.[15] Flaherty recalled from his days on City Council's Planning Committee that residents of Oakland, home to the

University of Pittsburgh and Carnegie Mellon, and affluent Shadyside and Squirrel Hill were the real "watchdogs" over the planning process beginning in the mid-1960s.[16]

By the 1970s, in Pittsburgh and other large cities, disparate groups of local activists—African Americans who came of age with the Black Power movement, young liberals who worked with Great Society programs, Left intellectuals, and white-collar gentrifiers—formed a loose neighborhood movement. Its members rejected the centralized planning and technocratic expertise typical of New Deal liberalism, trusting neither the government nor corporations. Politicians with roots in the neighborhood movement formed coalitions among white-collar professionals, blue-collar white ethnics, and black activists. Paradoxically, Nixon's 1973 moratorium on federal funding for HUD housing programs and his subsequent termination of urban renewal and Model Cities programs permitted the rapid expansion of block improvement associations, neighborhood federations, community revitalization projects, and nonprofits such as Neighborhood Housing Services. By 1977, forty-three city governments, including Pittsburgh, had formally recognized neighborhood organizations as part of the local governing process.[17]

By 1978, when the South Side Chamber of Commerce compiled a guide to help business owners find funding for historically sensitive building improvements, the Planning Department had begun to privilege conservation and rehabilitation as the city's primary approach to neighborhood development. Planners believed that the approach would attract new residents to Pittsburgh: "More and more people are evaluating and investing in our neighborhoods," they noted. "The attraction of high housing value, a sense of history, a strong and stable community, a shorter work trip, proximity to regional sports and cultural opportunities, plus the realization that urban problems affect suburban areas also combine to influence a still small but growing number of individuals and families." Even as planners sought to attract new residents to Pittsburgh, they assured residents that city officials remained primarily concerned with "retaining our existing residents and maintaining our housing stock and neighborhoods for both the existing and future residents." Echoing the Carter administration's national focus on self-help and voluntarism, Richard Caliguiri's planners marshalled privatist ideology to persuade residents that individual investment decisions, rather than public social programs, would remake the city: "The success of these programs and the future of the neighborhoods and the City depends on you, the individual, who must decide to reinvest in your homes and businesses," planners contended.[18]

South Side residents had reason to doubt the city's commitment to existing residents in the early 1980s, by which point the mayor's office had eliminated nonessential services in the neighborhood and Caliguiri focused his
attentions and residents' tax dollars on downtown construction projects. Caliguiri's austerity program for the neighborhoods reflected national trends, as
Reagan reduced federal spending on central cities. South Side civic organizations heeded planners' call for a partnership-based approach to redevelopment, if only to ensure that neighborhood residents received basic services.
As neighborhood planning moved toward the public-private partnership
model at the heart of Renaissance II, South Side civic groups remained attentive to the needs of existing residents and the businesses that served them.
The South Side Chamber of Commerce, for instance, bought street cleaning
equipment and hired a part-time cleaner to maintain the East Carson Street
business district, privatizing what a few years earlier had been an essential
public service.[19]

Shortly after LTV shuttered the South Side Works, the small business
owners and service providers who controlled the Chamber created the
SSLDC to do what the city government had not: produce historically sensitive planning guidelines for the South Side. The SSLDC represented not
so much a public-private partnership as the privatization and decentralization to the neighborhood level of planning and economic development. The
organization received only nominal support from the city government; it
was sustained instead by donations from the Chamber and its members. The
SSLDC immediately set out to draft an economic development plan for the
South Side, where both income and population had declined between 1960
and 1980. Commercial vacancy rates had skyrocketed, reaching 40 percent
by 1985. East Carson Street and residential areas showed signs of physical
deterioration.[20] While the neighborhood may have been in decline according
to the Planning Department's indicators, Carlson recalled that "the neighborhood and residential community here remained strong even when the
storefronts were vacant on Carson Street." In November 1983, the SSLDC
and Landmarks secured a national historic district designation for East Carson Street between Ninth and Twenty-Fourth Streets, which provided a 25
percent tax credit for property owners who carried out historically sensitive
renovations. The historic district designation, according to Carlson, "helped
us create a theme and a method of marketing the area" and reinforced the
economic development strategy underway in the neighborhood since 1968.
The SSLDC entered its second full year of operation in early 1984 with two
staffers and a paltry $70,000 budget ($30,000 of which came from the city's

community development funds and the rest from private contributions), but Carlson claimed that he could barely manage to return the calls he received from people interested in buying or renting space on the South Side.[21]

In the 1984 *Business Times* feature on the South Side's resurgence, Carlson indicated that the SSLDC and the South Side had reached a crossroads. The SSLDC had initially resisted gentrification, which Carlson underscored when he insisted, "we don't want to change the ethnic mixture that exists." He told the paper, "we're proud of the churches that sell pierogies on Fridays, and the small bars on the side streets that exist just as they have 20 years ago." In spite of his efforts to emphasize how much the neighborhood had stayed the same, Carlson also pointed out that "it's definitely not the same South Side as 30 years ago when the mills were booming and a Saturday night meant walking up and down Carson Street."[22] Existing businesses and long-time residents had not been forced out by newcomers, but the composition of the neighborhood commercial district had changed to include shops and restaurants that the SSLDC hoped would make East Carson Street a regional, rather than neighborhood, attraction.

In 1985, the National Trust for Historic Preservation selected the South Side to participate in its Main Street Urban Demonstration Program, which provided three years of technical assistance for preservation planning and façade restorations and bolstered the South Side's preservation "theme." Between 1985 and 1990, the SSLDC reported, more than $12 million in private investment had created 400 new jobs in the East Carson Street business district. 110 new businesses opened, 28 expanded, 131 undertook façade renovations, and 64 more pursued expansive rehabilitation projects. Only 52 businesses moved out of the neighborhood or closed.[23] Tellingly, the businesses that moved or closed typically had served the residential population, while new businesses such as specialty shops, arts and antiques stores, and gourmet restaurants were oriented to regional rather than neighborhood services. The South Side's residents may well have patronized the new establishments, but they were not the target audience.

Historic preservation had been long established as the South Side's engine of economic and physical development when, in 1985, a phalanx of civic, religious, educational, and social service organizations with very different constituencies and economic interests came together to establish the South Side Planning Forum and produce a neighborhood plan. These included the Brashear Association (a former settlement house that provided community social services); Friends of the Carnegie Library (South Side branch); the South Side Antiques, Arts and Crafts Association (which represented the arts community); the South Side Chamber of Commerce (which represented the business community); the South Side Community Council (which represented residents); the SSLDC; and the South Side Slopes Neighborhood Association. While the SSLDC described the Planning Forum as "the collective voice of the community on the issues pertaining to planning policy," the community meeting from which the Planning Forum emerged had only seventy attendees, and the subsequent meeting to determine the mission and activities of the task force attracted only forty people.

Initially, like the SSLDC, the Planning Forum's neighborhood-based planning efforts remained attuned to the interests of existing residents. Planning Forum member Randy Rayl told a reporter that South Side residents and business owners had originally begun the planning process because they were concerned that control over neighborhood development might otherwise "get away from us."[24] Main Street program director and Planning Forum member Caroline Boyce insisted that "we must make sure that as things progress here, we have clothing stores for the residential community, the drugstores, the shoe repair shops and five-and-ten stores." All the community development groups involved with the Planning Forum wanted to keep housing affordable for the neighborhood's disproportionately elderly residents.[25] This model remained tenable only as long as residential and commercial vacancy rates remained high; as vacancy rates declined, competition emerged over space and resources.

The Planning Forum's vision for economic development shared much with the growth coalitions' plans for postindustrial Pittsburgh, and planning efforts on the South Side remained exemplary of the type of "partnership" the city government hoped to foster in the neighborhoods. Civic groups and individual property owners organized, planned, and largely privately financed redevelopment, which allowed the Caliguiri administration to devote its resources to downtown projects. Public officials began to show greater interest in the South Side when LTV fully divested from the South Side Works. The 110-acre mill site located between East Carson Street and the Monongahela River occupied over 10 percent of the South Side's land area, including a mile and a half of riverfront property. In 1985, workers produced the mill's last steel slab; in 1987, LTV laid off all remaining employees and announced its intention to begin site demolition. Tri-State, the Steel Valley Authority (SVA), Landmarks, the mayor's office, and the SSLDC each proposed land use alternatives for the site, ranging from reindustrialization to a history museum to a riverboat gambling complex.[26] Between 1987 and 1994, the mill site embodied the struggle between the region's workers, city residents, public officials, and civic leaders over what Pittsburgh would become and which groups would control its development.

In 1986, as part of Strategy 21, the State of Pennsylvania authorized $750 million for a steel retention study. Tri-State organizers Mike Stout and Charles McCollester worried that state officials would produce a "broad, general study recounting the ills of the steel industry" and use it to undermine reindustrialization efforts. Tri-State members successfully lobbied state representatives to require an engineering assessment as part of the study and to concentrate on the portions of the mills that might feasibly reopen. Tri-State was particularly concerned about the electric furnaces on the South Side, which the organization believed represented the region's best possibility for reindustrialization. In 1987, anticipating a positive assessment from the steel retention study, Tri-State activists joined with state officials to secure funding to restart the furnaces.[27]

Six Mon Valley state representatives urged Pennsylvania's Public Utilities Commission to release development funds it was required to expend in the Pittsburgh region to the SVA or to an employee-owned corporation to restore the South Side Works to productive use. In a joint letter to the Public Utilities Commission, the representatives wrote that, while they understood that many of the steel mills were undeniably closed for good, they retained hope that "with the proper investment and application of technology that some of these older mills can become competitive."[28] The Pittsburgh City Council also urged the Public Utilities Commission to fund a feasibility study for South Side reindustrialization, and, in August 1987, the Public Utilities Commission awarded $590,000 to the SVA.[29] In January 1988, Arthur D. Little and Hatch Engineering released the state-funded steel retention study, which determined that the South Side Works electric furnace was "the only facility which represents a realistic, potentially viable, stand-alone business opportunity." More importantly, the consultants had identified a domestic market for semi-finished steel slabs, which could be produced on the South Side if a new continuous caster was installed. They estimated that, with an initial investment of $220 million for the caster and facility modernization, the mill would be able to produce 1.6 million tons of steel slab a year and provide 410 secure jobs, a far cry from the 8,500 at the mill in the 1960s.[30]

In a show of solidarity with the SVA's reindustrialization plans, South Side community leaders, unemployed steel workers who hoped to work in the revived mill, and sympathetic state representatives appeared together at the public announcement of the formation of a buyout committee for the site.[31] The SVA outlined a plan to purchase the electric furnaces, modernize them, install a continuous caster, and lease the facility to a worker-owned cooperative. The SVA also promised South Side community organizations an equity share in the mill and a voice in site redevelopment for their cooperation. Noting that "Pittsburgh's South Side is coming alive," the SVA projected that the revitalized mill would create more than 300 family-wage union jobs and 500 additional jobs in support industries, increase local tax revenues by $400,000 a year and state income and sales tax revenue by $700,000, and provide a stable tax base for local schools. Tri-State activists had tried to undermine Caliguiri's development agenda in the early 1980s, but, by the 1990s, SVA members recognized that they had to market their project as compatible with the growth coalition's postindustrial vision for the city if they were to have any chance of success. Declaring that "South Side Steel will be a part of South Side's revival," SVA board members opined that "South Side Steel would be ideal for a National Park Service plan to have visitors view a working steel mill. Coupled with Carson Street's high energy and historic flavor, it would be a showcase for the best of Pittsburgh's two worlds: 'Iron City' and 'Renaissance II.'"[32]

LTV officials initially supported reindustrialization, indicating both their willingness to sell the furnaces and to cooperate with efforts to return the mill to operation. Shortly after the release of the steel retention study, however, LTV changed course and announced that it planned to raze the entire mill site. The company was no longer interested in facilitating the electric furnaces' return to productive use.[33] By this point, Landmarks had joined Tri-State and the SVA in advancing reuse plans for the site. Earl James, director of programs and preservation services for Landmarks, described his organization's vision for the South Side works as "history and development occurring at the same place." James saw the Landmarks plan as compatible with the SVA's desire to reindustrialize part of the facility because Landmarks was primarily concerned with preserving the Bessemer building (one of only two left in the country) and the iconic smokestacks along the Monongahela, which were not part of the SVA's reindustrialization plan. Galvanized by Landmarks's proposal, the Pittsburgh City Council nominated the South Side Works as a local historic site in March 1988 in an effort to halt LTV's planned demolition and buy time for the SVA to assemble financing.[34]

While the City Council and Landmarks pursued the historic designation (ultimately overturned), the SVA's reindustrialization plans slowly unraveled. In 1989, on the advice of the United Steelworkers, the SVA hired Cole Tremain, formerly a plant manager at Republic Steel and a vice president at LTV, to create a business plan for the revitalized furnaces. Tremain immediately set about securing customer commitments for South Side Steel.[35] His business plan elicited interest from a consortium that included U.S. private investors, a Brazilian steel group, and a German industrial conglomerate. In 1991, Tremain's deal with the consortium fell apart because a confluence of events made the reindustrialization plan suddenly less viable: industrial credit tightened after the savings and loan crisis in the late 1980s, steel prices declined, new investment opportunities opened in East Germany after the fall of the Berlin Wall, and, most important, LTV remained intransigent. Although the property appraised at only $8 million, LTV refused to sell it to the SVA for less than $35 million because it did not want to create competition for its remaining steel investments.[36] With the temporary historic designation rescinded and no remaining barriers to demolition, LTV cleared a third of the site in 1990 and, in 1991, began to tear down the remaining buildings and structures.[37] As site clearance proceeded, all hope of reindustrialization disappeared because private capital undercut the community-based plan for neighborhood and industrial revitalization.

After the SVA reindustrialization bid failed, SSLDC members rejected industrial uses for the mill site, which they deemed "increasingly obsolete, uneconomical, and dysfunctional in terms of community character and potential."[38] The SSLDC decision to advocate against manufacturing uses reflected a shift in its members' perceptions about who composed the South Side "community." To complement its own economic development activities on East Carson Street, the SSLDC wanted to convert the mill site for "housing, stores, restaurants; courtyards, plazas and open space; entertainment and recreational facilities; maybe a museum." The organization hoped to open access to the riverfront and create "something new; something different; something we don't have now; and something we may never again get as good an opportunity to have."[39] Executive director Rebecca Flora pointedly noted that "the industrial past of the South Side's riverfront is not one that we hope to continue into another generation of uses."[40]

The SSLDC's planning study for the redevelopment of the South Side Works revealed that the interests of the SSLDC and the wider South Side community had diverged. The SSLDC's members had initially encouraged a mix of businesses for existing as well as for imagined future residents. Under Flora, the organization began to promote neighborhood development guidelines that treated long-term residents like tourist attractions, part of the South Side's old-world charm. The SSLDC stressed the need to open the South Side to "new residential markets that are not incompatible with the existing South Side population but that are sufficiently different to provide for a more balanced socio-economic growth in the community," while retaining the neighborhood's character and continuing to serve existing residents. To meet these goals, the SSLDC advocated for the construction of predominantly owner-occupied housing for "middle and upper-middle income young families" on the LTV site. The SSLDC also encouraged retail uses that would attract a regional consumer base, rather than primarily serve neighborhood needs.[41]

As the SSLDC held meetings to discuss the site's reuse, the mayor's office stepped in and decisively settled the question of who would control the redevelopment of the South Side Works. With the mill permanently shut down and the possibility of reindustrialization foreclosed, city officials took a renewed interest in land use on the South Side. In March 1994, Mayor Tom Murphy announced he had arranged to acquire the site from LTV. Despite significant private interest in the site and the city government's long-standing policy of promoting private redevelopment in the neighborhoods, Murphy opted to purchase the property through the URA because he thought it was the best way to ensure that the mayor's office gained control over the city's largest undeveloped riverfront site. "One of the reasons we moved quickly was that we feared 20 different individual interests that would not benefit the South Side," Murphy said. "I think that LTV could easily have sold the site off piecemeal, but I would much rather have us control the development." Former URA chairman Jack Robin told a *Pittsburgh Post-Gazette* reporter that the site had come full circle: in the 1940s, the URA had funded J&L's expansion of their steel-making facilities onto the land the city bought back for postindustrial redevelopment in 1994.[42]

Five years later, ground was broken for the SouthSide Works, an urban entertainment district that included shopping, dining, apartments, offices, and University of Pittsburgh medical and sports facilities. The SouthSide Works marketing strategy encouraged residents of suburban Mount Lebanon and Pittsburgh's elite Shadyside and Squirrel Hill neighborhoods—among the region's wealthiest residential areas—to "Come to the South Side, You Deserve a Night Out."[43] The site developer predicted that the mall would "be one of Pittsburgh's best marketing tools as we strive to create an exciting community that will entice university graduates from the University of Pittsburgh and Carnegie Mellon to stay in town." The Murphy administration clearly agreed: the mall was privately financed, but the city picked up the tab for $103 million in road construction, bridge renovations, and a parking garage—more money than it had invested on the South Side in the previous thirty years.[44]

When the SouthSide Works opened in 2002, the service-sector jobs created at chain restaurants and national retailers were largely low-wage, high-turnover positions that did not carry health insurance or retirement benefits. A few miles down the road, a mall had opened on the site of U.S. Steel's storied Homestead Works four years earlier, and similar projects had already been completed in Europe. A shopping mall replaced a steel mill on the outskirts of Sheffield in 1990. In 1996, a German developer had razed a defunct ThyssenKrupps steel mill in Oberhausen and built CentrO, billed as Europe's largest mall.[45] In the Ruhr, as in the Mon Valley, the family wage steel jobs that had once been a route to the middle class were long gone. The literal conversion of sites of production to sites of consumption became potent symbols of postindustrialism that obscured the human costs of economic restructuring with mid-priced clothing stores and chain restaurants.

Hazelwood, Pittsburgh's other urban steel center, was an entirely different story. In the 1960s, Hazelwood's Second Avenue business district thrived, with two supermarkets, several smaller groceries, drugstores, variety stores, and a movie theater.[46] Like the South Side, Hazelwood saw its population decline, initially due to suburban growth and, after 1968, because of incremental workforce reductions at the mill. In its 1950s heyday, the Hazelwood works employed 8,000 workers; by 1974, the number was 3,600. LTV shut down Hazelwood's furnaces in 1981 but kept its coke works operational until 1998, employing the last 750 steelworkers in Pittsburgh.[47]

Hazelwood lacked both an architecturally cohesive Victorian commercial district and an active Chamber of Commerce. While the South Side Chamber partnered with Landmarks in the late 1960s to establish historic preservation as the guiding principal for neighborhood revitalization and to tap into federal community development funds increasingly geared toward neighborhood conservation, Hazelwood's business owners were left to their own devices to cope with a dwindling consumer base. By the 1970s, several neighborhood businesses were boarded up. Flaherty recalled that Hazelwood had little influence with the City Planning Department or City Council during his mayoral tenure, a situation that changed little when Caliguiri came into office.[48] Like the South Side, Hazelwood was eligible for NCIP funds. City planners targeted its commercial district, in a very general way, for improvement in the early 1980s; but Hazelwood residents did not form a CDC capable of administering those funds until 1994.[49]

In stark contrast to the South Side, the redevelopment of Hazelwood's mill site preceded rather than followed neighborhood redevelopment. Because of Hazelwood's proximity to both downtown and Oakland and because LTV decisively shut down steel production in 1981, the 130-acre mill site on Second Avenue became central to the Caliguiri administration's efforts to showcase its postindustrial, high-tech vision for Pittsburgh. In 1983, the city purchased fifty-one acres of the Hazelwood mill site and transferred it to the Regional Industrial Development Corporation (RIDC) for conversion to the Pittsburgh Technology Center. In 1985, the RIDC estimated site acquisition, clearance, and infrastructure improvements at $9.5 million; by 1986, the redevelopment costs had skyrocketed to $25 million in local, state, and federal funds.[50] The Allegheny Conference helped secure funding from the Ben Franklin Partnership to convert the fifty-one-acre site to a tech-based industrial park for two projects of the joint University of Pittsburgh-Carnegie Mellon Advanced Technology Research partnership: the National Center for Robotics in Manufacturing and the Western Pennsylvania Biotechnology Center. The $98 million proposal for the two university programs required $14 million in new state funds (in addition to $2 million already committed), half a million of federal money, $3 million in local government funds, and $79 million of private money, and promised to create 1,100 new jobs.[51] The URA purchased the former hot strip mill in 1983 for $3.5 million and entered into an agreement with the RIDC to develop the site for technical businesses. In 1984, Metaltech, a new company launched by former National Steel and J&L executives, acquired an 8.5 acre parcel of land and equipment and reopened galvanized steel production in Hazelwood, initially with around forty employees. Some but not all of Metaltech's employees were former J&L workers, and the company hoped to employ up to eighty people if demand for its products increased.[52]

The growth partnership's visions of Pittsburgh's high-tech future were made manifest in the redevelopment of the Hazelwood Works. The site developer called the project "urban flypaper," designed to lure tech-oriented businesses to Pittsburgh by providing them with serviced land in an industrial park with ample open space and river access.[53] As a state representative from Pittsburgh's North Side, future mayor Murphy was one of the plan's biggest supporters, arguing that it would symbolize Pittsburgh's transition from the "steel age" to the "space age."[54] To city officials, the High Technology Center represented "the very real and visible transformation of a portion of the Pittsburgh economy from heavy metals to advanced technology." Local tech companies agreed. James Colker, president of Pittsburgh-based aerospace instrumentation company Contraves Goerz, was enthusiastic that the city and state governments supported high technology firms through "tax-exempt bonds, incubator buildings and parks, supportive tax structure and especially politicians who understand that businessmen aren't devils. Boy, that's nice."[55] Promoting the Technology Center to the *Chicago Tribune*, Penn's Southwest director Jay Aldridge described Pittsburgh as "two economies side by side. There's the traditional 19th Century economy that's in steep decline, and there's the 20th Century economy that's in steep incline." Penn's Southwest, he said, saw Pittsburgh "as basically a center for the exporting of knowledge." Carnegie Mellon's provost predicted that, in the future, "it's Silicon Valley for chips, it's Boston for electronics and it's going to be Pittsburgh for software."[56]

For Governor Dick Thornburgh, the Hazelwood site conversion was evidence that Pittsburgh was not "dwelling on the past." At the groundbreaking ceremony, Thornburgh glad-handed with Caliguiri, county commissioner Tom Foerster, State House speaker Leroy Irvis, Carnegie Mellon president Richard Cyert, and University of Pittsburgh chancellor Wesley Posvar. They singularly praised the high-tech research agendas of the University of Pittsburgh and Carnegie Mellon. A *Post-Gazette* editorial reported, "Suddenly, for this old steel town, knowledge has become its most precious commodity" and called Carnegie Mellon the clear "guiding light," with its strong research programs and "entrepreneurial" institutional values.[57] Thornburgh noted that the region's mill towns, too, were "undergoing a transition from the economy of yesterday to the economy of tomorrow." He echoed Cyert's use of the term "the new Pittsburgh" and praised the city for its highway and bridge improvements and its "impressively altered skyline." The Pittsburgh economy, he enthused, was headed in "an exciting new direction."[58] Like Caliguiri, Thornburgh said little about the impact of Pittsburgh's "new direction" on the region's, or Hazelwood's, residents, who had not been part of the conversation about the site's reuse. Moreover, none of the celebrants acknowledged that the seminal site of Pittsburgh's emerging knowledge economy stood next to a still-operating coke plant, a powerful reminder that, in the postindustrial Rust Belt, the new and old economies uneasily coexisted.

Residents of the neighborhoods downwind of Hazelwood were deeply concerned about the fumes wafting from the coke works. As the city and state funneled subsidies into the Technology Center, the rest of the Hazelwood Works either remained in use for coke production or stood vacant as the neighborhood continued to lose population and its physical condition declined. After LTV closed the coke works in 1998, one of LTV's suppliers proposed constructing a more environmentally friendly coking facility on the site and resuming smaller-scale coke production with approximately 200 workers.[59] The proposal generated conflict between Hazelwood's

Figure 12. Jones & Laughlin's Pittsburgh Works occupied both sides of the
Monongahela River on the South Side (left) and Hazelwood (right) neighborhoods,
ca. 1950. Courtesy of Detre Library & Archives, Senator John Heinz History Center.

remaining manufacturing workers and residents in adjacent neighborhoods. Framed as a debate over air quality, the conflict over the plant
reflected a renegotiation of whose interests would determine urban land
use. The most intense opposition to the coke works came from residents
of Squirrel Hill, and rationales provided for and against reindustrialization
reflected the obvious class dimension of the battle between residents of one
of the city's most exclusive neighborhoods and those from Hazelwood, one
of the poorest areas in Pittsburgh. Opponents articulated their opposition
as environmental concerns (shared by most residents of the city, who had
no desire to return to the smoke-filled skies of Pittsburgh's past), but they
also cited an "inefficient use of very valuable river front land" better suited
to nebulous "other uses"—and implicitly, a different workforce.[60] "I don't
think it's right to have to live all closed up," said suburban Munhall's Fran-
ces Harkins. "Making coke is inherently dirty. I commend the Sun Co. for

Figure 13. The site of the former Pittsburgh Works in 2014. The SouthSideWorks
is on the left; the Pittsburgh Technology Center is on the right. Photo reprinted
with the permission of the Regional Industrial Development Corporation
of Southwestern Pennsylvania.

its technology. But I don't think this (urban neighborhood) is the area for their plant."[61]

Public meetings generated emotional pleas from former steelworkers and their families to approve the coke plant and offer the possibility of well-remunerated manufacturing jobs. At a meeting at the Jewish Community Center in Squirrel Hill, twenty-year-old Kristy Kuhn, the daughter of a steelworker who had lost his job of thirty-two years when LTV closed the coke plant, asked how her father fit into the high-tech future the growth partnership promoted. "It's no fun now to see him worrying about how he'll support his family, how we'll finish college," Kuhn said through her tears. "People talk about the high-tech future. How can I be part of that future if I can't afford to finish college?" Supporters pointed out that this was the first manufacturing enterprise of significant size that had shown interest in locating in Pittsburgh in twenty-five years, and even Murphy, a staunch proponent of postindustrial Pittsburgh, testily remarked, "you can say 'we don't want coke, it's dirty. We want something else.' But I can tell you there isn't a long line of 'something elses.'"[62] Despite the mayor's support and political pressure from the United Steelworkers, the reindustrialization plan failed. Hazelwood's experience in 1998 echoed the mill town activists' earlier inability to prevent plant shutdowns, but with a meaningful difference: this time, the mayor and the coke company were on the workers' side. Rather than powerful corporate interests, steelworkers fought other urban residents over control of urban space and for a voice in the city's future development.

Following the announcement that LTV would shutter the plant, the *Post-Gazette* editorial board described the closing as a "sad development" for the 750 workers who would lose their jobs, but cheerily noted that "developers are waiting in the wings, and cleaner air will be a good dividend for a city reinventing itself in a post-industrial age."[63] A second editorial asserted, "Pittsburgh should remain a center of the steel industry, even if steel is no longer the backbone of Pittsburgh." What the *Post-Gazette*'s editorial staff meant was that the region's steel executives should continue to invest in steel and retain nonproductive corporate functions; whether continued investment provided manufacturing jobs in Pittsburgh was largely irrelevant to the city's emergent knowledge economy.[64]

After her organization helped defeat the coke works, Mary Lewin, a member of Squirrel Hill civic group Citizens Helping Our Community, told the *Post-Gazette* that the group's next step was to come up with a site plan that would complement other brownfield reuse projects in the city, one that would involve local residents in the planning process. "The citizens have a lot of good ideas," she said.[65] The citizens Lewin referred to did not include Hazelwood's African American residents or the region's manufacturing workers. In land use debates, residents of white-collar neighborhoods marginalized manufacturing concerns (and workers) in both the process and the outcome, facilitating a public discourse about redevelopment that reduced workers from "citizens" to "labor" without community ties or rights to urban space. Like the growth coalition, middle-class neighborhood organizations made it clear that the interests of the former steelworkers were not those of the new Pittsburgh. In a city where neighborhood-based planning and community control gained an almost intractable hold in the 1970s, Hazelwood's residents had little influence over neighborhood land use and little power to challenge the decisions of their more affluent neighbors.

Hamilton's Industrial District

In Hamilton, too, residents and public officials fought over land use in the city's industrial neighborhoods. At the same time that Copps and the Economic Development Commission began to pursue economic diversification, a new image for the city, and a public-private partnership based on the recommendations in the Lunchpail Report, the Planning Department and City Council implemented an innovative neighborhood-based planning model that frequently stymied economic development projects. Citizen participation in Canada was a very different prospect from that in the United States. While neighborhood-based groups emerged to challenge urban renewal plans in Canada, they never developed into the permanent government- and foundation-funded community development corporations that became prevalent in U.S. cities in the 1960s and 1970s.[66] Instead, neighborhood-based protest against or support for redevelopment plans in Hamilton typically involved a group forming around a specific issue and disbanding when the issue was resolved.

In 1966, under pressure from the Chamber of Commerce, the Labor Council, downtown business owners, and residents angry that Hamilton's outdated official plan meant that residential, commercial, and industrial areas had to compete for space, the City Council announced that it would develop a new official plan for the city. The council reorganized the Planning Department, tapped deputy director Robert Bailey to run it, and increased the department's budget. When the Planning Department began work on an official plan update, staff members held public meetings, a few people showed up, and residents complained privately to their councilors about indiscriminate high-rise construction, strip commercial developments, and traffic problems in residential areas.[67]

In 1971, Hamilton's frustrated planners developed a neighborhood-based planning process that was unique in Canada, eventually winning national awards for their efforts to involve residents in the planning process. To guide the preparation of the official plan, the planners worked closely with residents to prepare unofficial, resident-driven plans for many of the city's neighborhoods. Through the neighborhood plans, planners and residents together established guidelines for zoning and development, which the Planning Department subsequently incorporated into Hamilton's official plan in general terms. The individual neighborhood plans, while not formally approved by the province, guided the Planning Department's land use decisions and served as a check on unfettered development.[68] "It certainly appears that there is no way of stopping the citizen involvement in planning at this point," Bailey noted.[69] Not coincidentally, the City Planning Department became increasingly influential during the 1970s. "City controllers used to joke about 'the last man to the elevator' getting stuck with serving on Hamilton Planning Board," a *Spectator* article quipped. Senior councilor Ann Jones's 1973 request to sit on the Planning Board signaled a new interest in land use issues among councilors and suggested that "planning is 'where it's at' at city hall."[70]

Through Design for Development and the creation of regional municipalities, Ontario had, in the 1960s and 1970s, relegated Hamilton to the status of a regional manufacturing hub. Elected officials and residents alike chafed at the mandate to make more land available for heavy industry. Beginning in the 1970s, residents on the Mountain and in neighborhoods adjacent to downtown resisted the creation of new industrial land near their homes, which undermined city, regional, and provincial plans to decentralize industry and develop new areas. They did so through individual homeowners' associations rather than under the auspices of an organized, citywide system of neighborhood organizations as in Pittsburgh.

For Mountain residents, rapid transit, highway construction, and the decentralization of industry represented a threat to their quality of life and investments in their homes. Suburban-style residential and commercial development began in earnest on the Mountain after World War II, and by the 1970s many of Hamilton's manufacturing workers had relocated to the area. As James Cooke noted in a homeowners' association brief filed to protest industrial expansion on the Mountain, he and his neighbors moved to the Mountain to get away from the environmental hazards in the working-class neighborhoods near the harbor. "Now you are going to build factories along-side our houses," he complained to City Council. He and his neighbors had purchased property in neighborhoods zoned residential and agricultural and saw the Economic Development Commission's efforts to establish industry adjacent to their homes as a reason to abandon Hamilton for suburban juris-dictions.[71] Members of the Beach Community Council, which represented homeowners in the Beach Strip, a residential area nestled between Stelco and Dofasco on Hamilton Harbor, were similarly incensed about plans to build warehousing facilities on conservation land about one hundred yards from their homes. "No matter whether they paint them red, white, blue or purple, it's going to create rats and more smell, confusion, and noise," charged coun-cil co-chair Beth Dunk. Dunk cited widespread public support for maintain-ing the east end of the bay as a conservation area and charged that industrial waste from new warehousing facilities would increase pollution. "We haven't been able to swim in the lake for the last two years now," she complained.[72]

Residents, the mayor's office, and local aldermen also came into conflict over the procurement policy used to assemble industrial land. In an effort to attract new industries, the city, and later regional, government purchased land from private owners, often at inflated prices, serviced it, and sold it to industries for development. The approach created an indirect subsidy for industrial development because the city acquired and serviced the land with-out passing on the improvement costs to the buyer. In Hamilton, far more than in Pittsburgh, residents expressed outrage over city officials' desire to provide corporate welfare, arguing that industries should purchase land at market value and develop it directly, rather than receiving an indirect public subsidy.[73] When residents' property rights came into conflict with provincial development goals, however, provincial officials usually triumphed.

Battles between residents and their elected representatives over how to balance industrial expansion with the growth coalition's visions for postin-dustrial urban space and residents' desires to maintain their homes came into sharp relief in the neighborhoods near the mills. The North End was subject to many of the same pressures as Pittsburgh's South Side and Hazelwood, with one fundamental difference: Hamilton's mills did not shut down; rather, they expanded. Located adjacent to the city's primary industrial agglomera-tion, the neighborhood historically housed steel and other manufacturing workers. Italian, German, Portuguese, and Ukrainian immigrants and their descendants established working-class communities in Hamilton's North and East Ends in the first half of the twentieth century, while professionals and academics moved to Hamilton's West End.[74]

One of the city's earliest-settled neighborhoods, the North End was by the early 1960s an example of what midcentury planners described as "blighted." As industrial enterprises located along the harbor adjacent to the North End in the late nineteenth and early twentieth centuries, wealthier residents moved out and were replaced by manufacturing workers. Most of the neighborhood's modest one- and two-story homes dated from the late nineteenth and early twentieth centuries, and grand houses from the 1860s had been subdivided into apartments. Many of the residences had small yards, lacked driveways, and required minor maintenance or cosmetic improvements—all evidence of "blight" to midcentury planners.[75]

As suburbanization changed the residential composition of the city, Hamilton's planners began to imagine a thoroughly reconfigured North End. They envisioned a less industrial neighborhood more closely integrated with downtown, with the harbor developed for luxury residences and office space through a massive urban renewal project. Planners expected the North End to remain home to the blue-collar workers who had historically populated the neighborhood, but they thought it would also house the young professional workforce they hoped to attract. Hamilton's City Planning Department targeted the North End for redevelopment in 1958, and from the outset urban renewal plans for the North End and Jackson Square were linked in planners' minds.[76]

North End redevelopment conformed to a master plan approved by local and provincial officials, making it a very different prospect from the community-led revitalization of Pittsburgh's South Side or university-driven plans for Hazelwood. For the purposes of urban renewal, planners defined the North End as the 69-block area bounded by Wellington Street to the east, Strachan Street to the south, and the harbor to the north and west. City officials hired Toronto planning consultants Murray V. Jones and Associates to prepare a renewal plan that would "encourage renewed confidence and stability in the physical, social and economic characteristics of the North End neighborhood" and facilitate its return to one of Hamilton's most prestigious residential areas. The urban renewal study described the North End as an "island" isolated by industry to the east, the harbor to the west and north, and railroad tracks to the south. Yet the North End's geographical separation from the rest of the city, in consultants' estimation, had also "served to give the area a sense of identity and have contributed to its functioning as a partially self-contained community." The city government designed the renewal plan to realign the North End residential district with downtown, rather than with the harbor front industries. As had been the case with downtown

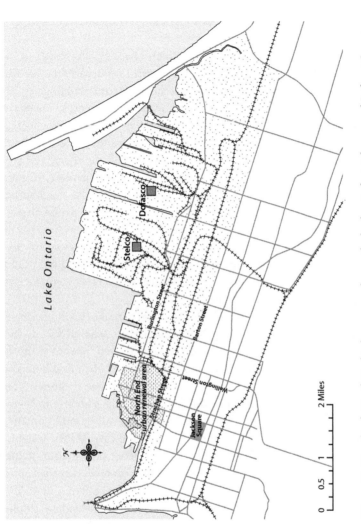

Figure 14. Hamilton's North End urban renewal area, the harbor industrial area, and Jackson Square.

development plans, public officials sought to meet the needs of both existing and imagined future residents.[77]

New development along James Street, the neighborhood's commercial district, figured prominently in the North End urban renewal scheme. The Murray Jones consultants described James Street's buildings as "almost invariably old" and characterized the North End's commercial enterprises as "purely local," with annual sales totaling only 30 percent of the average for the city. There were no theaters, bowling alleys, or other entertainment venues in the North End in 1961, which meant that all the spending by North End residents for leisure activities and most of their spending for personal services, repair services, and dining occurred outside the neighborhood.[78] The mayor's office hoped that the urban renewal project would attract new businesses, ranging from a grocery store to personal services, to serve neighborhood residents. Yet 54 percent of the residents interviewed by city officials said they preferred to remain in the North End and did not want to be relocated because of their proximity to work and downtown and the fact that they owned their homes outright.[79]

In the years between the city's 1961 decision to make North End renewal a priority and the completion of the North End Urban Renewal Scheme in 1968, city officials, private developers, and residents moved forward with various projects in the neighborhood. In 1962, six hundred North End homeowners packed a meeting with the Urban Renewal Committee to protest planned land expropriation. Dissatisfied with public officials' response to their concerns, neighborhood activists gathered more than a thousand signatures on a petition against the renewal plan.[80] The petition carried little weight, and, a few months later, the Hamilton City Council adopted interim guidelines for the urban renewal area, which were intended to meet two goals: improve the housing stock and boost the city's economy by spurring new development. The guidelines stipulated the clearance of "substandard" buildings; the creation of a Perimeter Road around the neighborhood to divert truck traffic away from residential areas; the construction of public housing, new schools, and a new park; and sewer and utility improvements.[81] Following the approval of the urban renewal plan, residents stopped organizing against it: when the Ontario Municipal Board (OMB) opened hearings to approve the plan, fewer than one hundred attended. Yet in letters to the editor of the *Spectator* and in public opinion surveys, North End residents continued to make it clear that they did not want to leave their homes and did not consider their neighborhood "blighted."[82]

From the outset of the renewal plan, Hamilton's planners imagined different types of residents coexisting in the North End, not in mixed-income developments but rather in spatially segregated areas designed to serve both existing and imagined residents—the same model used for downtown redevelopment. They reserved sections of the harbor front for private development, including residential, commercial, and retail uses. A publicly funded park, schools, and community center were intended to create a new neighborhood center one block east of the James Street commercial district. City officials hoped that these public expenditures, initially estimated at $9 million, would entice private developers to improve the neighborhood's housing stock for blue-collar and middle-class residents and to develop luxury housing on the harbor.[83] No incentives were available to private developers aside from zoning changes and serviced land, and Hamilton's city officials did not seek to displace the existing residential working class, opting instead to direct new white-collar residents to reclaimed land along the harbor.

The proposed Perimeter Road and a redeveloped harbor were integral to the city planners' vision for the North End. The Urban Renewal Department described heavy truck traffic through the neighborhood as "one of the most serious blighting influences." The success of the scheme for the neighborhood center hinged on the completion of the four-lane Perimeter Road and subsequent closure of John Street, which bisected the project area. Without the John Street closure, one school and a playground expansion would remain physically separated from the rest of the new neighborhood center.[84] In the late 1960s, planners had complained that industrial uses monopolized the waterfront, which limited public access, a situation they described as "understandable" but "in no way exemplary or admirable." A waterfront park at the harbor would provide a "vitally important" semiregional facility to bolster redevelopment efforts citywide, and the harbor represented the only viable location for such a park in proximity to downtown Hamilton. The park was slated to include five acres of existing open space, previously acquired by the city for an incinerator that was ultimately located elsewhere, and up to thirty acres of infill in the harbor.[85]

By 1965, city officials had selected clearance sites and had begun acquisition of substandard houses slated for demolition and those that stood in the path of the proposed Perimeter Road. Three years later, one of the new schools, a public housing facility for the elderly, and a privately developed high-rise were finished, the neighborhood center neared completion, and additional public housing was underway. Residents as well prepared their properties for urban renewal. The Hamilton Urban Renewal Department reported that it received over 250 inquiries a year from North End home-owners inquiring about aid for home repairs and asking whether making repairs would affect the status of their homes in the urban renewal plans, suggesting that residents were not interested in leaving their homes or the neighborhood. The Murray Jones consultants spotted evidence of "extensive repainting plus numerous instances of re-roofing, porch repairs and general clean-up," as well as four instances where houses slated for demolition in the 1964 plan were completely renovated by 1968, presumably in an effort to stave off the city's wrecking ball.[86]

The Murray Jones consultants had assured city officials that the North End would attract three hundred privately developed high-rise apartment units per year, based on population predictions and extrapolations from recent high-rise construction citywide. They estimated that the renewed North End would house nearly 12,000 people, a 40 percent increase over 1961.[87] By the end of the decade, however, only one apartment complex had materialized, and by 1971 the federal government had terminated its financial support for the North End urban renewal project. The loss of federal funds (half of the project funding) came on the heels of planners' revised renewal scheme, which called for an additional $19 million over ten years and excluded fund-ing for the Perimeter Road, which the city had abandoned after expropri-ating and demolishing 300 homes at a cost of nearly $1.3 million.[88] Federal retrenchment did not diminish city officials' interest in stimulating private redevelopment in the North End, but it did restrict their investment to the $9.2 million initially allocated for the project, a far cry from their revised estimate.[89] The elimination of federal urban renewal funds marked an impor-tant difference between redevelopment in the North End and on Pittsburgh's South Side: because South Side community groups received limited public funding and were left largely to their own devices until the 1990s, the more ad hoc nature of South Side redevelopment made it relatively impervious to the vagaries of federal urban development funding. In Hamilton, the loss of federal funds for North End urban renewal undermined planners' ability to realize their goals.

Around the same time the federal government terminated urban renewal funds, North End residents began to mount a serious challenge against the plan. By 1969, North End residents had collectively spent over $100,000 on home improvements. When planners tested a building code demonstration program in the North End in 1970, residents complained that overzealous building inspectors misled them as to the number of home repairs necessary to meet building codes and as to the amount of time they had to make repairs. They denounced the imposition of a minimum standards bylaw that only applied to homes in the urban renewal area and not elsewhere in the city, calling it "discrimination against these north end people."[90]

The same year, Planning Board chair John Miller expressed frustration with what he saw as efforts by North End residents to hinder development that planners deemed important to the city as a whole. When a group of residents protested the potential expropriation of their homes for a high-rise luxury housing development on the harbor, Miller told them that the city would not allow the interests of "a few" residents to prevent changes that public officials believed were in the long-term "best interests of the city," and he suggested that "perhaps the strong arm of the city may have to be exercised." City planning director Bob Bailey informed residents that the city government would step in to persuade them to sell once a developer had acquired at least 80 percent of the land required for any project that the planners wanted to see completed. Bailey responded to residents' queries about whether he represented their interests or those of potential developers with a terse "both."[91]

In addition to tension over demonstration programs and expropriation, North End residents and city officials disagreed over whether the urban renewal program was by any measure successful. Urban renewal chairman Lloyd Berryman insisted, "Even among people forced to move, 99 percent have bettered themselves."[92] Residents disagreed, and, in 1972, North End residents surveyed by the City Planning Department expressed displeasure about the loss of retail enterprises that were relocated or forced out by renewal activities, said they needed a supermarket or shopping center in the neighborhood to replace local markets that had closed, and indicated that they wanted more recreational and park facilities—all of which had been promised to them as part of the urban renewal project.[93] City officials blamed the federal funding freeze, the poor design of both the public housing and the single high-rise project, and the lack of private development for the North End scheme's failure to make good on planners' promises. Alderman Bill McCulloch insisted that the city had undertaken public projects "in good faith" and that "we did what we could to stimulate private commercial building but they did not take us up on it." As far as he was concerned, market forces had determined the North End's fate, and "if you believe in our system, the free enterprise system, then you have to accept that."[94]

In 1977, the North End Residential Organization (NERO) conducted an independent survey of residents' attitudes about the renewal program, by that point underway for nearly twenty years. Residents were less convinced than McCulloch that the invisible hand of the market was to blame for the outcome of the North End renewal program. More than 80 percent of those surveyed described themselves as dissatisfied with the course taken by the city. While the majority of respondents agreed that the renewal program had diminished a sense of "community spirit" and cohesiveness, their primary complaint, as it had been five years earlier, was that the city government relocated local businesses, including a hardware store and grocery stores, out of the neighborhood commercial district in anticipation that private developers would establish higher-end shops, a shopping center, and a chain grocery store. The shops and mall were never built, and the grocery chain abandoned its plans to build in the North End when the high-rise apartment complexes described in the renewal plans failed to materialize.[95]

The NERO survey found that residents remained angry with what they saw as an inequitable financial burden imposed on North Enders by the city government. NERO director (and North End resident) Alice Lupton recalled that the 1970 building code demonstration project had since been introduced citywide, but that the North End had been "the guinea pig and it got pretty rough treatment." Residents whose homes the city government had expropriated and demolished for the Perimeter Road project, which it subsequently abandoned, charged that they had been ejected from their homes for no reason and underpaid for their properties.[96] Lupton condemned planners for their lack of attention to the needs of North End residents. "Planners work with a map and a bunch of pins and they stick them here and there and they don't really think of the people who live there," she said. "They don't see them as human beings."[97]

As had been the case with Jackson Square, North End residents did not particularly object to the city government's plans to recast Hamilton as a postindustrial city or even to the creation of luxury housing in the neighborhood. Instead, residents' outrage centered on city and provincial officials' failure to deliver the neighborhood services and physical improvements detailed in the urban renewal scheme. At least one city official concurred with the residents: assistant building commissioner Rashmi Nathwani said that, in his estimation, the North End had not experienced significant new construction because of the renewal scheme. He characterized the North End as an unattractive financial risk to developers because of its low residential population and "unflattering" reputation as a declining neighborhood, factors exacerbated by the failed renewal project.[98] Copps, however, had very few tools with which to make the neighborhood more appealing to private sector developers. Unlike Pittsburgh's city officials, who ultimately stepped

Figure 15. Hamilton's North End and harbor industrial area in 1973,
largely unchanged by the urban renewal scheme. Courtesy of Local History
& Archives, Hamilton Public Library.

in to coordinate South Side redevelopment and advance lucrative incentives
to developers, Hamilton's city officials could no more offer capital subsidies
in the North End than they could downtown. And while Hamilton's elected
officials remained attentive to the needs of the North End's existing residents,
their concern did not translate to improved neighborhood services for working-class residents.

At the outset of the planning process, urban renewal officials expected
the North End to return to its historic prominence as a fashionable residential district.[99] This did not happen. Despite the project's failure to
achieve its original goals, McCulloch insisted that the urban renewal program had been indisputably worthwhile. "While there was a lot of harm
done to individuals," he said, "the overall beneficial effect was worth the
effort."[100] It was not entirely clear for whom he believed the "overall effect"
had been beneficial. Whereas, on Pittsburgh's South Side, gentrification in
the early 1990s served the interests of the young white-collar workers city
officials and civic leaders sought to attract, North End development did

not, in the end, create luxury housing or attract young professionals. The North End remained primarily working-class and continued to house new immigrant groups as they arrived in the city—but they had a longer trip to the grocery store.

With the North End renewal plan underfunded and widely judged a failure, city officials shifted their attention to the North End's enclaves. Artifacts of unregulated development in the nineteenth and early twentieth centuries, the enclaves were residential pockets scattered throughout an otherwise heavily industrialized area north of Barton Street. E. G. Faludi first proposed the rezoning of the enclaves for industrial use in his 1947 plan for the city.[101] Twenty years later, city officials had made little progress toward that goal. In 1968, the OMB approved an official plan amendment to rezone ten residential enclaves as industrial and gradually relocate residents, ostensibly to create more serviced land for industry and to move people out of blighted living conditions. "The close proximity of industrial and residential land uses North of Barton Street has resulted in mutual conflicts," the City Planning Department's 1969 annual report noted. Planners contended that the mingling of industrial and residential land uses subjected residents to "inordinate concentrations of air pollution, noise, industrial traffic" and that "the successful operation of industry is impeded by crowded residential streets and lack of space for expansion."[102] The new zoning designation did not force residents to move, but it allowed the city to expropriate land and made it illegal for residents to rebuild homes if they burned down or to acquire new mortgages or insurance policies on the buildings. With those possibilities foreclosed, it was impossible to sell the homes for residential use.[103]

Public officials had a conflicted relationship with the residential enclaves. The Planning Department dealt with the enclaves on a case-by-case basis, sometimes siding with residents, sometimes with industry. Provincial programs administered by the city made public financing available to property owners in some of the enclaves to rehabilitate their homes, an obvious conflict with the city's plan to eliminate the enclaves incrementally. Moreover, city officials' informal policy toward clearing the area of residents for industrial expansion stopped short of expropriation, and the city government typically purchased homes only when their owners listed them for sale. Piecemeal property acquisition meant that the city held oddly sized parcels that were not always suitable for transfers to industry until adjacent properties were also acquired. As a result, even though industrial land was technically available, it was easier and less expensive for companies to build warehouse and shipping facilities away from the harbor—sometimes as far away as neighboring Burlington.[104]

To compete with Burlington for new light industrial land uses, Hamilton planners eventually recommended pursuing a "politically unpalatable" alternative, whereby the city would either purchase residential properties outright for a price slightly above market value or establish a phased expropriation program.[105] Even as the Planning Department contemplated a more aggressive clearance policy, however, a 1974 rezoning proposal saved two hundred homes in the eight-block area west of Sherman Avenue North and north of the Barton Street commercial area from removal for industrial expansion. City Council had zoned the area for heavy industrial uses in the 1950s, but few residents seemed to take notice until Lupton and NERO warned them in the early 1970s that industrial expansion might occur near their homes. Alderman Pat Valeriano noted that residents were questioning "why they should bother to keep their homes in good shape, if the city was going to buy the land for more factories." City planners surveyed residents, asking whether they preferred to remain in their homes or sell to the city for future industrial expansion. Residents overwhelmingly indicated that they wanted to stay in their homes, and city councilors duly introduced an official plan amendment to downzone the neighborhood from heavy industrial to residential. Two years later, in another section of the enclaves, the city moved forward with plans for an industrial park established as part of the 1969 official plan, which required changing an existing residential designation to heavy industrial and expropriating two blocks of homes.[106]

Enclave rezoning plans suggest that the mayor's office and the Economic Development Division's concern for regional industrial expansion increasingly tempered the City Council and Planning Department inclination to side with residents. While, in the first case, the Planning Department and City Council worked quickly to meet the preferences of existing residents, in the second case, they dismissed residents' desires to remain in their homes as impossible. "The city has no business coming in and telling some old pensioner he has to get out of the house he's been living in all his life just because some industry wants to come in here," John Moroz, who had lived in the neighborhood for half a century, complained. "You're not working for the people, you're working for industry." McCulloch testily responded, "that's possible." He said the decision to create an industrial park had been made six years prior and that residents had little recourse aside from selling their property to the city. Moroz and another resident protested that the city's policies were forcing out long-time residents. "If the city comes in and buys up houses on either side of me and the tenants let them run down," said Bob Baxter, "you're forcing me out." McCulloch dismissed Moroz and Baxter's concerns: "that may be true but legally we have the right to do so."[107] In this instance, the city government intended to sell the expropriated land to Dofasco for parking, rather than industrial operations.

In 1977, Copps's successor Jack MacDonald made it clear that his office intended to privilege the land requirements of manufacturers over the residential preferences of the people living in the enclaves. MacDonald acknowledged that the city government's decision to encourage industrial expansion was at odds with residents' desires to stay in their homes, but he spuriously argued that resistance to leaving the enclaves was more about economics than neighborhood ties, claiming that residents believed they would not be paid enough to make it worthwhile to relocate. As a solution, he proposed a housing exchange in which federal, provincial, and city funds would be used to purchase comparable homes for residents elsewhere in Hamilton.[108] That the residents would eventually move was not up for negotiation as far as the mayor's office was concerned, because city officials thought that manufacturers might relocate because of lack of available land. "A prudent manufacturer must be thinking of expanding 5 to 10 years down the road," MacDonald said, "and the fact that there is room for expansion is inducement to stay in Hamilton."[109] MacDonald's concern over the enclaves undoubtedly also reflected a Planning Department study which suggested that the $200,000 generated annually by residential taxes on the properties in one enclave alone would yield more than $1 million for the city in industrial taxes.[110] In Hamilton's 1980 official plan, city officials downplayed their role in determining the future of the enclaves, noting vaguely, "the private market is gradually evolving the most economical use of this area."[111]

By the mid-1980s, as the recession deepened and unemployment became a pressing political problem, the enclaves turned into a flashpoint between the heads of the City Planning Department and the Regional Economic Development Department and between residents and city officials. Emerging conflict over the enclaves exposed fractures among members of Hamilton's ad hoc growth partnership. Hamilton's city councilors adopted an official plan amendment for a cluster of residential enclaves in the Normanhurst and Keith neighborhoods, which would downzone part of the area north of Barton Street from heavy industrial to light and limited heavy industrial uses. The regional council signed off on the proposed plan amendment with little fanfare. The City Council sought the zoning change to protect residents in the enclaves from establishment of heavy industry near their homes; the amendment did not affect any industrial uses already present in or near the area.[112]

Hamilton's manufacturers went on the offensive. Representatives of harbor-front industries, including H.H. Robertson, Union Gas Limited, Otis Elevators, Firestone Canada, Nella Cutlery, and Fred Hall and Son, together with the Hamilton and District Chamber of Commerce, approached the Regional Economic Development Committee to protest that the proposed downzoning threatened their future expansion, as well as their ability to sell the land.[113] The downzoning fight represented a pivotal moment of newfound business activism in Hamilton; before the Normanhurst and Keith downzonings, local manufacturers had displayed little inclination to strongarm the city over its development plans. When local CEOs finally took an organized interest in land use planning, it was to protect industrial property rather than to eliminate it, as had been the case with Pittsburgh's corporate elite. Two of the complainants, Union Gas and H. H. Robertson, were in the throes of expansion, and their representatives threatened to halt construction and potentially move out of Hamilton's industrial area if the downzoning moved forward. Representatives for Stelco and Proctor & Gamble, whose properties were unaffected by the proposed zoning change, also expressed concern about the plan. Stelco's lawyer issued a statement calling downzoning "frightening to industry" and intimated that, if Stelco had to worry about limits to its future expansion, it might decide to shift its facilities out of the city—a potent threat in light of the company's long-planned construction of a new facility an hour south of Hamilton in Nanticoke.[114]

Similarly, when Hamilton's regional councilors shifted course to support corporate interests over those of the residential working class, they protected potential industrial expansion instead of a shift to non-productive activities. Four of the region's mayors, including Hamilton's Bob Morrow, sided with the manufacturers. They expressed concern that the downzoning would cost the region much-needed manufacturing jobs. Morrow lambasted his City Planning Department for "running in conflict" with regional economic development goals and accused planners of being "out of touch with present [economic] realities." The mayors of suburban Ancaster and Stoney Creek joined Morrow in attempting to reassure businessmen that their interests were of foremost concern. Ancaster mayor Ann Sloat apologized to manufacturers, telling them, "we aren't looking after you very well." Stoney Creek mayor Bill Sears described the proposed downzoning as cutting "our own throats." Chamber of Commerce president Alec Murray accused city officials of creating a hostile business environment. "If the city can't take care of existing industry, how is it going to get any new ones?" he asked. Murray also decried the "loss of property rights" that he believed was implied in the downzoning. "If you expropriate a man's zonings," he argued, "you expropriate without compensation." Jim Thoms, Hamilton's city planning director, countered that zoning was not a property right, but rather a privilege that government granted and could take away at will.[115]

Despite interventions from some of the region's mayors, the regional council did not achieve a quorum on the issue and refused to reverse its earlier endorsement. Morrow promised the regional officials and the manufacturing executives that he would prevail upon city planners and council members to reconsider the downzoning in light of industry's concerns and expressed his own belief that urban planning in the enclaves had for too long favored residential over industrial interests.[116] The City Council, however, was disinclined to "bow down to the captains of industry and give them everything they want," as one North End councilor said. Thoms was frustrated that Hamilton's manufacturers were mounting an intense and expensive campaign against a land use designation that did not affect any of their existing or proposed activities.[117] Revealing conflict between city planning and regional economic development officials, Economic Development Division director Don Cole sided with the angry CEOs.

Because all official plan amendments were subject to approval by the OMB, provincial officials stepped in to settle the fight between the City Planning and Regional Economic Development Departments. The official plan amendment proposed to ban only the twenty-one most noxious uses (out of four hundred possible), and City Council, the manufacturers, and the OMB volleyed the proposed amendment back and forth until City Council withdrew it in 1988. While many aldermen believed that the vote on the amendment represented a choice between the interests of residents and those of corporations—one described it as a vote between human rights and property rights—Morrow's contention that "when it comes to existing industries, we just can't afford to fool around" ultimately carried the day.[118] The City Council gave in, noting that the zoning change affected property values and that "if we take property rights away from these companies by downzoning we are sending out a very strong message."[119] Regional officials' decision to drive out longtime residents to satisfy manufacturers' demands for guaranteed land for potential future expansion exposed the tension between the growth coalition's postindustrial imagination, the continued presence of heavy manufacturing on Hamilton Harbor, and the provincial mandate to expand industrial development. The outcome of the minor drama, in which business owners protested downzoning not because it conflicted with any planned expansion but rather to assert their property rights, suggests the extent to which Hamilton's city government by the 1980s, like Pittsburgh's had for decades, saw no viable option but to commit itself to serving corporate interests.

CHAPTER SIX

Marketing Postindustrialism

In a surprising boost to the growth coalition's postindustrial plans, Rand McNally's *Places Rated Almanac* declared Pittsburgh "America's Most Livable City" in February 1985.[1] Mystified by the supposed "livability" of a gritty steel town with a devastated manufacturing sector, the national press and late night talk show hosts made sport of the designation; on the *Tonight Show*, Johnny Carson cracked, "Pittsburgh is kind of like Newark, but without the cultural advantages."[2] Journalists, comedians, and the region's unemployed manufacturing workers may have questioned Rand McNally's metrics, but elected officials and civic leaders were thrilled by the long-awaited public relations boost. The Greater Pittsburgh Convention and Visitors Bureau snatched up hundreds of copies of *Places Rated*, ordered stationery emblazoned "Most Livable City," and advertised Pittsburgh's ranking on billboards across the country. The designation "came at a time when we didn't have anything else new or dramatic to sell," recalled bureau executive vice president Bob Imperata. "There was no hook out there for Pittsburgh, and this was the hook we were looking for."[3]

Hamilton, too, was looking for a hook. Just three years before Pittsburgh's public relations triumph, the *Hamilton Spectator* ran its "Pittsburgh Solution" feature. "It's a steel town trying to reduce its dependency on declining heavy industry and a lunchbucket image. It's a football town that would also like to be known for its universities and symphony orchestra," the article began. "And it must face the problems associated with a declining population and an unemployment rate high above the national average." The author might have been describing his hometown, but, as he quickly informed readers, his subject was "How Steel City USA handles the problems we face in Hamilton."[4] The two cities grappled not only with similar urban decline but also faced the same kind of image problem.

In 1880, the smokestacks that punctuated Pittsburgh's rivers and Hamilton's harbor had been symbols of wealth and power; by 1980, they were emblems of environmental degradation and urban decay. To bolster their efforts to materially transform the physical, social, and economic geography of their cities, Pittsburgh's and Hamilton's city officials and civic leaders launched marketing campaigns designed to shed their steel town images. The sort of urban marketing they engaged in had a long history. While some scholars suggest place promotion with the goal of "selling" places to visitors and investors began with the Hanseatic League, or perhaps Leif Ericsson, more useful precedents date from the nineteenth-century United States.[5] From New York to San Francisco, land grants from the U.S. government for railroad expansion spurred intense place-marketing campaigns in the 1850s. Cities and towns competed for rail stops, and the railroads aggressively advertised in newspapers and through self-produced brochures and maps. Local boosters, usually prominent businessmen, competed to host state universities or become county seats. At the end of the century, ambitious cities in the West promoted monumental architecture, infrastructure projects, and cultural institutions through promotional materials and advertising campaigns. Businessmen, newspapermen, and local elected officials worked together to market cities, typically in an ad hoc way that produced eclectic and uncoordinated symbols and images. In Atlanta and throughout the "New South," boosters printed scores of promotional brochures and advertisements designed to showcase urban growth and opportunities for industrial investment. By the 1930s, chambers of commerce in a host of southern cities promoted wide-ranging state and local subsidies for industrial development; twenty years later, boosters publicized "good business climates."[6]

The tug-of-war between cities for jobs, industry, residents, and tourists intensified in the face of government retrenchment in the 1970s, and the institutional arrangements of place promotion changed. Nineteenth- and early twentieth-century businessmen had sold their cities as sites of production. As basic industry declined in places like Pittsburgh and Hamilton, entrepreneurial city officials worked with civic leaders to market cities as spaces of consumption.[7] Growth coalitions adapted corporate branding strategies to turn cities into commodities they could sell to investors and consumers. Controlling a city's image, and commodifying certain kinds of spaces, was a political project with an ideological function. It allowed local elites to claim representational authority over the city, promote postindustrial redevelopment as uniformly beneficial for corporations and for existing and future residents, and at the same time sideline groups who challenged their activities.[8]

Scholars have dated the origins of urban branding to the 1975 New York fiscal crises and the efforts of the city's growth partnership to sanitize New York for investors and tourists.[9] They describe urban branding, along with the attack on organized labor, austerity policies, and corporate welfare programs that accompanied New York City's mid-1970s restructuring, as a marker of nascent neoliberal urbanism.[10] Like anti-unionism, fiscal reform, and public subsidies for private industry, however, urban branding was not entirely new. It was, instead, an intensification and reorientation of tactics that had for decades formed the basis of an emergent postindustrialism.

Together with government retrenchment, corporate welfare, downtown facelifts, and neighborhood makeovers, urban branding was part and parcel of regional economic restructuring. Central business district makeovers, lively and affordable residential areas, and a range of culture and leisure activities became part of a postindustrial product marketed to potential investors, to young professionals, to tourists, and to regional residents. City officials and civic leaders in Pittsburgh and Hamilton—and the advertising executives they hired—"gilded the smokestack" with carefully crafted symbols of clean, harmonious, resolutely middle-class cities, places without labor conflict, distressed neighborhoods, or industrial detritus.[11] Their counterparts in struggling North Atlantic manufacturing centers like Bilbao, Turin, and Newcastle did the same.[12] On both sides of the Atlantic, advertising campaigns for declining manufacturing centers promoted new downtown office buildings, knowledge industries, positive business climates, gentrifying neighborhoods, museums, sports, and shopping. Edinburgh, for instance, began to promote retail, culture, and tourism in the 1970s, emphasizing the city's early modern history and trying to attract service jobs while downplaying industrial restructuring.[13] When the steel crisis hit Piombino, Tuscany's "Little Manchester," local elites sought to sell it as an agricultural rather than industrial center, in part by aligning Piombino with regional wine tourism rather than trade unionism.[14]

Urban branding was both material and symbolic, a way for growth partnerships to create new mental maps of the cities they were physically reconfiguring. In Pittsburgh, the growth coalition hired consultants and began to develop a consistent post-steel image for the city in the 1960s, well before New York City's bankruptcy was on the horizon. With an eye toward successful branding campaigns for "global" cities such as New York, in the 1970s and 1980s public officials worked with local corporations, media outlets, and advertising firms to compete for jobs and residents by selling Pittsburgh as a postindustrial utopia for young, well-educated professionals. In Hamilton, public-private cooperation for place promotion, like that for urban renewal, was ad hoc. Conflict over how to represent the city deepened fractures in the loose coalition between city planners, regional economic development officials, mayors, and businessmen in the 1980s, and Hamilton struggled to establish a consistent urban brand.

Urban Boosterism

Members of Pittsburgh and Hamilton's growth coalitions were not the only people pondering the future of urban development in the two cities in the 1960s. In 1961, University of Nebraska architecture professor Patrick Horsbrugh traveled to Kingston, Ontario, to present a paper at a symposium on "The Canadian City," convened by the Canadian Federation of Mayors and Municipalities. Born in Ireland to Scottish parents and educated in England, Horsbrugh embodied the North Atlantic crossings that shaped postwar planning theory and practice. In his youth, he spent time in India, where his parents had grown up, and South Africa, where an uncle had settled with his American wife. Horsbrugh served in both the British and Canadian armed forces during World War II. At the end of his military service, he volunteered in a planning department in Yorkshire, where he worked on the Middlesbrough Survey and Plan to rebuild what he described as "England's Pittsburgh" after the war. He studied architecture in London and Rome before enrolling in the landscape architecture program at Harvard. By 1961, he had gained an international reputation for his work on ambitious modernist housing schemes in London and for his trenchant critique of the planning and design of Chandigarh, India's post-independence architectural showpiece.[15]

At the Canadian City symposium, Horsbrugh talked about a speech Hamilton mayor Lloyd D. Jackson delivered at a Community Planning Association of Canada conference. Jackson had cataloged the natural, cultural, and architectural features that established the city's "civic distinction," including parks, a botanical garden, and the city's zoo, symphony, and sports teams. "These are the things that are remembered, these are some of the ingredients that establish one city as being different from another, that maintain pride of place among inhabitants and reputation among travellers," Horsbrugh argued.[16] He told his listeners that, as Canada's municipal officials began to compete with each other and with newly built suburbs for residents, urban image and marketing would become increasingly important.[17]

Three years later, Horsbrugh went to Pittsburgh. The city had received federal Community Renewal Program funds to finance an image study, and the mayor's office hired Horsbrugh to provide design advice and develop a marketing scheme for Renaissance Pittsburgh.[18] Horsbrugh declared Pittsburgh a "City of Contrasts." While it was small in size, he suggested, it boasted the same amenities as larger cities like Philadelphia and New York. Perhaps with his experience in Middlesbrough in mind, he linked Pittsburgh's image to regional economic development, provided a host of suggestions for attracting and retaining industry, and urged city officials to sell Pittsburgh as a city with a diverse industrial base.[19]

The year 1964 turned out to be a watershed for marketing Renaissance Pittsburgh. In January, the Allegheny Conference, the Pittsburgh Regional Planning Association (PRPA), and the Regional Industrial Development Corporation (RIDC) issued a joint policy statement based on the PRPA multivolume *Economic Study of the Pittsburgh Region*, released the previous year.[20] The Economic Analysis Policy Group (EAPG), the ad hoc committee that formulated the policy statement, included the usual suspects: the presidents, chairmen or vice chairmen of the boards of Pittsburgh National Bank, U.S. Steel, Jones & Laughlin, Mellon Bank, Duquesne Light, Westinghouse, and other area corporations; former mayor David Lawrence; the president of the Mellon Charitable Trust; the presidents of Duquesne University and the Carnegie Institute of Technology (later, Carnegie Mellon University); and the presidents of the United Steelworkers and Pittsburgh Typographical Union. The policy statement enumerated the ways that business and labor, in particular, might help promote Pittsburgh. Businesses, EAPG urged, should modernize their facilities and strengthen their research and development programs, particularly in collaboration with area universities. Likewise, businessmen should seek to "publicize the good points" of the region, with the goal that "selling the advantages of the Southwestern Pennsylvania area becomes a built-in and normal role for representatives of Pittsburgh's industries as they travel throughout the country and the world."[21]

EAPG members believed that improving Pittsburgh's image rested on strengthening what the growth coalition would eventually come to refer to as the region's "business climate." They lamented the city's "undesirable reputation" for militant unionism, particularly after a bitter national steel strike in 1959, and described labor leaders' cooperation as central to regional promotion plans. The group cautioned that an unfavorable image of Pittsburgh persisted nationally and had a "discernible adverse impact" on regional economic development. More than in other places, EAPG members contended, labor-management relations in Pittsburgh carried "special responsibilities." The foundation of any regional economic development plan, in their view, should be "positive and well-publicized actions" focused on promoting the "productivity and flexibility" of the region's labor force or the "enlightened labor and management climate consistent with the need for competitive and profitable enterprises."[22]

Horsbrugh's analysis of Pittsburgh's image problem, issued a month after the policy statement, echoed the PRPA recommendations. Horsbrugh focused more on the urban landscape than on labor relations and found that perceptions of Pittsburgh, inside and outside the city, did not reflect the improved environmental conditions and physical redevelopment associated with the first Renaissance. He advised the city government to undertake a study of white-collar versus blue-collar employment patterns "to determine whether the existing conditions represent an encouraging future, or whether the changing industrial patterns require greater emphasis on office adminis-tration and efficiency." Horsbrugh urged the mayor's office to compile a list of Fortune 500 corporations with headquarters or branch offices in Pittsburgh and use the list to make it "a matter of deliberate planning policy" to target and attract new corporations.[23]

Horsbrugh also recommended a long-term advertising campaign designed to market Pittsburgh as a city with a diverse local economy in order "to overcome the prevailing impression of Pittsburgh as a place of gloom." Pittsburgh was popularly perceived as "a dour place, a place only of work, hard work, and of hideous envirium," he wrote. "This opinion will continue unless it is challenged by dramatic ideas and dynamic efforts." He contin-ued, "Who thinks of Pittsburgh in terms of sunlight? Yet this condition has become, once more, a reality. Who thinks of Pittsburgh as a place of night life, summer or winter? Yet this can be. Who thinks of Pittsburgh as a CITY SPECTACULAR? Yet the ingredients exist."[24] Horsbrugh's study underscored, for city officials, that Pittsburgh's national reputation did not reflect the city's current physical and social conditions. They ultimately rejected Horsbrugh's suggestion that they market Pittsburgh as the "City of Contrasts" or "City of Light" in favor of the homegrown "Renaissance City," but they embraced the spirit of his recommendations.

The same year that the EAPG released its statement and Horsburgh filed his report, Doubleday published Stefan Lorant's *Pittsburgh: The Story of an American City*. The book was a decade in the making and became a cen-tral promotional tool for the first Renaissance. In 1954, department store magnate, civic leader, and Frank Lloyd Wright patron Edgar Kaufmann had summoned Lorant to Pittsburgh to discuss the production of a "de luxe" book that would chronicle the city's past and its recent rebirth. Lorant, like Horsbrugh, had a career that spanned the Atlantic. Born in Hungary, Lorant had worked as a filmmaker and editor in Berlin and Vienna. After six months in prison for his opposition to Hitler, he fled to London, where he published a memoir, edited a succession of picture magazines, and served as an advisor to Henry Luce. He moved to the United States in 1940 and wrote popular histories like *Pittsburgh*, often with the support of wealthy benefactors.[25]

Kaufmann was deeply troubled that Americans thought of Pittsburgh as a smoky industrial center. He was "inordinately proud of his native city, very much in love with it, and he wished the whole world could know what a wonderful place it was," Lorant recalled. At Kaufmann's behest, Lorant explored the region for a few days before agreeing to write the book, and he came away impressed by its "buoyancy of civic spirit." He extolled the clean air, flood and pollution controls, slum clearance projects, and construction, park, and transportation projects then underway. Most of all, he praised the city's redevelopment partnership, whose members had "shelved their personal and political differences" and joined together to work for the common good. Pittsburgh's first Renaissance was "democracy at its best," he wrote. Kaufmann died not long after Lorant began his research, and the Allegheny Conference and Pittsburgh's foundations stepped in to finance the project.[26]

When *Pittsburgh* was finally published in 1964, it became one of the growth coalitions' most powerful marketing tools. The book, more than 500 pages long with over 1,000 illustrations, chronicled 200 years of Pittsburgh's history through the eyes of prominent scholars such as Henry Steele Commager and Oscar Handlin. The photos that accompanied the text featured manufacturing sites, corporate headquarters, headshots of local CEOs, executives and labor leaders smiling and shaking hands, and desolate tenements razed to make way for pristine, modernist apartment buildings.[27] Like Horsbrugh, Lorant depicted contemporary Pittsburgh as a city of harmonious contrasts. He told the stories of the men and women who had made Pittsburgh a mighty industrial center in the nineteenth and early twentieth centuries and ended with a fairy tale rendering of the city's rebirth after World War II. "And when the smoke and smog had gone—and the streets, Rivers and Hills of the city emerged," read one photo caption, "Pittsburgh presented itself as one of the most beautiful places in the land."[28]

In the book's closing chapter, Lawrence narrated the story of Pittsburgh's Renaissance from the point of view of the growth coalition, praising public-private cooperation for Golden Triangle redevelopment and urban renewal in the Hill District and East Liberty. The former mayor's frustration over Pittsburgh's poor image bled through in his reflections on the Renaissance. "Pittsburgh's great effort has been to remake itself, to change as fast as it can from the environment of the old nineteenth-century technology into the sleek new forms of the future," Lawrence noted. "The city welcomes tomorrow, because yesterday was hard and unlovely." Pittsburgh was "proud and self-confident," he wrote, and "used to good notices in the national magazines and the international press." But there was, he conceded, "one sure irritant"—a reference to Pittsburgh's smoke-filled past. "No Pittsburgher," Lawrence declared, "will be patient with the ignoramus who has not learned that times have changed."[29] Lawrence's annoyance that Pittsburgh had not yet shaken its image as "The Smoky City" became a common lament for city officials and civic leaders, who expressed similar concerns over the next five decades.

In 1966, Duquesne Light sponsored a brochure that promoted Pittsburgh as "the pivot point for profit," a "dynamic market" where industry and services could find skilled labor, cutting-edge scientific research, ample raw materials, and eager consumers. Pittsburgh, according to the brochure, represented different things to different people. For some, what made Pittsburgh "pivotal" was the "ever-changing skyline of the Golden Triangle, with its 20th Century skyscrapers." For others, it was the "progressiveness of having industry and suburbia in close proximity," which the brochure characterized as a "most comfortable arrangement." The proximity of industry, represented by photographs of sterile industrial parks rather than steel mills, to suburban idyll reinforced Lorant's sketch of Pittsburgh as a city on the rise. Pittsburgh, in the already-entrenched Renaissance narrative, had replaced heavy industry and smoke-filled skies with scientists, engineers, and medical researchers through the determination and hard work of dedicated civic leaders. "Pittsburgh is profit," the brochure promised its readers, "but it is also a nice place to live."[30]

By the next decade, the growth coalition was engaged in a national public-relations campaign designed to sell Pittsburgh for what it might become, rather than what it was. Its members marketed the city's postindustrial transformation and the public-private partnership that facilitated it alongside the Steelers, the rivers, and the universities. The *New York Times* reported that the old shot-and-a-beer Pittsburgh had given way to a "new" Pittsburgh, and compared the city's elite Shadyside neighborhood favorably with Washington, D.C.'s Georgetown. "The young women pouring out of the new office buildings look and dress like their miniskirted counterparts in

New York and Chicago and San Francisco," the reporter noted approvingly. "If there is a babushka left in the city, it apparently stays in Polish Hill or one of the other ethnic neighborhoods."[31] The reporter, like the Allegheny Conference, described white-collar workers as the "real" Pittsburgh, while the city's blue-collar workers were a lingering vestige of bygone days who added local color to central city neighborhoods increasingly marketed to young professionals.

When they spoke to the national press, Pittsburgh's businessmen cast the region's population loss between 1960 and 1970 as an advantage for the city. The *Times* described Pittsburgh as wearing downtown's "Golden Triangle like a silk shirt, self-consciously hiding its dirty fingernails under ruffled cuffs," and noted the "ancient image of Pittsburgh as a grimy steel town, spitting fire and smoke" was "almost, but not quite a libel now." Locals "point[ed] with enthusiasm to a shift from manufacturing to non-manufacturing employment, a change that they are confident heralds a new era of white-collar stability for Pittsburgh as a service and distribution center."[32] Following the *Times*, other national media outlets promulgated official narratives of Pittsburgh's revitalization, eagerly chronicling the shift from heavy industry to commercial and financial services and the wholesale remaking of urban space for "residents more likely to be engineers or professors than steelworkers," as a reporter characterized Pittsburgh in the early 1980s.[33]

Under the direction of the Allegheny Conference, efforts to promote a new image for the Pittsburgh region intensified in the 1970s. In 1973 the Allegheny Conference established a separate promotional agency, Penn's Southwest, to sell Allegheny, Armstrong, Beaver, Butler, Fayette, Greene, Lawrence, Washington, and Westmoreland counties. Penn's Southwest's was charged with improving Pittsburgh's image nationally and locally and coordinating promotional activities that would encourage businesses to relocate to Southwestern Pennsylvania. Reflecting its corporate roots, the agency's first two presidents were Mellon Bank chairmen, and it shared most of its board members with the Allegheny Conference. Penn's Southwest also partnered with the governor's office, the Pennsylvania Department of Commerce, the Regional Industrial Development Corporation (RIDC), chambers of commerce throughout the region, corporate leaders, and local, state, and federal elected officials to achieve its mandate. Penn's Southwest's directors initially sought to secure any new enterprise for the region but quickly shifted their focus to light industry, high technology, and research and development to reflect civic leaders' (and the state government's) changing ideas about what types of economic activities should dominate the region's economy.

Executive Director Jay Aldridge carried out an agenda established by the organization's corporate board members, who sought to provide economic development incentives and induce local governments to cut public services in the name of efficiency. When Aldridge retired in 1996, after running the organization for twenty-four years, the *Pittsburgh Post-Gazette* reported the "tall and courtly" director and his staff had long had a "'trench coat' existence, flying off to meet with prospects around the globe but rarely reporting back to the public on their activities."[34] Public accountability may not have been Aldridge's chief concern, but in its first four years Penn's Southwest's issued press releases on sporting events, cultural amenities, and the region's "lifestyle" to 3,500 national newspapers and invited members of the national media to town, which resulted in "several fine articles which detailed the physical and economic change of the region." The agency held seminars for regional firms on stimulating foreign trade, delivered a bimonthly newsletter touting the region's advantages to 12,000 executives nationally, and prepared over 350 customized presentations on the region for corporate leaders. It also sponsored advertisements in national publications on relocating to Southwestern Pennsylvania and produced a guidebook on regional leisure and cultural opportunities for corporations to distribute to their employees.[35]

Penn's Southwest wanted to induce a "favorable business climate" and market the region "on the basis of those attributes." To Aldridge, this meant maintaining infrastructure, establishing "stable taxes and efficient government," and providing a "quality of life" that would appeal to white-collar workers.[36] Staffers and board members alike lamented increasing interurban competition in which "national magazines display advertisements extolling the attractions of one or another state, major news media feature stories about the recent spectacular economic growth of the 'Sunbelt,' and various groups of 'raiding parties' are reported to be visiting both here and abroad for the purpose of enticing business to settle in their home area." The agency's first president, Mellon Bank chairman James H. Higgins, derided "the siren song of the Sunbelt" and argued that the best way to combat South's poorly unionized labor force and low taxes was through a well-coordinated marketing campaign that advertised Pittsburgh's quality of life and competitive advantages, such as stable tax rates and the availability of utilities and serviced land.[37]

In Hamilton, too, concern over the city's steel town image influenced the direction of redevelopment plans. In the 1890s, Hamilton's boosters touted the city as the "Birmingham of Canada"; in the early twentieth century, they described it as the "Pittsburgh of Canada."[38] By the 1960s, however, Hamilton's growth coalition was worried about the city's steel town moniker. A

1967 National Film Board of Canada documentary, *Steeltown*, caused a furor with its portrayal of Hamilton as dirty, polluted, and overrun by impoverished immigrants. Mayor Vic Copps and civic leaders were incensed at the unflattering depiction of the city, and the *Ottawa Citizen's* report on Hamiltonians response to the film likely added fuel to the fire. "Poor, poor Hamilton," the *Citizen* taunted. "Ontario's ugly duckling had been offended again. . . . It must be galling to be ugly and to feel duty-bound to pretend that you're beautiful."[39]

When consultants for Arthur D. Little & Company submitted the "Lunchpail Report" in 1968, they too cited Hamilton's "lunch bucket" image as the biggest impediment to commercial expansion. Residents and visitors alike described Hamilton as "solid, but uninteresting and unexciting," a perception that, in large part, reflected Hamilton's proximity to "more cosmopolitan" Toronto. The consultants interviewed bank managers, financial journalists, and advertising executives in Toronto to assess their perceptions of Hamilton. While some businessmen characterized Hamilton as "progressive," they most strongly associated the city with the smoke they saw when driving past on the highway. Hamilton's residents and those in neighboring cities used phrases like "a workingman's city" and "a 'lunch pail' economy" to describe Hamilton. For the consultants, a workingman's city carried only negative connotations: old-fashioned and rundown, representing the past rather than the future. "The city lacks flair and style," they wrote. "The stores are not in attractive or impressive buildings generally; selection is somewhat limited; the attractions in the downtown are relatively few."[40]

The Lunchpail Report concluded that Hamilton's "deficiency in commercial activity" was almost entirely a reflection of negative attitudes about the city and that "only a well-planned and intelligently designed program to enrich the social life of the city will change people's conceptions." The consultants stressed that changing negative perceptions of Hamilton required more than "advertising, slogans, and other public relation devices." Instead, they urged public-private cooperation to plan and carry out social and cultural events, such as an international music festival, which would "create a new image that emphasizes progressiveness and modernity." For the consultants, downtown urban renewal was a better signifier of Hamilton's future than the heavily industrialized harbor. "As a long-term goal," they advised, "policy action must be taken to create an image of Hamilton that more accurately symbolizes the city. The 'lunch bucket' should become a symbol of the past. The modernity of the Civic Square development should be utilized to provide a symbol of the future."[41]

A year later, Jack Moore outlined a new economic development strategy for the city, inspired in part by his trip to Pittsburgh. "Without trying to downgrade Hamilton's industrial image—which has served the city well for more than half a century," he said, "we would like to build on the city's image as a commercial and educational center and eventually, as a cultural center." The *Hamilton Spectator* business editor predicted the emergence of a "newer and bigger Hamilton" in the 1970s, reporting that "the lifeblood of the city is shifting—from manufacturing to a service economy—a shift that will become more pronounced and more dramatic before the next decade is out."[42]

With the Lunchpail Report in hand and Moore's reflections on his Pittsburgh visit likely in mind, Copps tried to figure out how to change Hamilton's "lunch bucket" image. In the absence of serious public policy alternatives or substantial private funding, he rejected the consultants' suggestion that a public relations campaign alone would not be effective. In 1972, the city published a book, *Pardon My Lunch Bucket*, to commemorate the 125th anniversary of Hamilton's incorporation. *Pardon My Lunch Bucket* had much in common with Lorant's *Pittsburgh*. Most of the book focused on Hamilton's past, while the text and accompanying photos reinforced the postindustrial image that city officials and civic leaders increasingly sought to project. Copps's foreword reflected the city government's precarious position between the provincial mandate to attract and promote heavy industry and his own desire to project an image of a diversified economy.[43]

Elaborate, full-color photos in *Pardon My Lunch Bucket* highlighted the region's natural beauty, leisure activities, and recent redevelopment projects. The cover showed construction workers at a downtown building site, but little of the text and few of the images selected to represent Hamilton featured heavy industry or blue-collar workers. Photos of the steel mills were historical, not contemporary, leaving readers with the impression that they were part of Hamilton's past rather than its present. The conclusion flashed forward to the year 2000 to offer a glimpse of the future the growth coalition hoped to make possible. In Hamilton's imagined future, the Ambitious City rivaled Toronto. It hummed "with activity at night as people cluster in front of the new theaters and nightclubs," downtown so completely altered by high-rise apartment and office buildings that present-day residents would not recognize it.[44]

Hamilton's elected officials wanted to attract white-collar jobs, but they did not speak as derisively about Hamilton's existing residents as Richard Caliguiri did about Pittsburgh's. The constituent members of Hamilton's ad hoc partnership recognized that, even though they emphasized "new economy"

Figure 16. Hamilton's promotional book, *Pardon My Lunch Bucket*, emphasized
the downtown construction boom and Hamilton's emerging role as
a commercial center. City of Hamilton, 1972. Courtesy of the City of Hamilton.

jobs and workers in their efforts to market the city, they also had to retain a
manufacturing labor force to work in the harbor front industries. Instead of
going on the attack, Copps adopted a defensive tone: "So Hamilton has industry. So what?" he asked in his introduction to *Pardon My Lunch Bucket*. A
strong industrial base meant stable, well-paying jobs, he wrote. "I don't particularly mind Hamilton being called a lunchbucket town," Copps insisted.
A mere five paragraphs later, however, he challenged detractors to come and
see the "new" Hamilton. "If they're at all observant," he charged, "they'll see
that the lunchbucket image, like the smoke from the steel companies, is fading away. This city is turning from blue-collar to white-collar, particularly as
technology advances and the burgeoning service industry continues to grow."
Copps concluded happily that "the old lunch-bucket, like the glass milk bottle
of a few years ago, is destined to become a museum piece."[45]

A few years later, the Chamber of Commerce produced promotional
materials focused on downtown redevelopment and the rapid expansion

of the residential and commercial areas on the Mountain. The Chamber declared that Hamilton had changed more in the past fifteen years than at any other point in its history. "Today's Hamilton has kicked the lunch-bucket image," claimed Chamber officials, shortly after pointing out that the "New Hamilton" was still Canada's largest steel producer. Despite this fact, Hamilton was "no longer the grim, heavy-industry town it was once said to be," in no small part because of the "combined private-and-public" downtown facelift.[46] City profiles published in 1979 and 1983 also reflected the Chamber's desire to showcase the "new" Hamilton, while making sure that manufacturers knew they were still welcome in the city. Photos featured high-tech industries, rather than steel mills, and in panoramic vistas of downtown taken from the Mountain, the familiar plumes of smoke from the mills were conspicuously absent.[47]

As city officials reimagined Hamilton as a postindustrial place, Ontario's provincial government launched new industrial attraction schemes that undermined the growth coalition's visions for the future. Local economic development officials may have looked to Pittsburgh for models, but provincial officials saw U.S. Rust Belt cities as competition for scarce resources. In the 1960s and early 1970s, Southern Ontario towns such as Hamilton, Burlington, Oakville, and London housed 80 percent of Canada's foreign manufacturing investment. By 1979, Ministry of Industry and Tourism officials had come to believe that the province should shift its focus to attracting capital-intensive high technology manufacturing instead of basic industry, which "required aggressive promotion of Ontario as an attractive business location with competitive economic and social advantages."[48] By the end of the decade, Ontario officials had adopted economic development language from boosters in the U.S. Sunbelt and began to talk about creating a positive business climate—language that usually signaled attacks on organized labor and corporate welfare packages.

Provincial officials understood that Ontario's manufacturing centers were in competition with U.S. and European cities for new industry and commercial services. As they had in regional economic development, provincial ministries took the lead in marketing Ontario's cities to domestic and international corporations, inviting them to "do business" in Ontario. Ministry officials recognized that the range of subsidies available to corporations from state and local governments in the United States far surpassed those available in Ontario. The biggest obstacle, they noted, was a lack of "municipal freedom" for cities in Ontario versus the "dynamic role" played by local governments in the United States, which could offer incentives to developers.[49]

In 1979, the ministry hired an advertising firm to study industrial attraction programs in North America. The consultants determined that, in the United States, states and individual cities sponsored large-scale advertising campaigns intended to spur tourism and industrial development.[50] Ministry officials worried that U.S. states and cities used "creative approaches" not available in Canada, such as making political commitments to ensure private sector profitability through financial incentives and countering inducements offered by other jurisdictions.[51]

The ministry set out to compete with U.S. cities on their own terms, investigating incentive programs, studying promotional literature, and buying advertising space in the same periodicals and trade publications as U.S. states. Industrial promotion had long been an area of the economy in which the provincial government saw itself as having a legitimate role, but promotion efforts intensified and changed course in the 1970s. Rather than merely providing a consultative mechanism, Ministry of Industry and Tourism officials began to actively target certain sectors. The ministry established a "hard-nosed, practical and aggressive" comprehensive marketing plan through a new Industrial Promotion Group.[52] The industrial promotion plan was supposed to "speak more directly to the needs of the potential investor" than prior initiatives and to marshal municipal as well as provincial resources.[53] For the ministry, the imagined "potential investor" was a multinational corporation. Much of the new marketing campaign was devoted to demonstrating that Ontario offered better investment opportunities than the U.S. Sunbelt, and ministry officials drew heavily on a 1979 report that described Ontario's manufacturing climate as more analogous to booming Texas, Florida, and Georgia than to declining Michigan, Pennsylvania, and New York.[54] With its new industrial promotion plan, the provincial government jumped into international interurban competition for industry.

Dynamic Pittsburgh

As Ontario's provincial officials grew increasingly concerned about industrial competition, in Pittsburgh the growth coalition's coordinated but intermittent promotional efforts coalesced into a full-fledged branding campaign after Caliguiri became acting mayor in 1977. The mayor's office, the Allegheny Conference, the Allegheny County government, the local media, and the Chamber of Commerce began to work on complementary marketing campaigns to promote their shared vision for postindustrial Pittsburgh. During Caliguiri's first year in office, the utility company Duquesne Light published a brochure, *Living in Pittsburgh*, which it had developed with guidance from the Flaherty administration and the Allegheny Conference. *Living in Pittsburgh*, like most of the growth coalition's previous marketing efforts, targeted corporate executives who might relocate their companies to Pittsburgh. Pittsburgh, as the brochure described it, was "provincial" in a good way—friendly and manageable, but not an "outpost." It depicted the region's upscale urban and suburban neighborhoods, and featured photos of Steelers games, the ballet, and the elite Duquesne Club. Profiles of recent transplants

Two votes for city living

Betty and Robert Dickey are the only people on these pages who experienced the smoke-dark years: she is a fifth-generation Pittsburgher, he a fourth. Then you could tell how long the snow had been laying, he says: slice into a snowbank and count the daily soot lines. "It looked like a Napoleon." Under clear skies now, they live in the city, a walk from the University of Pittsburgh and Carnegie-Mellon, on a street of nineteenth-century homes. He is Chairman and President of Dravo. "For people who like to be involved in the affairs of the city, it's easier. I complain and honk my horn if it takes more than fifteen minutes to get to the office. Coming back from downtown on a Sunday evening, we must make it in six or seven minutes."

Figure 17. Dravo President and CEO Robert Dickey and his wife Betty were featured in *Living in Pittsburgh*, a promotional publication targeted to corporate leaders the growth coalition hoped might relocate to Pittsburgh. Photo reprinted with the permission of Duquesne Light Company.

to the city focused on middle-class and wealthy white families, including some who had relocated from European capitals.[55]

Living in Pittsburgh appeared the same year as Milton Glaser's I♥NY campaign. Glaser's iconic pop-art logo, originally commissioned to promote New York State, quickly became a symbol of elite-led efforts to rebrand New York City in the wake of a near-bankruptcy and decades of intense racial and labor conflict.[56] It was a central aspect of a larger branding campaign designed, as Miriam Greenberg has shown, to market a "cleaned-up" New York "as a safe and exciting city for the 'average' white, middle-class consumer."[57] I♥NY marked a shift from the diverse institutional arrangements of traditional boosterism to urban branding strategies that linked the city's image to its economic restructuring.[58] The runaway success of the I♥NY campaign made urban branding a first-line response to fiscal and urban crises in declining North Atlantic cities. Within a decade, civic leaders in Glasgow and Amsterdam had commissioned slogans designed to emulate I♥NY. The "Glasgow's Miles Better" logo, which remains in use, featured Mr. Happy from the Mr. Men children's books. Like I♥NY, it won national and international awards. ("Amsterdam Has It" proved less durable.)[59]

The brand that Pittsburgh's city officials and civic leaders tried to sell to the world in the 1980s reflected the influence of New York's successful symbolic clean-up. Shortly after I♥NY appeared, Pittsburgh's growth coalition launched a series of marketing campaigns that promoted a unified postindustrial brand. Duquesne Light reworked 1977's *Living in Pittsburgh* into 1980's *Seven Pittsburghs: Discoveries by Some Younger Settlers*. *Living in Pittsburgh* had marketed the region to executives of multinational corporations and to small business owners who would live in elite neighborhoods like Pittsburgh's Shadyside or suburban Fox Chapel and Mount Lebanon. *Seven Pittsburghs* instead promoted the city's shift to "new economy" jobs and trendy urban living. The brochure promoted the displacement of the city's residential working class by knowledge workers from outside the region. It profiled members of what Richard Florida would later dub the "creative class" and self-consciously positioned Pittsburgh as an alternative to New York, Boston, and San Francisco.[60]

The jobs, neighborhoods, and culture and leisure activities that attracted the seven Pittsburghers profiled in detail in the brochure sent a clear message about which groups local officials and civic leaders wanted in the city: educated professionals whose spending habits and tax dollars would support the cultural district, fine dining establishments, and downtown boutiques. They were also people who were likely to gentrify downtrodden blue-collar neighborhoods. A finance worker and his young family had purchased and restored a house in the North Side's Mexican War Streets, for instance, and he compared Pittsburgh's real estate prices favorably to those in New York. "This development on the North Side—the Mexican War streets, Allegheny West and Manchester—is mostly a function of outsiders coming in," he noted approvingly. "People from the East Coast or just outside the city; not very many native Pittsburghers."[61]

Seven Pittsburghs also represented the city as a culturally rich alternative to other, more distressed, northern cities. Glossing over the region's often-violent labor history, it promoted instead the city's entrepreneurial spirit, top-notch research universities, cultural institutions, and sports teams. A Carnegie Mellon robotics professor, originally from England, liked the "energy" of New York and London but chose to live in Pittsburgh, he said, because it "provides a stimulating working environment for people who are in the middle-class intelligentsia bracket" and offered "world-class" art museums and theatre. A young art conservator who had relocated from Ohio characterized her former home as "Midwestern" and found Pittsburgh to be more like East Coast cities. Young people in Pittsburgh, she said, were less "staid" than those in Cleveland.[62]

Pittsburgh was also home to a black middle class, the brochure intimated, rather than the urban ghettoes typical of its competitors. A young black Harvard graduate who had grown up in Washington, D.C., said he had left Boston after graduating from college because it lacked a "young, black, married middle-class." He reported that he and his wife had decided to put down roots in Pittsburgh because of the friendliness of the people, both white and black.[63] His story suggested that Pittsburgh lacked the racial conflict present in other eastern and midwestern cities. The same civic and political leaders who managed the city's brand had been heartened that the 1968 uprisings in Pittsburgh's predominantly African American Hill District and Homewood were short-lived and less violent than those in other northern cities.[64] They glossed over the widespread arson and property damage born of years of rage over residential segregation and lack of economic opportunity. In the utopian Pittsburgh portrayed in marketing materials, middle-class residents, young and old, black and white, harmoniously populated the symbolic space of the postindustrial city.

The year after *Seven Pittsburghs* appeared, Penn's Southwest launched *Dynamic Pittsburgh*, a major print advertising campaign in the *Wall Street Journal* aimed at national business leaders. Undoubtedly influenced by New York City's successful rebranding, the campaign represented the culmination of a joint effort by the Allegheny Conference, Penn's Southwest,

A House Of Their Own

The Schweitzers come home to their old house made new. The addition to the family turned out to be a young man named Kristian.

Suburban Philadelphia was for growing up, Washington, D.C. and Europe for college, New York for marrying a beautiful Danish girl and looking for a job. At that point in Neal Schweitzer's migrations, the chance for management training in international banking made Pittsburgh the end of the rainbow. For a job he wanted, he would have gone, he says, to Hoboken.

"We only spent three days here, and we found an apartment that was a lot better than our experience in New York City. Two hundred and forty dollars. Between Shadyside and Point Breeze. Beautiful little area. Nice little gingerbread on the houses. Lots of trees and close to the park. Two hundred forty bucks. My God!" He recites some Pittsburgh apartment rentals: $350 for a 'pretty nice' apartment, $450 for a 'beautiful' one. "One can't touch that in any other major East Coast city or Chicago.

"The neighborhood was a nice place to start off. Mostly out-of-towners, lots of junior executive types. I remember, the bus was nicknamed the Cocktail Cruiser—all these young bankers, lawyers, corporate types, reading their Wall Street Journals.

"It was a place to meet a lot of people. A lot of parks, the golf course in Schenley Park—cross-country skiing in the winter there. Oakland is right down the street, with all the big universities. I don't know what I considered Pitt to be, maybe just a big community college. It's a fabulous university. Their night school's as big as their day school, and their *staff*—they have a *Danish* teacher at Pitt, which is unheard of in most other cities. Actually teaches four or five students who are interested in Danish. They really have it stocked."

They found a reason to move on: "We heard of this package over on the North Side." The city had set up a program to revive a rundown neighborhood by getting the once fine old homes restored. "Because of the package that was offered, 8½% financing, 5% down, we bought a reasonably good house. At the same time we took down a second mortgage for rehabilitation. Then put the contractor and all the subs to work, June of last year. Our mortgage is in the range of what an efficiency apartment would cost in New York. Taxes are cheap over here in the inner city; they put a three-year moratorium on tax increases when you go in the program."

"This development on the North Side—the Mexican War streets, Allegheny West and Manchester—is mostly a function of outsiders coming in. People from the East Coast or just outside the city; not very many native Pittsburghers. We bought on Sherman Avenue, which had virtually no development. Since that time, in a year, about eight houses have gone, on a street of maybe fifty. They're mostly young families and singles—that would be up to forty, I think—buying houses over there and fixing them up."

The North Side is separated from downtown Pittsburgh only by a river. Neal Schweitzer walks to work, twenty minutes. The neighborhood is still predominantly lower income. "Lots of nice people over in our neighborhood. Some of the old-time Pittsburghers keep an eye out on the apartment—people who have raised big families. People are very friendly. I was putting a skylight in the bathroom, and two guys came over and were just watching. Then it was 'Hey, let me give you a hand? Do you need a hand?' One is not on guard as much as in the cities I have grown up in or lived in. They have a good sense of guarded optimism here, versus guarded pessimism in other cities. People just aren't as tough to meet here. They actually come up and speak to you as you're walking down the street, rather than looking at the pavement."

In the fall, his training complete, Neal Schweitzer expects to be transferred to another country. How would he feel about some day moving *back* to Pittsburgh? "We've been talking recently. A year ago we didn't think we'd ever come back to Pittsburgh. I think I have changed a lot—changing my mind-set to have a son or daughter. It strikes one as a nice place to raise a family. Great school system in some sections. Because the housing market is reasonably priced, because the neighborhoods are really nice...Nice place to grow up for a kid."

But that's all far in the future. Meanwhile, there's the house. Restoring the interior, the contractors did the initial rough cut, then Neal and Kirsten took over. "This last weekend I was working on the house and fixing. Doing floors and getting the nursery ready. My wife is pregnant. I'm tired. This city has worn me out."

Figure 18. Neil Schweitzer praised Pittsburghers "guarded optimism," friendliness, and can-do attitude when his family's story was featured in the *Seven Pittburghs* promotional brochure. Photo reprinted with the permission of Duquesne Light Company.

and the city government to promote physical and cultural redevelopment and business, residential, and recreational opportunities in the nine-county region. Jay Aldridge managed the campaign and hired New York advertising firm Creamer, Inc., to design it. Local CEOs sponsored or cosponsored the eighteen ads in the series. The twenty-one participating corporations, all headquartered in Pittsburgh, principally reflected Pittsburgh's traditional industrial base rather than the knowledge economy the ads promoted. The sponsors included Westinghouse, Pittsburgh and Lake Erie Railroad, Heinz, Joy Manufacturing, Pittsburgh National Bank, Dravo, U.S. Steel, Jones & Laughlin, National Steel, Mobay Chemical, Alcoa, Rockwell International, Mine Safety Appliances, USAIR, Mellon Bank, Pittsburgh Plate Glass, Equibank, Gulf Oil, and H. H. Robertson. After their run in the *Wall Street Journal*, Penn's Southwest collected the ads into a brochure that it used as a business recruitment tool.[65]

Dynamic Pittsburgh, more than any other promotional activity undertaken in support of Renaissance II, revealed the growth coalition's ideas about what constituted Pittsburgh's postindustrial brand. The early ads focused on the preponderance of Fortune 500 companies headquartered in the region; on its industrial and economic diversity, skilled workforce, prestigious universities, and research and development facilities; on its corporate building campaigns; and on easy transportation to and from the region. The first ad in the series, sponsored by Gulf Oil, described Pittsburgh as "a region where big business thrives. And emerging businesses can grow." The second, sponsored by PPG Industries, hyped the $4.5 billion construction boom under Renaissance II; the third, sponsored by Mellon Bank, highlighted 150 foreign companies that had moved into the "cosmopolitan" Pittsburgh region. While many ads depicted industrial workers on the job, those workers were engaged in light industrial or high tech production, not the heavy manufacturing that was, by 1981, in sharp decline. Only the ad co-sponsored by the Consolidated Coal Company and Joy Manufacturing prominently featured smokestacks, and it promoted energy, not the steel industry.[66]

Many of the ads featured striking photos of the Golden Triangle and corporate headquarters, but they also incorporated Pittsburgh's cultural institutions, the region's history, its residential neighborhoods, its sports teams, and outdoor recreation such as golf, white water rafting, and skiing. A Dravo-sponsored ad used images of a new townhouse, lovingly restored historic homes, and Station Square to underscore that Pittsburgh was a "charming place to live and work." U.S. Steel's ad portrayed a post-steel city. In it, Pittsburgh was a "vigorous region" with "hard-working, skilled people as diverse

Dynamic Pittsburgh

Few other American skylines have changed so dramatically since WWII—and now Pittsburgh is renewing itself again. It's a fresh, vibrant place to live and work.

Figure 19. A PPG-sponsored ad for the *Dynamic Pittsburgh* campaign promoted Renaissance II and the city's business-friendly policies. Reprinted with the permission of the Allegheny Conference on Community Development and its Affiliates.

as democracy itself." The accompanying images were of a rugby game, Russian dancers, and ethnic food. The ad touted the "charm" imparted by the region's ethnic roots and the work ethic of its skilled labor force. It also linked the immigrant groups that had "originally settled the region" to a new group of settlers: the international banks and corporations that had more recently moved in. In a departure from earlier promotional materials, members of the hard-working, colorful ethnic groups depicted in the photos were service, high tech, and cultural workers, not immigrant factory workers.[67]

The year after the campaign ran in the *Wall Street Journal*, Penn's Southwest president (and Mellon Bank CEO) David Barnes reported that it had attracted "a great deal" of national attention and had persuaded "worthwhile business organizations" to "take a closer look" at the Pittsburgh region. "Several," he said, had made a "commitment to join us."[68] While *Dynamic Pittsburgh* certainly never gained the cultural currency of the I♥NY campaign, Pittsburgh's growth coalition coordinated and financed a cohesive branding campaign that successfully sold the physical redevelopment, cultural attractions, and leisure activities that marked the city as a postindustrial space. They cast blue-collar workers and neighborhoods as part of the city's old-world charm, rather than as a vital part of the contemporary labor force or local economy—a Rust Belt version of Disney's "Its A Small World," a variation on a theme park.[69]

Capitalizing on the favorable press generated by *Dynamic Pittsburgh*, the Pittsburgh Media Group (PMG), formed in 1980, launched a complementary marketing campaign after the ads ran. Created to sell the Pittsburgh market to national advertisers, PMG included representatives of the *Pittsburgh Press*, the *Pittsburgh Post-Gazette*, and local radio and television stations. PMG promoted Pittsburgh's redevelopment, arts, industry, commerce, universities, and hospitals in a film, *Renaissance Pittsburgh*; a brochure titled "Pittsburgh: A Place Worth Investing In"; and through city tours for advertisers. Like *Dynamic Pittsburgh*, PMG's campaign sought to attract new businesses and white-collar professionals to the city by demonstrating that business interests drove development decisions and that the city and state governments collaborated with corporate leaders to create a positive business climate. PMG praised the Allegheny Conference's "comprehensive blueprint" to "ensure jobs for future generations" and gathered retail sales data to demonstrate that Pittsburgh's residents bought what advertisers were trying to sell. The group also sought to dispel what it saw as common myths about Pittsburgh, such as the idea that the city had "a predominance of low-income families."[70]

Dynamic Pittsburgh

A vigorous region, originally settled by 29 ethnic groups. Hard-working, skilled people as diverse as democracy itself. It's a friendly, productive place to live and work.

21

Figure 20. U.S. Steel ad for the *Dynamic Pittsburgh* campaign showcased skilled workers and "ethnic" pursuits such as Russian dance and Italian cooking. Reprinted with the permission of the Allegheny Conference on Community Development and its Affiliates.

One outcome of the early 1980s public relations blitz was a glowing pro-file of Pittsburgh in *U.S. News & World Report*. Caliguiri told the magazine, "Pittsburgh is going to counter the conservative mood of other cities. The attitude of business and government is upbeat." The article described the growth coalition's plans to redevelop the Golden Triangle as "nothing short of spectacular." Renaissance II, according to the magazine, would "speed the city's shift from steel town to cosmopolitan center for business, education, medicine and entertainment." In the *U.S. News* assessment, the local labor market was buoyant: while the metropolitan area had lost 23,000 manufac-turing jobs between 1970 and 1980, service sector jobs increased by 111,000, "giving the area a healthy 10 percent gain in employment" overall. Three years later, the *New York Times* offered a similarly rosy assessment of the "new" Pittsburgh, praising Pittsburgh for its declining number of steelworkers, increasing number of high-tech companies, temperate climate, first-rate golf courses, expansive downtown redevelopment projects, excellent nightlife and cultural institutions, and top-ranked universities and hospitals.[71] Both articles reflected reporters' tacit acceptance of the narrative of modernization and progress presented in press kits and left the impact of lost manufacturing jobs on the region's residents entirely unexamined.

The region's workers were more skeptical of the growth coalition's rebranding efforts than were reporters for national news outlets. The mill town activists who challenged the growth coalition's plans for physical rede-velopment also undermined Pittsburgh's emerging postindustrial brand. In determining which kinds of activities would represent Pittsburgh's future, the growth coalition sought to erase from view the city's industrial past and the economic violence that postindustrialism visited on the region's blue-collar workforce. Downtown's gleaming headquarters buildings and the South Side's Station Square and Victorian historic district may have supported Caliguiri's version of the Renaissance, but the mill towns told a different story. When Southwest Pennsylvania's steel industry collapsed, the social and economic consequences of plant closures were indisputably more severe in single-industry towns like Homestead, Duquesne, and McKeesport than in the city and its suburbs. In these places, a plant closing affected the entire town, and with no remaining tax base to draw on, city governments had little hope of attracting new industry or undertaking extensive economic development.[72]

When the mill town economies collapsed, devastating images of uneven regional development threatened to undermine the recovery the growth coalition worked to market. Caliguiri's second Renaissance required a sym-bolic reimagining of Pittsburgh not as the historical "Pittsburgh district"—the city and its steel-making and coal-mining hinterlands—but as the city and its middle-class suburbs. Marketing materials recast Pittsburgh as a white-collar place flush with corporate headquarters, cultural enterprises, shopping, dining, and nightlife, and firmly situated industrial decline and the social problems of disinvestment in the discursively, if not physically, distant mill towns. In casting off a long-held regional identity, the growth coalition washed its hands of responsibility for mill town residents and regional manufacturing workers, most of whom worked for companies headquartered in Pittsburgh, deposited their savings in banks headquartered in Pittsburgh, paid taxes that disproportionately supported the city, and spent part of their paychecks downtown. The editor of *Pittsburgh Magazine* bemoaned this schizophrenic state in 1984, suggesting that the region might adopt Janus as its symbol, with one face turned forward toward Renaissance Pittsburgh, the other turned back toward the economically devastated mill towns.[73]

As Penn's Southwest, the Allegheny Conference, and the mayor's office tried to brand Pittsburgh as a postindustrial place, DMS activists set out to disrupt the idea that Pittsburgh had a good business climate. City officials and corporate public relations personnel typically refused to comment on DMS's actions, presumably in the hope that, if they ignored DMS, it would either fade away or generate so much negative opinion through its activities that it would become inconsequential. Several local executives wrote letters to the editors of local papers, pleading with them to stop covering DMS. David Roderick accused the mill town activists of "committing murder to our community image" by painting an unfavorable picture in the national media and scaring away new jobs.[74] DMS members were unmoved by Roderick's complaint, blasting back: "Scaring whos[e] jobs away? You don't think for a minute he's talking about good paying UNION jobs do you?"[75] The *Pittsburgh Post-Gazette* ran an editorial castigating "steel worker groups" for their 1983 Mellon Bank boycott, accusing the region's labor activists and clergy of attempting to block investment that helped workers in other countries. "Surely the welfare of the working people and the unemployed in every nation should be of concern to union people here, just as it should be to churches which preach the worth of the individual everywhere," the editorial board scolded. "That, ultimately, is what is at stake in an endeavor to punish a Pittsburgh corporation for doing business abroad."[76] A month later, the *Pittsburgh Business Times* reported that an unidentified New England company had decided not to move into the region because of DMS's activities and cautioned area workers against radicalism: "Tax laws and labor costs become minor considerations when stacked against the peace of mind and physical safety of the very people who make site location decisions."[77]

While it is impossible to determine how many companies chose to locate elsewhere because of DMS's persistent attacks on corporate leaders, Roderick's and the local editorial boards' responses suggest DMS was more than a minor irritant to growth coalition members. A local executive recalled, "I was personally involved with a large company trying to get them to move to Pittsburgh at the time the dissident steelworkers were demonstrating, picketing executives' houses, and disrupting church services, and the people I was trying to encourage to come to Pittsburgh heard of those incidents on television and decided to locate elsewhere."[78] By 1985, *Business Times* editors castigated recalcitrant corporate executives for hindering regional promotional campaigns by ignoring DMS. Under the guise of trying to broker a truce between workers and management, the editors insisted, "Whatever your view of [DMS], they are succeeding in damaging Pittsburgh's chances of attracting new business. They are even making a lot of the city's existing corporate lynchpins uneasy." The "feigned disinterest of the corporations," they wrote, had prolonged the conflict and created a "double negative for a city trying to improve its image nationwide."[79] In the end, much as labor activists ultimately lacked the power and resources to halt the growth coalition's redevelopment plans, they also lacked the ability to fundamentally disrupt the symbolic imagery of Pittsburgh's postindustrial rebirth.

In 1984, PMG sponsored a luncheon in Manhattan for New York executives and New York-based travel agencies. Caliguiri, Steeler Lynn Swann, Carnegie Mellon president Richard Cyert, Allegheny International CEO Robert Buckley, and representatives from Pittsburgh's major news outlets promoted Pittsburgh as a good place to live, work, and visit. PMG also induced Carnegie Mellon Drama Department alums who worked on Broadway to praise Pittsburgh at the luncheon. Actress Barbara Feldon called Pittsburgh the most romantic city she had ever been in. Other speakers described Pittsburgh as a "world-class city" and suggested that the Sunbelt's image was "a bit better than is deserved." A Pittsburgh advertising executive proclaimed that Pittsburgh was "no longer Steel City" but had become "a diversified city of the future." Reflecting his often-stated desire to replace blue-collar residents with white-collar workers, Caliguiri declared that he wanted to tear every picture of Pittsburgh's smokestacks out of the country's textbooks.[80] For him, blue-collar workers, like the factories that employed them, were an inconvenient reminder of an industrial past the growth coalition hoped to erase.

When Pittsburgh received the Most Livable City designation a year later, comedians and columnists may have mocked it, but the *New York Times* praised the city for the honor. "Anyone who knows the Pittsburgh of the 1980's knows that this mountainous city of the Three Rivers is not what it once was," the *Times* reported. "With its breathtaking skyline, its scenic waterfront, its cozily vibrant downtown, its rich mixture of cultural and intellectual amenities, its warm neighborhoods and its scrubbed-clean skies, it is no longer the smoky, smelly, gritty milltown of yesteryear."[81] For the growth coalition, the Most Livable City designation represented a triumph of decades of rebranding efforts. The Greater Pittsburgh Chamber of Commerce published a commemorative brochure, "Celebrate Pittsburgh," which assured Pittsburgh's residents that they had "every reason to celebrate and to pat yourselves on the back for Rand McNally's ranking of our area as America's most livable." Pittsburghers had achieved a quality of life that was "fast becoming the envy of cities, large and small, across the land." The Chamber claimed, in a moment of extraordinary cognitive dissonance, "the last 40 years have been a time of constant progress and towering achievement. Only decades ago, the city was a symbol of industrial grime, its smoky skies as famous as its steel. But, through years of commitment and cooperation the people of Pittsburgh reclaimed their town from that image and built it into a model American city, a glittering riverside jewel."[82]

In a few short years, Pittsburgh's growth coalition had turned the city into a commodity, packaged for consumption by tourists, suburbanites, and imagined new residents. Christopher Marquis, a Pittsburgh-based reporter for the *Christian Science Monitor*, described the Most Livable designation as "a long-awaited lift by business leaders, who envision a swankier 'service sector' Pittsburgh," an urban vision that required Pittsburgh to disown "parts of itself." Like many of the region's manufacturing workers, Marquis understood that the mill towns "shared everything with Pittsburgh except recovery" and were "left out" of the region's postindustrial brand. "As the nation's economy veers from making products to trading services, old cities understandably want a fresh start," Marquis wrote. "But abandoning people who built our cities because they don't fit into our plans (unlike the ever-malleable young professional), is nothing but a sellout. Today, that is Pittsburgh's shame." Pittsburgh was only "livable," he pointed out, because the mill towns were "dying quietly." Marquis rebuked the growth coalition for "catering to a certain 'kind' of resident and spurning another" and for suggesting that former residents "who can't find a place in the 'New Pittsburgh' should leave."[83] Marquis's was a voice in the wilderness; by the end of the decade, the *Times* called

Renaissance II "America's most promising post-industrial experiment" and declared Pittsburgh the "spiritual capital" of the Rust Belt.[84]

The postindustrial product advertised in marketing campaigns was rooted in processes that remade sites of production for a service economy and altered the relationship between the city and its suburbs, mill towns, and hinterlands. In the afterglow of the Most Livable designation, the city's second Renaissance looked like a resounding success. Twenty-five years later, however, a *Pittsburgh Post-Gazette* reporter noted that civic leaders could not pinpoint any "tangible benefits" from the designation or the hundreds of thousands of dollars they spent to capitalize on it. "The *Pittsburgh Press* sold more than 11,000 T-shirts that year boasting of the No. 1 ranking," the reporter noted wryly, "but it might have been better if 11,000 fewer people left the area."[85] The Rust Belt's "spiritual capital" had come to resemble the neoliberal city critics on the Left had anticipated since the 1970s: a social and physical landscape in which manufacturing workers were anachronistic and the middle class was increasingly hollowed out.

More Than a Lunch Bucket Town

Even though Hamilton did not share Pittsburgh's population losses in the early 1980s, as the *Hamilton Spectator* pointed out, it did have a similar image problem. In 1978, at around the same time the provincial Ministry of Industry and Tourism decided to jump into the fray with the U.S. Sunbelt for new jobs, an economic study struck a blow to the notion that Hamilton's lunch bucket image was "fading away." Two years after Mayor Vic Copps's premature retirement, Toronto consultants Currie, Coopers & Lybrand submitted an "Action Plan for Economic Growth" to the regional government. The study characterized Hamilton as a militant union town with a poor image and an unstable political structure.[86] In response to the action plan, the regional government turned its Economic Development Division (EDD) into a formal department instead of a standing advisory committee and set staffers to work on regional promotional efforts.[87] EDD staffers coordinated public relations efforts in the region and served as liaisons between developers, businessmen, and all levels of government.[88] EDD produced a marketing plan that included a strategy for industrial development as well as a promotional scheme for tourism and conventions, which reflected city officials' attempt to balance their provincial mandate to pursue new industry with their own desires to attract more white-collar residents.[89]

Hamilton's growth coalition spent far less time parsing the benefits of dissociating the city from its larger region than did Pittsburgh's. Doing so would have been of little use: the regional steel industry was located entirely within city limits and only a few miles from downtown, and provincial policies mandated that Hamilton serve as a manufacturing hub for Southern Ontario. In contrast to Pittsburgh's promotional efforts, where industry and the blue-collar workforce were entirely hidden from view, Hamilton's marketing materials sometimes presented the region's unionized industrial workers as a selling point. EDD's marketing plan, for instance, targeted union executive members and shop stewards, as well as corporate executives and relocation specialists. Staffers designed a brochure around the theme "Life in Hamilton-Wentworth Has Everything," which was supposed to demonstrate that the region was a desirable and profitable location for corporate expansion, location, or relocation. EDD's promotional materials were supposed to "stress the prospect's reasons for relocation," rather than the region's reasons for trying to attract new businesses, and to make sure corporate executives knew that "red tape gets cut quickly in Hamilton-Wentworth." Regional, national, and provincial tourism officials coordinated their efforts and consistently depicted Hamilton as the hub of Ontario's Golden Horseshoe.[90]

EDD's efforts were not enough to dispel the popular image of Hamilton as a smoky steel town. In 1982, emulating nearby Buffalo, New York's, "Talking Proud" campaign, Hamilton's City Council sponsored a $500 slogan contest amid "bitter counter-attacks" between aldermen. Some council members thought that a catchy slogan would improve Hamilton's image locally and nationally. Other councilors worried, to the contrary, that the slogan contest would damage Hamilton's image because it drew attention to the problem. All of them seemed to conflate concern over Hamilton's image with public perceptions of the council's performance. "I'm very disappointed in the way Hamilton is going," said Alderman Pat Valeriano. "We haven't been the ambitious city for a number of years. I'd like to see more enthusiasm, to see the people motivated." Other aldermen accused Valeriano and the Chamber of Commerce of "knocking the council" instead of promoting the city. Alderman Jim Bethune complained, "the Chamber of Commerce should be very active in a positive sense," rather than "throwing roadblocks in our way as far as getting anything done." As far as Bethune was concerned, the "Ambitious City" slogan was just fine. "The more we get up in council and the more leaders in the community get up and knock it, it is creating the stigmatization of negative attitudes which filter down to the public," charged Alderman Fred Lombardo. "All we're doing is throwing egg on our own faces." Vince Agro

insisted that the council needed to listen more carefully to its critics, saying, "I think we've made all kinds of mistakes."[91] The disagreement within
City Council over how to promote the city reflected a larger problem: the ad
hoc nature of Hamilton's public-private cooperation and the lack of a formal
partnership through which to pursue a branding campaign meant the city
and regional governments and the Chamber of Commerce worked independently to promote overlapping, but not entirely cohesive, visions of the city.

None of the region's promotional efforts had achieved demonstrable success by the time the *Hamilton Spectator* ran a five-part investigative series
on "Hamilton's Image" in October 1984. *Spectator* reporters determined that
the primary problem facing the city was residents' assumptions that outsiders held negative views of Hamilton. According to the reporters, Hamiltonians believed that "outsiders pictured Hamilton as a city where the bomb had
already dropped."[92] Elected officials and civic leaders worried about outsiders'
perceptions of their city, but outsiders did not, in fact, seem to think about
Hamilton. The vice president of a Toronto media-buying company joked to
the *Spectator*, "Hamiltonians are extremely self-conscious if they think that
anyone outside of Hamilton gives them much thought at all." He added,
"Hamilton has no image. We don't have to think of it." A businessman who
had relocated from Toronto to Hamilton in 1982 said that "Hamilton's image
doesn't have any moxy. It doesn't sparkle." He complained, "they're not interested in sex appeal down at City Hall." More problematic for the city, national
advertisers classified Hamilton as part of the Toronto market, and executives
of international businesses, such as Amstel Breweries (which had recently
located in Hamilton) were likely to know that Hamilton existed only if provincial officials directed them there. The *Spectator* concluded that, despite
local concern, "bordering on neurosis," about Hamilton's image, "most people outside this area give it very little thought."[93]

In the mid-1980s, the city government continued to come under attack
for hindering rather than helping promote Hamilton's image as a postindustrial city. A CBC reporter voiced the sentiments of many in the city when
he commented that, since Copps had left office, "we've never had a towering
mayor. If he was still in City Hall it would be an entirely different Hamilton
today." Alderman Paul Cowell charged, "Council is giving a very negative
image. We're seen as a group of unprofessional people who don't know what
we're doing." Mayor Bob Morrow implied that the regional, rather than city,
government was at fault, saying Hamilton's image would not change without
a coherent regional economic development policy that signaled strong leadership and a sense of identity to business leaders. Yet, as the *Spectator* pointed

out, city and regional officials seemed to have forgotten they had commissioned just such a plan six years earlier: the Currie, Coopers & Lybrand study that cost taxpayers $25,000. The reporter took a dim view of the regional government's refusal to commit an economic development strategy to paper, asking, "how are we being sold?"[94]

The answer was that Hamilton was being sold inconsistently because of factious relationships among growth coalition members. The Chamber and the mayor's office hoped to promote the region as a location for corporate headquarters and emphasize white-collar jobs and residents, while EDD director Don Cole said that "the image I want to project for Hamilton is that it's a blue collar town with a lot more to offer." He took a pragmatic approach to economic development as Hamilton began to recover from the recession and layoffs. Cole dismissed his predecessor John Morand as "a booster who operated in an atmosphere of hype." Instead of showcasing "pretty pictures of flowers and castles," Cole was determined to market the region's labor pool and land availability. He concentrated on the Toronto market and largely abandoned European advertising. Cole also reallocated half of the region's $15,000 direct mailing budget to subsidize the Chamber of Commerce's "Operation Toronto" program, which brought Toronto executives to Hamilton to tour the city in the hope of attracting new commercial service jobs.[95] Cole's promotional plans emphasized Hamilton's regional role; his was perhaps the only realistic approach at a time when the provincial government mandated that Hamilton function as a regional center and precluded local officials from offering capital subsidies that might have allowed the city to more effectively engage in interurban competition.

Despite Cole's resistance to pretty pictures of flowers and castles, regional officials ran an ad in facility planning magazines in the United States and Canada that featured just that: a bouquet of pink begonias sprouting from a hardhat, which invited business owners to discover "The Beautiful Side of the Hard-Headed Facts." After the ad first ran in 1984, the *Spectator* reported that "the competition for expanding or relocating businesses is frantic among states, provinces, cities and regions" and that Hamilton-Wentworth had joined the "tiger pit" of cities selling "a pro-business attitude, great quality of life, no red tape, cheap land and ideal location." Once again, the city's growth coalition saw no alternative but to try to compete with U.S. cities, particularly Sunbelt cities, despite Hamilton's heavily unionized workforce and inability to offer corporate welfare programs. The regional government settled on the flowers growing from a hard hat as the symbol of the "new" Hamilton because, according to the region's manager of business development, "we

Figure 21. Hamilton-Wentworth's economic development officials invited potential investors to see "the beautiful side of the hard-headed facts." Regional Municipality of Hamilton-Wentworth, ca. 1985. Courtesy of the City of Hamilton.

wanted to project the fact that we are a labor town and that we're not ashamed of that." But, he pointed out, "the other side of Hamilton-Wentworth is beautiful countryside and a wonderful quality of life. It would be wrong to hide our labor side, and incorrect to say it's all we are."[96]

The hard-hat-as-planter image featured prominently in Hamilton-Wentworth's promotional materials for the rest of the decade. A 1985 brochure paired the image with the tag line "Talk About a Great Place," and the 1987 version demanded, "Look at Us Now."[97] Much like the promotional materials sponsored by Duquesne Light in Pittsburgh, the brochures featured profiles of local businessmen, though the focus remained on executives and plant managers rather than on young professionals in "new economy" jobs, few of which had materialized. The brochures stressed the range of residential options—rural, urban, and suburban—available in the region, lauded state-of-the-art technology, and promoted McMaster University, Mohawk College, and Hamilton's natural beauty and cultural attractions. The promotional materials even rehabilitated steel as a clean industry that was "as high-tech as anything you will find in Silicon Valley." In striking contrast to the Dynamic Pittsburgh campaign and Hamilton's own marketing materials from the 1970s, the hard hat brochures featured photographs of steel mills alongside those of cultural and leisure pursuits. On the back cover of the 1985 brochure, regional chairwoman Ann Jones assured businessmen that "elected and staff people at both the regional and municipal levels will do everything possible to streamline every step of the way, from site search to start-up." Morrow echoed her promise, attesting "you can be sure of 100% cooperation."[98] Two years later, new regional chairman William L. Sears went farther, saying regional and municipal officials would "do everything possible to assure a continued viable economic climate." For good measure, his vow was translated into Japanese, Chinese, Italian, and German.[99]

By 1986, Hamilton's economy had rebounded, and the public discord between elected officials and Chamber of Commerce representatives had receded. The *Spectator* announced that Hamilton was booming. Record highs for new construction included the completion of Copps Coliseum, Stelco and Dofasco expansions, and three hospital expansions, as well as a revived building program in the downtown core and cosmetic improvements in neighborhood commercial districts.[100] The *Spectator* ran a five-part series on "the New Hamilton" in October 1986 that promoted professional service jobs and new restaurants, 500,000 square feet of new office space constructed downtown since 1982, an unemployment rate below the national and provincial average, and a local economy fueled by a "new spirit of entrepreneurialism."[101] Morrow told the paper that the early 1980s recession had hurt the city, "But with our location, the beauty of the city, the Escarpment, the bay, the lake, I like to think the new Hamilton has just begun."[102] The regional government proclaimed, "Hamilton-Wentworth now provides cultural, institutional, commercial, environmental, sports and recreational services and facilities to a hinterland area." Moving forward, Hamilton's promotional materials would be "aimed at major population centers in neighboring regions." Any new marketing effort, regional officials stipulated, should focus on attracting young managerial and professional workers. That mandate represented the realization of the provincial government's vision for Hamilton rather than city officials', one in which industry and postindustrialism uneasily coexisted.[103]

In 1988, Hamilton's regional government approved an "extensive" marketing campaign in Pittsburgh. Regional officials hoped to capitalize on the historical similarities between the two cities, their diversification efforts, and their downtown redevelopment. The EDD contacted Penn's Southwest and targeted Pittsburgh businesses through a direct mail program in an effort to identify companies interested in establishing Canadian branch plants or in joint ventures with Canadian companies.[104] Pittsburgh sent a delegation of executives to Hamilton two years later to discuss improving trade links and forming "strategic alliances" between the two cities, and, in 1991, Hamilton officials stopped in Pittsburgh on their way back from a trade show in New York to meet with the Chamber of Commerce and the Pittsburgh High Technology Council.[105]

In Hamilton, however, place promotion never coalesced into a branding campaign; it remained in the realm of urban boosterism and, like public-private cooperation in the region, was an ad hoc enterprise. The city government, regional government, and the Chamber of Commerce independently produced marketing materials that presented a plurality of alternative visions for a postindustrial future, some more and some less inclusive of the residential working class. Promotional efforts, like mill neighborhood redevelopment, exposed fractures within the loose coalition between the public and private sectors. Lacking the capacity for urban branding and absent a public-private partnership through which to conduct such a campaign, Hamilton's city government and Chamber of Commerce worked independently to promote the city and region, but both continued to function in a booster mode. In part because of Hamilton's proximity to Toronto and in part because of poorly coordinated marketing efforts, Hamilton's elected officials and civic leaders opened only a regional, rather than national, discussion about the city's image. By the end of the 1980s, primary metals manufacturing still accounted for half of the region's manufacturing employment and 30 percent of the city's total jobs, making the growth coalition's claims that Hamilton was no longer a steel town untenable. Despite decades of efforts by Hamilton's political and civic leaders to emulate Pittsburgh's brand—to replicate the signs and symbols, as well as the material changes, that marked Pittsburgh as postindustrial—the growth coalition was unable to shed the city's industrial image.

Cities for Whom?

In 1968, Stelco dealt a blow to budding plans for postindustrial Hamilton when corporate leaders moved the company's headquarters to Toronto. In 1991, Stelco returned to Hamilton; Canada's largest steel company could no longer afford the prestige of a Toronto address. Two and a half decades later, Stelco was run from Pittsburgh. U.S. Steel purchased Stelco in 2007, renamed it U.S. Steel Canada, and raised the American flag over the mill on Hamilton harbor. Dutch conglomerate ArcelorMittal had acquired Dofasco the previous year. The foreign acquisitions of Hamilton's steel producers were poorly timed. In the wake of the 2008 recession, U.S. Steel temporarily shut down its Canadian operations, laid off nearly 3,000 workers, and became enmeshed in a bitter labor dispute. ArcelorMittal seized the opportunity to briefly ramp up production, but by 2011 the company had halted expansion plans and eliminated 700 jobs. In October 2013, U.S. Steel announced it would permanently cease steel production in Hamilton at the end of the year.[1]

Shortly before U.S. Steel confirmed the shutdown of Hamilton's blast furnaces, former Pittsburgh mayor Tom Murphy arrived in Hamilton to give a lecture on Pittsburgh's postindustrial rebirth. MGI Media, a Hamilton-based media company with a particular interest in urban marketing, sponsored the talk in conjunction with a local arts and music festival. MGI Media printed posters that invited residents to "hear the story of Pittsburgh's remarkable transformation from a depressed rustbelt city to an example of prosperity and livability as told by one of the leaders that made it happen." Murphy, a self-described "public entrepreneur" and since 2006 a senior fellow at the Urban Land Institute, a Washington, D.C.-based real estate industry think tank, has spent much of his post-mayoral career advising cities from Baton Rouge to Moscow about urban revitalization strategies.[2] In Hamilton, he spoke to around a hundred residents (local politicians were notably absent from the event) about Pittsburgh's rebirth. Murphy pulled out old saws about public-private partnerships and advised his audience to elect city leaders with long-term vision, rather than functionaries who focused on fixing potholes. He touted Pittsburgh's new economic base, built on "eds and meds" rather than manufacturing. Forty percent of Pittsburgh's workers were employed in technology industries, he told his listeners, and only 10 percent in manufacturing. He credited his own administration for much of that shift and was particularly self-congratulatory about his foresight in purchasing and redeveloping mill sites along the waterfront.[3]

Not long after Murphy's lecture in Hamilton, the *Pittsburgh Post-Gazette* ran the first installment in a four-week series called "30 Years, 30 Changes," which detailed Pittsburgh's economic, cultural, social, and spatial transformation since 1983. Pittsburgh had finally earned its Most Livable City designation, noted one of the articles, in no small part because "bustling offices, shops and restaurants" had replaced derelict mills along the Monongahela River. Health and education sectors provided a "more stable economy" than the manufacturing corporations that once dominated Pittsburgh, thanks, Murphy told reporters, to Strategy 21 and the Ben Franklin Partnership.[4] U.S. Steel had once been the region's largest employer; by 2013, it had fallen out of the top ten, which was topped by University of Pittsburgh Medical Center, the Allegheny Health Network, and the University of Pittsburgh.[5] The economic restructuring that occurred in the 1970s and 1980s, the *Post-Gazette* reported, "while painful for those tied to old blue-collar jobs that no longer exist," had allowed city officials to reclaim Pittsburgh's waterfront for recreational uses. Downtown, there was talk of a third Renaissance.[6]

In the second decade of the twenty-first century, much as it was in the 1960s and 1980s, Pittsburgh remains an international model for urban regeneration. It regularly tops annual "livability" lists, the number and types of which have proliferated since Pittsburgh's first such designation in 1985. In recent years, Pittsburgh has been named the top city for geeks by *Wired* magazine, the country's number-one sports city by *Sporting News*, the best place to buy a home by *Forbes* magazine, a top city for culture hunters by *New York Magazine*, one of the nation's most walkable cities by the Brookings Institution, and one of the best urban makeovers by *Lonely Planet*. However, Pittsburgh's elected and civic leaders remained anxious about the city's steeltown image. Craig Davis, president and CEO of VisitPittsburgh, Allegheny County's tourism website, told the *Post-Gazette* that, despite Pittsburgh's high standing in a host of national rankings and its 2012 designation as one of

National Geographic Traveler's twenty top destinations, "we still have somewhat of a perception issue among people who've never been here."[7]

Hamilton, too, has earned a host of superlatives in recent years: London's
Financial Times named Hamilton one of the top ten large cities in North
America; *Site Selection Magazine* called it one of the five best places to invest
in Canada; and Canada's Real Estate Investment Network named it the third
best place to invest. In 2012, Ontario's Ministry of Research and Innovation
featured Hamilton in its *Ontario Business Report*. The ministry dubbed Hamilton the "comeback kid of Canadian cities" and pointed out that Hamilton's
unemployment and commercial vacancy rates were lower than national and
provincial averages. Yet, as in Pittsburgh, Chamber of Commerce members
and city officials continued to fret about Hamilton's reputation as an "old
economy 'has been.'" They self-consciously littered their praise for Hamilton's
economic diversification with rejections of the city's industrial past. "We're
not Steel Town anymore," insisted one local executive, "we're about education
and health services and transportation and the arts." Even the steel production that remained in Hamilton was, as the head of ArcelorMittalDofasco
liked to say, high-tech, high-value-added, advanced manufacturing—the
type that employed few blue-collar workers.[8]

In his lecture on postindustrial Pittsburgh, Murphy called Hamiltonians
to action: "Envision Hamilton as it could be, not as it was," he exhorted. "You
can make it happen. You can kick the door down."[9] Hamilton had, in fact,
already become more like Pittsburgh. The fortunes of Hamilton's manufacturing industries—and workers—in the twenty-first century resembled those
of Pittsburgh in the 1980s, due in large part to the adoption of the 1994 North
American Free Trade Agreement, which cost Canada's steel industry many
of its historic trade and tariff protections. The elections of Mike Harris as
premier of Ontario in 1995 and Stephen Harper as prime minister in 2006
pushed Canada in an increasingly neoliberal direction. Harris cut social
programming by 22 percent and income taxes by 30 percent, introduced a
"workfare" program, eliminated industrial assistance and job training programs, cut public jobs, slashed budgets for infrastructure improvements, and
attempted (more or less unsuccessfully) to sell off provincially owned enterprises. Despite significant protest from local officials, Harris realigned the
roles and responsibilities of the provincial state and municipal governments
and devolved oversight of and some funding for a host of social services to
the local level. Harper pursued similar policies at the federal level.[10]

Public-private partnerships proliferated as Canada's political culture changed in the 1990s and 2000s. McMaster University became more

entrepreneurial, opening an Innovation Park to serve as an incubator for start-ups and an Innovation Factory "to connect new and expanding businesses with commercialization experts, entrepreneurs and strategists." Perhaps most importantly for public officials and civic leaders, the "out-of-town creative class" had "discovered" Hamilton. Attracted by Hamilton's proximity to Toronto and comparatively inexpensive real estate, small businesses and young families moved into "creative districts" around Hess Village and James Street North—the neighborhoods the Central Area Planning Committee had targeted for just such development three decades earlier. One "real estate refugee" from Toronto said he had moved to Hamilton because "it's never been a suburb of anything."[11]

A month after his talk in Hamilton, Murphy was back in Pittsburgh for Carnegie Mellon's "Remaking Cities Congress," held by the university's Remaking Cities Institute to mark the twenty-fifth anniversary of the 1988 Remaking Cities conference. In 1988, British and American planners and economic development officials converged on Pittsburgh to address the common problems facing their industrial centers. As he had twenty-five years earlier, Prince Charles served as keynote speaker, though, in 2013, he spoke via pre-recorded video rather than in person. The 1988 conference, with its near-exclusive focus on U.S. and UK cases, was intended to produce a blueprint for the future of industrial cities. Attendees participated in design charrettes centered on "New Economic Opportunities for Cities," "The Evolving Metropolis," "Preservation and Development of Neighborhoods and Housing," "Creating New Partnerships for Development," and "Urban Futures—Developing a Vision for the City of Tomorrow." In the Mon Valley mill towns, they were met with the specter of hulking, empty factories, abandoned industrial areas, and thousands of unemployed manufacturing workers.[12]

By 2013, most of the factories were gone, and so were most of the people who had worked in them: many had long ago moved to find work, some had aged into government pensions, and still others had died. The three hundred urban specialists who participated in the congress came to Pittsburgh not to rehash the future of industrial centers but to discuss the future of postindustrial cities. In 1988, mayors, heads of public development agencies, architects, planners, and academics attended the conference. Speakers were more diverse in 2013 and reflected the degree to which public-private partnerships had come to dominate urban development on both sides of the Atlantic. Plenary speakers (so-called thought leaders, in the parlance of congress organizers) included private-sector urban policy consultants, representatives from think tanks and philanthropic foundations, and people with job titles

participants would have found incomprehensible twenty-five years earlier—
"innovation policy officer" for the European Commission, or "special advisor
to HRH the Prince of Wales on global urbanism."[13]

The workshop themes were different, too. Postindustrialism remained a
largely North Atlantic phenomenon, but by 2013 it was so widely accepted as
an urban development model that nearly every session title included some
variation on the term. Case studies from Bilbao and Milwaukee were the
focus of "Re-Positioning the Post-Industrial City in the Global Economy."
"Post-Industrialism and the Physical City" paired speakers from Buffalo and
the Ruhr Valley. Examples of "The 21st Century City as Innovation Hub"
were drawn from the Manchester/Liverpool and the Toronto/Hamilton/
Kitchener/Waterloo regions. "Urban Systems, Infrastructure, and the Post-
Industrial City" highlighted the experiences of Rotterdam and New Orleans,
while "Planning and Social Innovations for Post-Industrial Cities" featured
Turin and Detroit. Murphy spoke at a morning session devoted to "The Pittsburgh Story," its title an homage to Stephan Lorant's seminal book.[14]

Murphy was not the only former Pittsburgher back for the congress. Former Carnegie Mellon professor Richard Florida, who had led a workshop on
public-private partnerships at the 1988 conference, returned to give a plenary address. In 2013, Florida held several titles: director of the University
of Toronto's Martin Prosperity Institute; global research professor at New
York University; founder of a global consultancy, the Creative Class Group;
and founder and director of *The Atlantic Cities*. His website described him as
"perhaps the world's leading urbanist."[15] In his influential 2002 book *The Rise
of the Creative Class* and subsequent works, Florida urged cities to adopt public policy packages designed to attract the so-called "creative class"—a motley
crew of artists, academics, tech workers, lawyers, and stockbrokers. Florida
adapted Daniel Bell's post-industrial society thesis for a new century when
he described "creativity" as a new phase of capitalist development and told
public officials they needed to attract "creatives" if their cities were to remain
competitive in the global economy.[16]

Florida had a complicated relationship with Pittsburgh. In 2004, after
seventeen years at Carnegie Mellon, he left town in a huff, having described
the city as "trapped in the culture of a bygone era" in *Creative Class*. He told
local papers that Pittsburgh was a "conventional, Organization Man, corporate-driven city" run by out-of-touch executives from their posh seats in the
Duquesne Club.[17] As Florida admitted in an article publicizing the congress,
however, Pittsburgh provided the basis of his ideas about how to transform
cities.[18] The cultural and recreational amenities Florida recommended, in

concert with a public policy program that privileged "flexible" labor, market-based solutions to urban problems, and local government-led gentrification in an effort to reclaim the city for the middle class, reflected the tactics that since the 1960s had shaped the physical redevelopment agendas of Pittsburgh's—and Hamilton's—growth coalitions, as well as their fetishization of high tech, white-collar workers.

The policy packages the Creative Class Group peddled to political leaders in declining manufacturing centers around the world opened a new chapter in postindustrialism in the early twenty-first century. The concept of a creative economy rested on neoliberal principles in a way Bell's work did not and could not have in the 1970s. Jamie Peck, one of Florida's most incisive critics, has characterized the creative cities thesis as the "the mobilization of new regimes of local governance around the aggressive pursuit of growth-focused development agendas."[19] Creative cities, Peck argues, work "with the grain of extant 'neoliberal' development agendas, framed around interurban competition, gentrification, middle-class consumption and place-making."[20] What Florida acknowledged and Peck did not was that postindustrial Pittsburgh helped generate the framework in which neoliberal urbanism functioned in North Atlantic cities. The consulting package Florida sold to public officials in Michigan, Ontario, Cape Town, Dublin, Brisbane, Forth Worth, and scores of other places was merely the most recent conduit for postindustrial policy circulation.

The American Institute of Architects, which cosponsored the congress, ran a reflection on the event in one of its publications. *AIArchitect* managing editor Zach Mortice praised Florida, writing that the congress made it clear that cities must become more equitable, not merely for moral reasons but "with the recognition that moving impoverished service-sector residents to Florida's prized 'creative class' is the best strategy for igniting urban economies." Mortice identified "a wide range of tools" that could be used to build creative economies, most of which Pittsburgh's leaders, and city officials throughout the North Atlantic who hoped to emulate Pittsburgh's postwar transformations, had deployed for decades: civic leadership, entrepreneurial innovation, and good design.[21] While the language congress participants used to talk about cities shifted and the policy instruments available to them had expanded significantly since the 1960s, the core problems of attracting residents, remaking urban space for new uses and residents, and fixing local economies remained painfully familiar.

Like Florida, Alan Mallach, a senior fellow at the National Housing Institute and the Center for American Progress, participated in the 1988 conference and returned for the congress. The pressing question for the twenty-first century was no longer whether manufacturing centers would survive—they had, and many had thrived. Instead, Mallach said, policymakers should ask, "for whom?" "We are not only creating a society with vast inequalities, we are institutionalizing these inequalities into the very fabric of American society," he argued. "That is part and parcel of the revitalization story. Can we somehow change [this] progressive institutionalization of inequality?"[22] Mallach's critique echoed decades of complaints from critics on the Left that neoliberal urban policies constituted an attack on unions, had hollowed out the middle class, and had narrowed access to urban space, to civic life, and to political expression.

For growth coalitions in Pittsburgh and Hamilton, and more recently for Florida, his clients, and his acolytes, successful urban transformation meant an outcome like Pittsburgh's, where local elites directed redevelopment through a decades-long public-private partnership and where local land use and economic development decisions reflected the emergence of increasingly neoliberal policies at the state and federal level. Measuring the success of postindustrialism in terms of efforts to retain, retrain, and support existing residents, particularly working-class residents, suggests that, in the 1980s, Hamilton was the real success story. In Hamilton, a more pluralistic political culture balanced competing claims from local business elites and working-class residents, and public officials worked to accommodate the interests of both groups. But more recent evidence suggests that Hamilton's pluralism was unsustainable.

Ontario Common Front (OCF), an organizing campaign against austerity and retrenchment founded in 2010 by the Ontario Federation of Labor and a coalition of ninety labor and community organizations, reported in 2012 that Ontario, among all Canadian provinces, had the fastest-growing rates of poverty and income inequality and spent the least on public programs and social services. The OCF blamed provincial and federal tax policies that privileged corporations and wealthy individuals over the commonweal.[23] Local leaders were pleased that Hamilton's unemployment rates were lower than provincial and national averages, but their statistics masked the fact that 30,000 of the city's half-million residents were part of the "working poor"—employed, but not earning enough to live without public assistance. A quarter of Hamilton's children and almost half of its recent immigrants lived below the poverty line.[24]

In Pennsylvania, income gaps widened even as the state's economy grew in the 1990s and early 2000s. There, as elsewhere in the United States, the incomes of the wealthy rose while middle-class incomes and those of the

Figure 22. A *Pittsburgh Post-Gazette* cartoon poked fun at the Mills Company's
Pittsburgh Mills mall in suburban Tarentum and highlighted the lack
of job opportunities for blue-collar workers in the region.
©2005 Rob Rogers/Pittsburgh Post-Gazette. Reprinted with permission.

working poor stagnated or fell. Between 1979 and 2013, productivity in Pennsylvania increased by 61 percent while wages languished. Over the same
period, median wages increased only once, between 1995 and 2000.[25] In 2010,
nearly a quarter-million residents of the Pittsburgh metropolitan area lived
below the poverty line, though the region's 12 percent poverty rate was three
points lower than that for the United States as a whole.[26] Poverty rates and
unemployment levels, as they had been in the 1980s, were higher outside

the city limits than within them and higher for African Americans than for whites.[27] After the 2008 recession, Pittsburgh had the highest rate of poverty among working-age African Americans in the forty largest metropolitan areas in the United States, and more than 25 percent of the region's African Americans lived below the poverty line.[28]

The persistent inequality that has taken root in North America since the 1980s is not limited to Rust Belt cities, of course, but it is in former manufacturing centers where the depths of the problem are most visible. A *Post-Gazette* cartoon satirized the 2005 conversion of an Allegheny Ludlum steel mill in suburban Tarentum to the Pittsburgh Mills mall, laying bare the employment options facing many middle-aged workers. The cartoon showed a steelworker who had traded in his hard hat for an apron to sell pretzels in the mall's food court. The Pittsburgh Mills project was only the most recent of several mill sites-to-mall conversions, including those on the South Side and in Homestead. In 2011, the *New York Times* ran a story about the plight of middle-aged blue-collar workers in the Rust Belt. An Illinois steelworker, laid off at forty-eight, served a brief stint as a math teacher, after which he was unable to find a job that "was neither demeaning nor underpaid."[29] The article exposed a harsh reality for many former manufacturing sector employees in Pittsburgh and Hamilton and for their counterparts in Bilbao and Glasgow and Duisburg: as plant shutdowns continue in North Atlantic manufacturing centers, workers whose skills do not match the high technology, high finance "new economy" are increasingly shut out of jobs with living wages and benefits and pushed toward persistent unemployment or poorly compensated service-sector positions.

ABBREVIATIONS

An asterisk denotes collections that were unprocessed when research was conducted.

ACCD: Allegheny Conference on Community Development Records, Detre Library & Archives, Senator John Heinz History Center, Pittsburgh, Pennsylvania.

CPB: Community Planning Branch General Files, Archives of Ontario, Toronto, Ontario.

DMS*: Denominational Ministry Strategy Papers, 1983–1989, University of Pittsburgh, Archives Service Center, Pittsburgh, Pennsylvania.

DRIE: Department of Regional Industrial Expansion Fonds, Series Al, Library and Archives of Canada, Ottawa, Ontario.

Dynamic Pittsburgh: Dynamic Pittsburgh Collection, 1973–1985, Detre Library & Archives, Senator John Heinz History Center, Pittsburgh, Pennsylvania.

Hamilton Clerk: Regional Minutes, City of Hamilton, Office of the Clerk, Hamilton, Ontario.

HUD: General Records of the Department of Housing and Urban Development, National Archives at College Park, College Park, Maryland.

IGP: Industrial Growth Promotion Files, Archives of Ontario, Toronto, Ontario.

IPB: Industrial Policy Branch Briefing Files, Archives of Ontario, Toronto, Ontario.

IUMSW: Industrial Union of Marine and Shipbuilding Workers of America Papers, University of Pittsburgh, Archives Service Center, Pittsburgh, Pennsylvania.

MI&T: Ministry of Industry and Tourism Committee and Task Force Files, Archives of Ontario, Toronto, Ontario.

MSUA: Ministry of State for Urban Affairs Fonds, Series B, Library and Archives of Canada, Ottawa, Ontario.

OEC: Ontario Economic Council Press Releases, Archives of Ontario, Toronto, Ontario.

Pease: Robert Pease Papers, Detre Library & Archives, Senator John Heinz History Center, Pittsburgh, Pennsylvania.

Shapp: Governor Milton J. Shapp Papers, Pennsylvania State Archives, Harrisburg, Pennsylvania.

SLGA: State and Local Government Archives Oral History Collection, University of Pittsburgh, Archives Service Center, Pittsburgh, Pennsylvania.

Thornburgh: Dick Thornburgh Papers, University of Pittsburgh, Archives Service Center, Pittsburgh, Pennsylvania.

Thornburgh FA: Finding Aid, Dick Thornburgh Papers, 1979–1987, Pennsylvania State Archives, Harrisburg, Pennsylvania.

Tri-State: Tri-State Conference on Mfg. (or Steel) Records, 1982–1993, University of Pittsburgh, Archives Service Center, Pittsburgh, Pennsylvania.

TTPP: Trade and Tourism Policy Project Files, Archives of Ontario, Toronto, Ontario.

NOTES

Introduction. Cities and the Postindustrial Imagination

1. J. H. Moore to John Grove, November 19, 1968, folder 7 Canada—1969–74, box 164, ACCD.

2. See Series XVI: Planning (1930–1981), Subseries 2: Planning Outside Allegheny County, PA, ACCD, as well as Robert C. Alberts, "The Shaping of the Point: Pittsburgh's Renaissance Park," *Western Pennsylvania Historical Magazine* 63, 4 (October 1980): 285–311; Roy Lubove, *Twentieth-Century Pittsburgh*, vol. 1, *Government, Business, and Environmental Change* (Pittsburgh: University of Pittsburgh Press, 1996); Jon C. Teaford, *The Rough Road to Renaissance: Urban Revitalization in America, 1940–1985* (Baltimore: Johns Hopkins University Press, 1990).

3. Arthur D. Little, Inc., *Commercial Development in Hamilton: A Report to the Hamilton Economic Development Commission* (Boston: Arthur D. Little, 1968), 1.

4. I use "post-industrial" to denote historical actors' usage of the term, and "postindustrial" or "postindustrialism" to signal my own use of the term as a historical and analytical category.

5. On metropolitan regional change after 1945, see Andrew Needham and Allen Dieterich-Ward, "Beyond the Metropolis: Metropolitan Growth and Regional Transformation in Postwar America," *Journal of Urban History* 35 (2009): 943–69.

6. Daniel Bell, *The Coming of Post-Industrial Society: A Venture in Social Forecasting* (New York: Basic, 1976); Lawrence Mishel and Jared Bernstein, *The State of Working America, 1994–95* (Washington, D.C.: Economic Policy Institute, 1994), 121; John H. Mollenkopf, *The Contested City* (Princeton, N.J.: Princeton University Press, 1983); Suleiman Osman, *The Invention of Brownstone Brooklyn: Gentrification and the Search for Authenticity in Postwar New York* (New York: Oxford University Press, 2012), 65–68; Saskia Sassen, "Economic Restructuring and the American City," *Annual Review of Sociology* 16 (1990): 465–90; Annette Steinacker, "Economic Restructuring of Cities, Suburbs, and Nonmetropolitan Areas, 1977–1992," *Urban Affairs Review* 34, 2 (November 1998): 212–40.

7. On European steel centers, see Philip Cooke, ed., *Rise of the Rustbelt: Revitalizing Older Industrial Regions* (London: Routledge, 1995); Joachim J. Hesse, ed., *Regional Structural Change and Industrial Policy in International Perspective: United States, Great Britain, France, Federal Republic of Germany* (Baden-Baden: Nomos, 1988).

8. On popular imagery of Great Lakes manufacturing centers, see Steven C. High, *Industrial Sunset: The Making of North America's Rust Belt, 1969–1984* (Toronto: University of Toronto Press, 2003), 5.

9. Bernard Weinraub, "Mondale, at Chicago Rally, Says Tide Is Turning in '84 Election," *New York Times*, October 31, 1984.

10. High, *Industrial Sunset*, 192.

220

Notes to Pages 5–6

11. Cooke, *Rise of the Rustbelt.*

12. See, for example, Alistair Cole and Peter John, *Local Governance in England and France* (London: Routledge, 2001); Cooke, *Rise of the Rustbelt*; Sara González, "Bilbao and Barcelona 'in Motion': How Urban Regeneration 'Models' Travel and Mutate in the Global Flows of Policy Tourism," *Urban Studies* 48, 7 (May 2011): 1397–1418; Michael E. Leary and John McCarthy, *The Routledge Companion to Urban Regeneration* (London: Routledge, 2013); Rebecca Madgin and Richard Rodger, "Inspiring Capital? Deconstructing Myths and Reconstructing Urban Environments, Edinburgh, 1860–2010," *Urban History* 40, 3 (August 2013): 507–29; John McCarthy and S. H. Alan Pollock, "Urban Regeneration in Glasgow and Dundee: A Comparative Evaluation," *Land Use Policy* 14, 2 (1997): 137–49; Libby Porter and Kate Shaw, *Whose Urban Renaissance? An International Comparison of Urban Regeneration Strategies* (London: Routledge, 2009).

13. In 1987, for instance, the *Journal of the American Planning Association* ran a special issue on Pittsburgh's redevelopment. On Renaissance I and II, see especially Lubove, *Twentieth-Century Pittsburgh*, vol. 1; Lubove, *Twentieth-Century Pittsburgh*, vol. 2, *The Post-Steel Era* (Pittsburgh: University of Pittsburgh Press, 1996). On Pittsburgh's twentieth-century urban and suburban history, see John F. Bauman and Edward K. Muller, *Before Renaissance: Planning in Pittsburgh, 1889–1943* (Pittsburgh: University of Pittsburgh Press, 2006); Allen Dieterich-Ward, *Beyond Rust: Metropolitan Pittsburgh and the Fate of Industrial America* (Philadelphia: University of Pennsylvania Press, 2015); Laura Grantmyre, "Visual Representations of Redevelopment in Pittsburgh's Hill District, 1943–1968," Ph.D. dissertation, University of Pittsburgh, 2014; Dale A. Hathaway, *Can Workers Have a Voice? The Politics of Deindustrialization in Pittsburgh* (University Park: Pennsylvania State University Press, 1993); Samuel P. Hays, *City at the Point: Essays on the Social History of Pittsburgh* (Pittsburgh: University of Pittsburgh Press, 1989); Mariel P. Isaacson, "Pittsburgh's Response to Deindustrialization: Renaissance, Renewal and Recovery," Ph.D. dissertation, City University of New York, 2014; Kent James, "Public Policy and the Postwar Suburbanization of Pittsburgh," Ph.D. dissertation, Carnegie Mellon University, 2005; Sherie Mershon, "Corporate Social Responsibility and Urban Revitalization: The Allegheny Conference on Community Development, 1943–1988," Ph.D. dissertation, Carnegie Mellon University, 2000; Edward K. Muller, "Downtown Pittsburgh: Renaissance and Renewal," in *A Geographic Perspective of Pittsburgh and the Alleghenies*, ed. Kevin J. Patrick and Joseph L. Scarpaci, Jr. (Pittsburgh: University of Pittsburgh Press, 2006), 7–20; Brian Robick, "Blight: The Development of a Contested Concept," Ph.D. dissertation, Carnegie Mellon University, 2011; Andrew Thomas Simpson, "Making the Medical Metropolis: Academic Medical Centers and Urban Change in Pittsburgh and Houston, 1945–2010," Ph.D. dissertation, Carnegie Mellon University, 2013; Joel A. Tarr, *Devastation and Renewal: An Environmental History of Pittsburgh and Its Region* (Pittsburgh: University of Pittsburgh Press, 2003); Joel A. Tarr, ed., *Pittsburgh-Sheffield, Sister Cities* (Pittsburgh: Carnegie Mellon University, 1986); Patrick Vitale, "The Atomic Capital of the World: Technoscience, Suburbanization, and the Remaking of Pittsburgh During the Cold War," Ph.D. dissertation, University of Toronto, 2013.

14. There has been little scholarly interest in Hamilton's twentieth-century history, and, as Steven High has noted, "one would be hard pressed to find a more under-researched topic in Canadian history than urban decline and revitalization." Steven C. High, "Introduction," *Urban History Review* 35, 2 (2007): 2. An edited collection and a few recent articles and dissertations address Hamilton's postwar urban physical and social development: Ken Cruikshank and Nancy B. Bouchier, "Blighted Areas and Obnoxious Industries: Constructing Environmental Inequality on an Industrial Waterfront, Hamilton, Ontario, 1890–1960," *Environmental History*

9, 3 (July 2004): 464–96; M. J. Dear, Lloyd George Reeds, and J. J. Drake, eds., *Steel City: Hamilton and Region* (Toronto: University of Toronto Press, 1987); John Eyles and Walter Peace, "Signs and Symbols in Hamilton: An Iconology of Steeltown," *Geografiska Annaler. Series B, Human Geography* 72, 2–3 (1990): 73–88; Barbara Fennessy, "Communities and Leaders at Work in the New Economy: A Comparative Analysis of Agents of Transformation in Pittsburgh, Pennsylvania, and Hamilton, Ontario," Ph.D. dissertation, University of Toronto, 2009; Robick, "Blight: The Development of a Contested Concept"; Margaret Rockwell, "The Facelift and the Wrecking Ball: Urban Renewal and Hamilton's King Street West, 1957–1971," *Urban History Review* 37, 2 (2009): 53–61; Allison Ward, "Guarding the City Beautiful: Liberalism, Empire, Labour, and Civic Identity in Hamilton, Ontario, 1929–53," Ph.D. dissertation, Queen's University, 2014; John C. Weaver, *Hamilton: An Illustrated History* (Halifax: J. Lorimer, 1982).

15. On uneven development, see especially Neil Smith, *Uneven Development: Nature, Capital, and the Production of Space* (New York: Blackwell, 1984); David Harvey, *Justice, Nature and the Geography of Difference* (Cambridge, Mass: Wiley-Blackwell, 1997); Charles W. J. Withers, "Place and the 'Spatial Turn' in Geography and in History," *Journal of the History of Ideas* 70, 4 (October 1, 2009): 639.

16. On efforts to diversify urban economies before the 1970s in the United States, see especially Bauman and Muller, *Before Renaissance*; David Koistinen, *Confronting Decline: The Political Economy of Deindustrialization in Twentieth-Century New England* (Gainesville: University Press of Florida, 2013); Samuel Zipp, *Manhattan Projects: The Rise and Fall of Urban Renewal in Cold War New York* (New York: Oxford University Press, 2010).

17. Bell, *The Coming of Post-Industrial Society*. Bell claimed to have coined the term "post-industrial society" in a 1959 speech, but sociologist David Riesman used the phrase a year earlier to describe a society organized around leisure rather than work. The term "post-industrial" dates to at least the 1920. On the history of the term, see Howard Brick, "Optimism of the Mind: Imagining Postindustrial Society in the 1960s and 1970s," *American Quarterly* 44, 3 (1992): 348–80.

18. Daniel Bell, "Notes on the Post-Industrial Society (I)," *Public Interest* 6 (1967): 24–35; Bell, "Notes on the Post-Industrial Society (II)," *Public Interest* 7 (1967): 102–18.

19. Norman Birnbaum, "The Coming of Post-Industrial Society: For People Who Have Everything: More Knowledge and Less Consensus," *New York Times*, July 1, 1973.

20. Robert Cassidy, "Where We May Be Headed: A Complex and Lengthy Report," *Chicago Tribune*, July 22, 1973.

21. Bell, "Notes on the Post-Industrial Society (I)," 25.

22. OECD Structural Analysis (STAN) Databases, extracted December 10, 2014. See also Hesse, *Regional Structural Change and Industrial Policy*; George Kozmetsky, *The Economic Transformation of the United States, 1950–2000: Focusing on the Technological Revolution, the Service Sector Expansion, and the Cultural, Ideological, and Demographic Changes* (West Lafayette, Ind.: Purdue University Press, 2005).

23. See Jefferson R. Cowie, *Stayin' Alive: The 1970s and the Last Days of the Working Class* (New York: New Press, 2010); David Harvey, *A Brief History of Neoliberalism* (New York: Oxford University Press, 2005); Laura Kalman, *Right Star Rising: A New Politics, 1974–1980* (New York: Norton, 2010); Judith Stein, *Pivotal Decade: How the United States Traded Factories for Finance in the Seventies* (New Haven, Conn.: Yale University Press, 2010).

24. See especially Barry Bluestone and Bennett Harrison, *The Deindustrialization of America: Plant Closings, Community Abandonment, and the Dismantling of Basic Industries* (New York: Basic Books, 1982).

25. For scholarly analyses of deindustrialization and postindustrialism, see especially ibid.; Cowie, *Stayin' Alive*; Howard Gillette, *Camden After the Fall: Decline and Renewal in a Post-Industrial City* (Philadelphia: University of Pennsylvania Press, 2005); High, *Industrial Sunset*; Guian A. McKee, *The Problem of Jobs: Liberalism, Race, and Deindustrialization in Philadelphia* (Chicago: University of Chicago Press, 2008); Sean Safford, *Why the Garden Club Couldn't Save Youngstown: The Transformation of the Rust Belt* (Cambridge, Mass.: Harvard University Press, 2009); Robert O. Self, *American Babylon: Race and the Struggle for Postwar Oakland* (Princeton, N.J.: Princeton University Press, 2003); Thomas J. Sugrue, *The Origins of the Urban Crisis: Race and Inequality in Postwar Detroit* (Princeton, N.J.: Princeton University Press, 1996).

26. Ash Amin, *Post-Fordism: A Reader* (Cambridge: Blackwell, 1994); Taylor C. Boas and Jordan Gans-Morse, "Neoliberalism: From New Liberal Philosophy to Anti-Liberal Slogan," *Studies in Comparative International Development* 44 (2009): 137–61; Pierre Bourdieu, "The Essence of Neoliberalism," *Monde Diplomatique*, December 1998, http://mondediplo .com/1998/12/08bourdieu; Susan Braedley and Meg Luxton, eds., *Neoliberalism and Everyday Life* (Montreal: McGill University Press, 2010); Wendy Brown, *Undoing the Demos: Neoliberalism's Stealth Revolution* (New York: Zone, 2015); Raewyn Connell, "Understanding Neoliberalism," in *Neoliberalism and Everyday Life*, ed. Braedley and Luxton, 22–36; Gérard Duménil and Dominique Lévy, *Capital Resurgent: Roots of the Neoliberal Revolution*, trans. Derek Jeffers (Cambridge, Mass.: Harvard University Press, 2004); Gérard Duménil and Dominique Lévy, *The Crisis of Neoliberalism* (Cambridge, Mass.: Harvard University Press, 2013); Simon Enoch, "Changing the Ideological Fabric? A Brief History of (Canadian) Neoliberalism," *State of Nature: An Online Journal of Radical Ideas*, October 16, 2007, http://www.stateofnature.org/?p=6217; Michel Foucault, *The Birth of Biopolitics: Lectures at the Collège de France, 1978–79*, ed. Michel Sennelart, trans. Graham Burchell (New York: Palgrave Macmillan, 2008); James Ferguson, "The Uses of Neoliberalism," *Antipode* 41, 1 (2009): 166–84; Terry Flew, "Letting Go of Neo-Liberalism (with Some Help from Michel Foucault)," paper presented at Queensland University of Technology, Brisbane, Australia, November 25, 2010; Marion Fourcade-Gourinchas and Sarah L. Babb, "The Rebirth of the Liberal Creed: Paths to Neoliberalism in Four Countries," *American Journal of Sociology* 108, 3 (2002): 533–79; Jean-François Lyotard, *The Postmodern Condition: A Report on Knowledge*, trans. Geoff Bennington and Brian Massumi (Minneapolis: University of Minnesota Press, 1984); Susan George, "A Short History of Neoliberalism: Twenty Years of Elite Economics and Emerging Opportunities for Structural Change," in *Global Finance: New Thinking on Regulating Speculative Capital Markets*, ed. Walden F. Bello, Nicola Bullard, and Kamal Malhotra (London: Zed, 2000), 533–79; Philip Mirowski and Dieter Plehwe, *The Road from Mont Pèlerin: The Making of the Neoliberal Thought Collective* (Cambridge, Mass.: Harvard University Press, 2009); Harvey, *A Brief History of Neoliberalism*; David Harvey, *The Condition of Postmodernity: An Enquiry into the Origins of Cultural Change* (New York: Blackwell, 1989); Philip Mirowski, *Never Let a Serious Crisis Go to Waste: How Neoliberalism Survived the Financial Meltdown* (London: Verso, 2013); Jamie Peck, *Constructions of Neoliberal Reason* (Oxford: Oxford University Press, 2013); Monica Prasad, *The Politics of Free Markets: The Rise of Neoliberal Economic Policies in Britain, France, Germany, and the United States* (Chicago: University of Chicago Press, 2006).

27. For a critique of the idea of neoliberalism as market orthodoxy, see Mirowski, *Never Let a Serious Crisis Go to Waste*, chap. 2.

28. See especially Harvey, *A Brief History of Neoliberalism*.

29. Michel Foucault's 1978–79 lecture series, *The Birth of Biopolitics*, popularized the term "neoliberalism" among academics. Foucault differentiated between liberalism as an attempt to balance state and market, public and private, and neoliberalism as a project designed to ensure that the "overall exercise of political power can be modeled on the principles of a market economy." Foucault, *The Birth of Biopolitics*, 131. On how scholars from different disciplines use the term, see Boas and Gans-Morse, "Neoliberalism," 138.

30. Flew, "Letting Go of Neo-Liberalism."

31. Ferguson, "The Uses of Neoliberalism," 171.

32. On historians' uses (or rejections) of neoliberalism, see Angus Burgin, *The Great Persuasion: Reinventing Free Markets Since the Depression* (Cambridge, Mass.: Harvard University Press, 2012); Nancy MacLean, "Southern Dominance in Borrowed Language: The Regional Origins of American Neoliberalism," in *New Landscapes of Inequality: Neoliberalism and the Erosion of Democracy in America*, ed. Jane Lou Collins, Micaela Di Leonardo, and Brett Williams (Santa Fe, N.M.: School for Advanced Research Press, 2008), 21–38; Bethany Moreton, *To Serve God and Wal-Mart: The Making of Christian Free Enterprise* (Cambridge, Mass: Harvard University Press, 2009); Elizabeth Tandy Shermer, *Sunbelt Capitalism: Phoenix and the Transformation of American Politics* (Philadelphia: University of Pennsylvania Press, 2013).

33. Cowie, *Stayin' Alive*; Niall Ferguson et al., eds., *The Shock of the Global: The 1970s in Perspective* (Cambridge, Mass.: Belknap Press of Harvard University Press, 2010); Kalman, *Right Star Rising*; Stein, *Pivotal Decade*.

34. On divergent paths to neoliberalism, see Fourcade-Gourinchas and Babb, "The Rebirth of the Liberal Creed."

35. Miriam Greenberg uses the term "testing grounds." Miriam Greenberg, *Branding New York: How a City in Crisis Was Sold to the World* (New York: Routledge, 2008), 27. On neoliberal cities, see especially Neil Brenner and Nikolas Theodore, *Spaces of Neoliberalism: Urban Restructuring in North America and Western Europe* (Malden, Mass. Oxford: Blackwell, 2002); Jason R. Hackworth, *The Neoliberal City: Governance, Ideology, and Development in American Urbanism* (Ithaca, N.Y.: Cornell University Press, 2007); Harvey, *A Brief History of Neoliberalism*; Bob Jessop, "Liberalism, Neoliberalism, and Urban Governance: A State-Theoretical Perspective," *Antipode* 34, 3 (2002): 452–72; Helga Leitner, Jamie Peck, and Eric S. Sheppard, eds., *Contesting Neoliberalism: Urban Frontiers* (New York: Guilford, 2007); Jamie Peck and Adam Tickell, "Neoliberalizing Space," *Antipode* 34, 3 (2002): 380–404; Jamie Peck, "Austerity Urbanism: American Cities under Extreme Economy," *City* 16, 6 (December 2012): 626–55; Tuna Tasan-Kok and Guy Baeten, *Contradictions of Neoliberal Planning: Cities, Policies and Politics* (Dordrecht: Springer, 2011); Timothy Paul Ryan Weaver, "Neoliberalism in the Trenches: Urban Policy and Politics in the United States and United Kingdom," Ph.D. dissertation, University of Pennsylvania, 2012; Rachel Weber, "Extracting Value from the City: Neoliberalism and Urban Redevelopment," *Antipode* 34, 3 (2002): 519–40.

36. Robert A. Beauregard, "Public-Private Partnerships as Historical Chameleons: The Case of the United States," in *Partnerships in Urban Governance: European and American Experiences*, ed. John Pierre (New York: Palgrave, 1998), 52–70; Brent Cebul, "Developmental State: Business, Poverty, and Economic Empowerment from the New Deal to the New Democrats," book manuscript (2015); M. V. Levine, "The Politics of Partnership: Urban Redevelopment Since 1945," in *Unequal Partnerships: The Political Economy of Urban Development in Postwar America*, ed. Gregory D. Squires (New Brunswick, N.J.: Rutgers University Press, 1989), 12–34; Gregory Squires, "Partnership and the Pursuit of the Private City," in *Urban Life in Transition*,

ed. Mark Gottdiener and Chris Pickavance (Newbury Park, Calif.: Sage, 1991), 239–59; Teaford, *Rough Road to Renaissance*.

37. Manuel Castells, *The Rise of the Network Society* (Malden, Mass.: Blackwell, 1996); Peter F. Drucker, *The Age of Discontinuity: Guidelines to Our Changing Society* (New York: Harper and Row, 1969); Marc Uri Porat and Michael Rogers Rubin, *The Information Economy* (Washington, D.C.: U.S. Department of Commerce, 1977); Barry Smart, "Editor's Introduction: Post-Industrial Society and Information Technology," in *Post-Industrial Society*, ed. Smart (London: Sage, 2011), 1: xxi–xlvi.

38. On European experiences with public-private partnerships, see Timothy K. Barnekov, Robin Boyle, and Daniel Rich, *Privatism and Urban Policy in Britain and the United States* (New York: Oxford University Press, 1989); Naomi Carmon, "Three Generations of Urban Renewal Policies: Analysis and Policy Implications," *Geoforum* 20 (1999): 145–58; Alan DiGaetano and Elizabeth Strom, "Comparative Urban Governance: An Integrated Approach," *Urban Affairs Review* 38, 3 (January 1, 2003): 356–95; H. V. Savitch, "The Ecology of Public-Private Partnerships: Europe," in *Partnerships in Urban Governance: European and American Experiences*, ed. John Pierre (New York: Palgrave, 1998), 175–86.

Chapter 1. The Roots of Postindustrialism

1. Arthur D. Little, Inc., *Commercial Development in Hamilton: A Report to the Hamilton Economic Development Commission* (Boston: Arthur D. Little, 1968), 77.

2. Ibid.

3. Ibid., 80, 84.

4. See, for example, Brent Cebul, "Developmental State: Business, Poverty, and Economic Empowerment from the New Deal to the New Democrats," book manuscript (2015); N. D. B. Connolly, *A World More Concrete: Real Estate and the Remaking of Jim Crow South Florida* (Chicago: University of Chicago Press, 2014); Andrew R. Highsmith, *Demolition Means Progress: Flint, Michigan, and the Fate of the American Metropolis* (Chicago: University of Chicago Press, 2015); Arnold R. Hirsch, *Making the Second Ghetto: Race and Housing in Chicago, 1940–1960* (New York: Cambridge University Press, 1983); Roy Lubove, *Twentieth-Century Pittsburgh*, vol. 1, *Government, Business, and Environmental Change* (Pittsburgh: University of Pittsburgh Press, 1996); Jon C. Teaford, *The Rough Road to Renaissance: Urban Revitalization in America, 1940–1985* (Baltimore: Johns Hopkins University Press, 1990).

5. Robert A. Beauregard, "Public-Private Partnerships as Historical Chameleons: The Case of the United States," in *Partnerships in Urban Governance: European and American Experiences*, ed. John Pierre (New York: Palgrave, 1998), 57–59. See also M. Christine Boyer, *Dreaming the Rational City: The Myth of American City Planning* (Cambridge, Mass.: MIT Press, 1983); Richard E. Foglesong, *Planning the Capitalist City: The Colonial Era to the 1920s* (Princeton, N.J.: Princeton University Press, 1986).

6. M. V. Levine, "The Politics of Partnership: Urban Redevelopment Since 1945," in *Unequal Partnerships: The Political Economy of Urban Development in Postwar America*, ed. Gregory D. Squires (New Brunswick, N.J.: Rutgers University Press, 1989), 14.

7. Cebul, "Developmental State," chap. 3; H. V. Savitch, "The Ecology of Public-Private Partnerships: Europe," in *Partnerships in Urban Governance*, ed. Pierre, 175.

8. Carl Nightingale, *Segregation: A Global History of Divided Cities* (Chicago: University of Chicago Press, 2012); Pierre-Yves Saunier, "Introduction: Global City, Take 2: A View from Urban History," in *Another Global City: Historical Explorations into the Transnational Municipal*

Moment, 1850–2000, ed. Pierre-Yves Saunier and Shane Ewen (New York: Palgrave Macmillan, 2008), 10.

9. Daniel T. Rodgers, *Atlantic Crossings: Social Politics in a Progressive Age* (Cambridge, Mass.: Harvard University Press, 1998); Saunier and Ewen, eds., *Another Global City*; Stephen V. Ward, "Learning from the US: The Americanisation of Western Urban Planning," in *Urbanism: Imported or Exported?* ed. Joe Nasr and Mercedes Volait (Chichester: Wiley-Academy, 2003), 83–106.

10. Beauregard, "Public-Private Partnerships."

11. Ibid.; Cebul, "Developmental State"; Levine, "The Politics of Partnership"; Gregory Squires, "Partnership and the Pursuit of the Private City," in *Urban Life in Transition*, ed. Mark Gottdiener and Chris Pickavance (Newbury Park, Calif.: Sage, 1991), 239–59; Teaford, *Rough Road to Renaissance*.

12. Teaford, *Rough Road to Renaissance*.

13. Levine, "The Politics of Partnership," 19–20.

14. Robert A. Caro, *The Power Broker: Robert Moses and the Fall of New York* (New York: Knopf, 1974); Connolly, *A World More Concrete*; Hirsch, *Making the Second Ghetto*; Christopher Klemek, *The Transatlantic Collapse of Urban Renewal: Postwar Urbanism from New York to Berlin* (Chicago: University of Chicago Press, 2011); Kenneth L. Kusmer and Joe W. Trotter, eds., *African American Urban History Since World War II* (Chicago: University of Chicago Press, 2009), part 2; Lubove, *Twentieth-Century Pittsburgh*, vol. 1; John H. Mollenkopf, *The Contested City* (Princeton, N.J.: Princeton University Press, 1983); Thomas H. O'Connor, *Building a New Boston: Politics and Urban Renewal, 1950–1970* (Boston: Northeastern University Press, 1993); Samuel Zipp, *Manhattan Projects: The Rise and Fall of Urban Renewal in Cold War New York* (New York: Oxford University Press, 2010).

15. Klemek, *The Transatlantic Collapse of Urban Renewal*; Naomi Carmon, "Three Generation of Urban Renewal Policies: Analysis and Policy Implications," *Geoforum* 20 (1999): 145–58; Nancy Haekyung Kwak, "A Citizen's Right to Decent Shelter: Public Housing in New York, London, and Singapore, 1945 to 1970," Ph.D. dissertation, Columbia University, 2006; Amy C. Offner, "Anti-Poverty Programs, Social Conflict, and Economic Thought in Colombia and the United States, 1948–1980," Ph.D. dissertation, Columbia University, 2012; Jon Pierre, ed., *Partnerships in Urban Governance: European and American Experience* (New York: Palgrave Macmillan, 1998); Zipp, *Manhattan Projects*.

16. Stanley H. Pickett, "An Appraisal of the Urban Renewal Programme in Canada," *University of Toronto Law Journal* 18, 3 (Summer 1968): 233–47.

17. Peter Shapely, "Governance in the Post-War City: Historical Reflections on Public-Private Partnerships in the UK," *International Journal of Urban and Regional Research* 37, 4 (2013): 1297.

18. Sam Bass Warner, *The Private City: Philadelphia in Three Periods of Its Growth* (Philadelphia: University of Pennsylvania Press, 1968).

19. J. B. Cullingworth and Roger W. Caves, *Planning in the USA: Policies, Issues, and Processes* (New York: Routledge, 2009), 45.

20. Klemek, *The Transatlantic Collapse of Urban Renewal*; Ward, "Learning from the US."

21. Michael Keating, "The Politics of Economic Development: Political Change and Local Development Policies in the United States, Britain, and France," *Urban Affairs Review* 28, 3 (March 1993): 373–96; Paul Starr, "The Meaning of Privatization," *Yale Law and Policy Review* 6 (1988): 6–41; Savitch, "Ecology of Public-Private Partnerships."

22. Rémi Dormois, Gilles Pinson, and Hélène Reignier, "Path-Dependency in Public-Private Partnership in French Urban Renewal," *Journal of Housing and the Built Environment* 20, 3 (September 2005): 243–56; Peter K. Eisinger, *The Rise of the Entrepreneurial State: State and Local Economic Development Policy in the United States* (Madison: University of Wisconsin Press, 1988); Pierre, ed., *Partnerships in Urban Governance*; Savitch, "Ecology of Public-Private Partnerships"; Hank V. Savitch and Paul Kantor, *Cities in the International Marketplace: The Political Economy of Urban Development in North America and Western Europe* (Princeton, N.J.: Princeton University Press, 2002); Jon C. Teaford, *The Rise of the States: Evolution of American State Government* (Baltimore: Johns Hopkins University Press, 2002).

23. Beauregard, "Public-Private Partnerships," 60–62; Levine, "The Politics of Partnership," 22.

24. Philip J. Ethington and David P. Levitus, "Placing American Political Development: Cities, Regions, and Regimes, 1789–2008," in *The City in American Political Development*, ed. Richardson Dilworth (New York: Routledge, 2009), 154–76; Bruce J. Schulman, *From Cotton Belt to Sunbelt: Federal Policy, Economic Development, and the Transformation of the South, 1938–1980* (Durham, N.C.: Duke University Press, 1994); Elizabeth Tandy Shermer, *Sunbelt Capitalism: Phoenix and the Transformation of American Politics* (Philadelphia: University of Pennsylvania Press, 2013).

25. On growth partnerships, see Beauregard, "Public-Private Partnerships."

26. Levine, "The Politics of Partnership," 22–23.

27. Shapely, "Governance in the Post-War City," 1299.

28. Charles Landry and Franco Bianchini, *The Creative City* (London: Demos, 1995), 52; Alistair Cole and Peter John, *Local Governance in England and France* (London: Routledge, 2001), 131–32. On differences between French partnerships and those elsewhere in Europe and North America, see Dormois, Pinson, and Reignier, "Path-Dependency in Public-Private Partnerships."

29. Landry and Bianchini, *The Creative City*, 52; Savitch, "Ecology of Public-Private Partnerships," 181.

30. Kim England and John Mercer, "Canadian Cities in Continental Context: Global and Continental Perspectives on Canadian Urban Development," in *Canadian Cities in Transition*, ed. Trudi E. Bunting and Pierre Filion (Toronto: Oxford University Press, 1991), 39.

31. Ken Cruikshank and Nancy B. Bouchier, "Blighted Areas and Obnoxious Industries: Constructing Environmental Inequality on an Industrial Waterfront, Hamilton, Ontario, 1890–1960," *Environmental History* 9, 3 (2004): 464–96; John C. Weaver, *Hamilton: An Illustrated History* (Halifax: J. Lorimer, 1982); M. J. Webber, "Regional Production and the Production of Regions: The Case of Steeltown," in *Production, Work, Territory: The Geographical Anatomy of Industrial Capitalism*, ed. Allen J. Scott and Michael Storper (London: Allen & Unwin, 1986); Harold A. Wood, "Emergence of the Modern City: Hamilton, 1891–1950," in *Steel City: Hamilton and Region*, ed. M. J. Dear, Lloyd George Reeds, and J. J. Drake (Toronto: University of Toronto Press, 1987), 119–37.

32. Richard Harris and Robert Lewis, "The Geography of North American Cities and Suburbs, 1900–1950: A New Synthesis," *Journal of Urban History* 27, 3 (2001): 262–93; Richard Harris, *Creeping Conformity: How Canada Became Suburban, 1900–1960* (Toronto: University of Toronto Press, 2004); Kent James, "Public Policy and the Postwar Suburbanization of Pittsburgh," Ph.D. dissertation, Carnegie Mellon University, 2005.

33. U.S. Department of Commerce, Bureau of the Census, Decennial Census of Population and Housing, 1950–2000.

34. Statistics Canada, Census of Population, 1951–2001.

35. Between 1951 and 1991, the Canadian census did not record race; in 1996, respondents were asked to identify themselves as one or more "visible minority." Ontario Ministry of Finance, "Visible Minorities and Ethnicity in Ontario," Census 2001 Highlights, Fact Sheet 6 (Toronto: The Ministry, 2003).

36. Actual numbers (rounded) were Pittsburgh, 26 percent; Detroit, 76 percent; Cleveland, 47 percent; and St. Louis, 48 percent. Campbell Gibson and Kay Jung, "Historical Census Statistics on Population Totals by Race, 1790 to 1990, and by Hispanic Origin, 1970 to 1990, for Large Cities and Other Urban Places in the United States," Population Division Working Paper 76 (Washington, D.C.: U.S. Census Bureau, February 2005).

37. U.S. Census, Decennial Census of Population and Housing, 1950.

38. Bob Gradek, *The Root of Pittsburgh's Population Drain* (Pittsburgh: Carnegie Mellon University Center for Economic Development, 2003), 2.

39. W. G. Peace and A. F. Burghardt, "Hamilton Today," in *Steel City: Hamilton and Region*, ed. M. J. Dear, Lloyd George Reeds, and J. J. Drake (Toronto: University of Toronto Press, 1987), 296.

40. Meg Luxton and June Shirley Corman, *Getting By in Hard Times: Gendered Labour at Home and on the Job* (Toronto: University of Toronto Press, 2001), 138.

41. Robert C. Alberts, *Pitt: The Story of the University of Pittsburgh, 1787–1987* (Pittsburgh: University of Pittsburgh Press, 1986); Charles M. Johnston, *McMaster University*, vol. 2 (Toronto: Toronto University Press, 1981); Lubove, *Twentieth-Century Pittsburgh*, vol. 1.

42. On regional planning in the 1920s, see John F. Bauman and Edward K. Muller, *Before Renaissance: Planning in Pittsburgh, 1889–1943* (Pittsburgh: University of Pittsburgh Press, 2006).

43. The Mellon fortune included major shares of Gulf Oil and Alcoa, as well as the family banking interests. Richard Austin Smith, "America's Biggest Fortunes," *Fortune*, November, 1957; Jean R. Haley, "Richard Mellon, Financier, Dies," *Washington Post*, June 4, 1970.

44. On the establishment and governing rules of the Allegheny Conference, see Sherie Mershon, "Corporate Social Responsibility and Urban Revitalization: The Allegheny Conference on Community Development, 1943–1988," Ph.D. dissertation, Carnegie Mellon University, 2000.

45. See, for example, the essays in Bert Altena and Marcel van der Linden, eds., *De-Industrialization: Social, Cultural, and Political Aspects* (New York: Cambridge University Press, 2002). See also Lubove, *Twentieth-Century Pittsburgh*, vol. 1; Joel A. Tarr, ed., *Pittsburgh-Sheffield, Sister Cities* (Pittsburgh: Carnegie Mellon University, 1986).

46. On Pittsburgh's environmental history, see Joel A. Tarr, *Devastation and Renewal: An Environmental History of Pittsburgh and Its Region* (Pittsburgh: University of Pittsburgh Press, 2003).

47. Thomas Winship, "Pittsburgh Mayor, Here, Tells of His City's Face-Lifting," *Washington Post*, October 10, 1951. Lawrence made the comments at the 1951 conference of the National Association of Housing Officials. Quoted in Chalmers M. Roberts, "Cooperation at All Levels Gives Life to Downtown Pittsburgh," *Washington Post*, February 4, 1952.

48. On Pittsburgh's first Renaissance, see Allen Dieterich-Ward, *Beyond Rust: Metropolitan Pittsburgh and the Fate of Industrial America* (Philadelphia: University of Pennsylvania Press, 2015); Laura Grantmyre, "Visual Representations of Redevelopment in Pittsburgh's Hill District, 1943–1968," Ph.D. dissertation, University of Pittsburgh, 2014; Lubove, *Twentieth-Century Pittsburgh*, vol. 1; Mershon, "Corporate Social Responsibility and Urban Revitalization"; Brian Robick, "Blight: The Development of a Contested Concept," Ph.D. dissertation, Carnegie Mellon

University, 2011; Patrick Vitale, "The Atomic Capital of the World: Technoscience, Suburbanization, and the Remaking of Pittsburgh During the Cold War," Ph.D. dissertation, University of Toronto, 2013.

49. Winship, "Pittsburgh Mayor, Here, Tells of His City's Face-Lifting."

50. Pittsburgh Regional Planning Association, *Economic Study of the Pittsburgh Region*, vol. 2 (Pittsburgh: University of Pittsburgh Press, 1963), 33.

51. Ibid., 9.

52. Pittsburgh Regional Planning Association, *Economic Study*.

53. Regional Industrial Development Commission, *1971 Annual Report* (Pittsburgh: RIDC, 1971), 2.

54. Jack Sholl, "Golden Triangle Completed," *Washington Post*, November 25, 1969.

55. On Hamilton's urban physical and social development, see the essays in Dear, Reeds, and Drake, ed., *Steel City*; Margaret Rockwell, "The Facelift and the Wrecking Ball: Urban Renewal and Hamilton's King Street West, 1957–1971," *Urban History Review* 37, 2 (2009): 53–61.

56. Robick, "Blight," 133–41, 164.

57. On Canada's housing and urban renewal legislation, see the essays in John R. Miron, ed., *House, Home, and Community: Progress in Housing Canadians, 1945–1986* (Montreal: McGill-Queen's Press, 1993).

58. "Copps Scores Victory After Only 2 Years in Hamilton Politics," *Globe and Mail*, December 5, 1962; Barbara Brown, "The Mayor of the Little People," *Hamilton Spectator*, October 17, 1988; Jane Coutts, "They're Remembering a Fighter," *Hamilton Spectator*, October 17, 1988.

59. Gordon Hampton, "Four Months into Office, Critic Now Peacemaker," *Hamilton Spectator*, April 13, 1963.

60. J. H. Moore to John Grove, November 19, 1968, folder 7 Canada—1969–74, box 164, ACCD.

61. Robert MacDermid and Greg Albo, "Divided Province, Growing Protests: Ontario Moves Right," in *The Provincial State in Canada: Politics in the Provinces and Territories*, ed. Keith Brownsey and Michael Howlett (Peterborough, Ont.: Broadview, 2001), 167.

62. See, for example, Ontario Economic Council, Press Release—Intergovernmental Relations, Toronto, April 14, 1977, RG 34-5-0-2 file, box 2, RG 34-5, OEC; Ontario Economic Council, Press Release—The Ontario Economy to 1987, Toronto, April 25, 1977, RG 34-5-0-2 file, box 2, OEC.

63. Gerald Hodge and Ira M. Robinson, *Planning Canadian Regions* (Vancouver: University of British Columbia Press, 2001), 326.

64. Speech Prepared for the Honorable W. Darcy McKeough, Minister of Municipal Affairs, re: Toronto-centered Region, May 5, 1970 (draft 3), 7–8, Metro Toronto-Centered Region April 22–29, 1970 file, box VK39, RG 19-59, CPB.

65. See "Ontario: Situation Analysis Report," ca. 1976, 7, File 1410-3, Part 2, Vol. 153, MSUA; John Robarts, *Design for Development: Statement by the Prime Minister of the Province of Ontario on Regional Development Policy* (Toronto: Government of Ontario, 1966).

66. City of Hamilton Planning Department, *Hamilton Area Regional Development Study* (Hamilton: City of Hamilton, 1968), 24.

67. David M. Freund, *Colored Property: State Policy and White Racial Politics in Suburban America* (Chicago: University of Chicago Press, 2007); Hirsch, *Making the Second Ghetto*; Thomas J. Sugrue, *The Origins of the Urban Crisis: Race and Inequality in Postwar Detroit* (Princeton, N.J.: Princeton University Press, 1996).

68. Stephen V. Ward, "The International Diffusion of Planning: A Review and a Canadian Case Study," *International Planning Studies* 4, 1 (1999): 67. See also Michael A. Goldberg and John Mercer, *The Myth of the North American City: Continentalism Challenged* (Vancouver: University of British Columbia Press, 1986); Klemek, *The Transatlantic Collapse of Urban Renewal*.

69. Richard Simeon and Ian Robinson, *State, Society, and the Development of Canadian Federalism* (Toronto: University of Toronto Press, 1990), 251.

70. Gregory S. Wilson, *Communities Left Behind: The Area Redevelopment Administration, 1945–1965* (Knoxville: University of Tennessee Press, 2009).

71. Lee-Anne Goodman, "Nixon Tapes Include Testy Trudeau Chat," *Toronto Star*, December 8, 2008; Pierre Elliott Trudeau, *Memoirs* (Toronto: McClelland & Stewart, 1993).

72. Quoted in Edith Iglauer, "Pierre Trudeau: Champion of a Just Society," *Americas* 53, 1 (January 2001), 56.

73. On the Trudeau administration and its critics, see especially John English, *Citizen of the World: The Life of Pierre Elliott Trudeau* (Toronto: Knopf Canada, 2006); Gregory J. Inwood, *Continentalizing Canada: The Politics and Legacy of the MacDonald Royal Commission* (Toronto: University of Toronto Press, 2005); David Milne, *Tug of War: Ottawa and the Provinces Under Trudeau and Mulroney* (Toronto: J. Lorimer, 1986); Trudeau, *Memoirs*.

74. On DREE and regional development in Canada, see P. E. Bryden, "The Limits of National Policy: Integrating Regional Development into the Federal Agenda," *American Review of Canadian Studies* 37, 4 (Winter 2007): 475–93; J. B. Cullingworth, *Urban and Regional Planning in Canada* (New Brunswick, N.J.: Transaction Books, 1987); R. Harley McGee, *Getting It Right: Regional Development in Canada* (Kingston-Montreal: McGill-Queens University Press, 1992); Gordon F. Osbaldeston, *Organizing to Govern: Getting the Basics Right* (London: University of Western Ontario, National Centre for Management and Research Development, 1993); Donald J. Savoie, *Reviewing Canada's Regional Development Efforts* (Ottawa: Royal Commission on Renewing and Strengthening Our Place in Canada, 2003).

75. Cullingworth, *Urban and Regional Planning in Canada*, 275; Savoie, *Reviewing Canada's Regional Development Efforts*, 153–54.

76. Savoie, *Reviewing Canada's Regional Development Efforts*, 155.

77. Ibid.

78. Denis Peloquin to Mark Jewett, et al., memo re: The Public/Private Redevelopment Corporation, July 10, 1975, File 1400-2, Vol. 151, MSUA; Donald J. Savoie, "The Toppling of DREE and Prospects for Regional Economic Development," *Canadian Public Policy* 10, 3 (1984): 329–30.

79. Cullingworth, *Urban and Regional Planning in Canada*, 277.

80. Notes for a Statement by the Honorable D. C. Jamieson, Minister of Regional Economic Expansion, to the House of Commons Standing Committee on Regional Development, March 28, 1974, File 121-1-2-1 (74–75), Vol. 145, Part 1, DRIE.

81. "Spatial Demographics Trends: Their Importance and The M[S]UA's Role," n.d. (ca. 1970), 23–24, File c-2105-C1, Vol.120, MSUA.

82. F. D. Millar to D. Ryan, memo re: Halifax Waterfront Project, April 15, 1975, File 1400-2, Vol. 151, MSUA.

83. Paul Scott to Doug Ryan, memo re: Dealing with the Private Developers, Appendix B, June 12, 1975, File 1400-2, Vol. 151, MSUA. On MSUA's public-private partnerships, see also Paul Scott, Draft Public/Private Interface, 1976, Vol. 151, File 1400-2, MSUA; Secretary to Minister, memo re: Public/Private Sector Model Development, May 28, 1975, 1, File 1400-2, Vol. 151, MSUA.

84. Millar to Ryan, April 15, 1975, MSUA; Scott to Ryan, June 12, 1975, MSUA.

85. Timothy J. Conlan, "The Politics of Federal Block Grants: From Nixon to Reagan," *Political Science Quarterly* 99, 2 (Summer 1984): 253–54.

86. Richard Nixon, "Address to the Nation on Domestic Programs," August 8, 1969, *American Presidency Project*, http://www.presidency.ucsb.edu.

87. Richard Nixon, "Special Message to the Congress on Sharing Federal Revenues with the States," August 13, 1969. *American Presidency Project.*

88. Ibid.

89. William R. Barnes, "Beyond Federal Urban Policy," *Urban Affairs Review* 40, 5 (May 2005): 581.

90. Allen E. Pritchard to Members of the Board of Directors, National League of Cities, March 1, 1973, re: National Policy Strategy Recommendations, 2, 6–7, U.S. Conference of Mayors folder, Office Files of Floyd H. Hyde, 1969–72, Records of the Office of the Assistant Secretary for Community Planning and Development, HUD.

91. Eisinger, *The Rise of the Entrepreneurial State*; Schulman, *From Cotton Belt to Sunbelt*; Teaford, *Rise of the States.*

92. Milton J. Shapp to Richard G. Marden, Executive Director, Pennsylvania League of Cities, April 19, 1971, folder 47/14, box 47, Subject Files, Shapp, and correspondence between Shapp and John D. Erlichmann, Nixon's Assistant for Domestic Affairs, between March and May 1971, in folder 46/41, box 46, Subject Files, Shapp.

93. On the development of block grants, see Conlan, "The Politics of Federal Block Grants."

94. On revenue sharing, see Conlan, "The Politics of Federal Block Grants."

95. "The State of the Department," November/December 1972, 34–39, 72–73, Files of Undersecretary Van Dusen folder, Finding Aids, Publications and Annual Reports, Non-Record Material Relating to RG 207, HUD.

96. Ibid., 21–22.

Chapter 2. Forging Growth Partnerships

1. Douglas E. Kneeland, "Pittsburgh: A Brawny City Puts on a Silk Shirt," *New York Times*, October 3, 1970. None of the local executives were identified by name.

2. City of Hamilton Planning Department, *City of Hamilton General Background Information* (Hamilton: City of Hamilton, 1971), 1.

3. Hamilton Economic Development Commission, *1971 Annual Report* (Hamilton: City of Hamilton, 1972).

4. City of Hamilton Planning Department, *City of Hamilton General Background Information*, 11.

5. On the fortunes of the international steel industry in the postwar period, see Donald F. Barnett and Jarvis Schorsch, *Steel: Upheaval in a Basic Industry* (Cambridge, Mass.: Ballinger, 1983); Anthony P. D'Costa, *The Global Restructuring of the Steel Industry: Innovations, Institutions, and Industrial Change* (New York: Routledge, 1999); Ray Hudson and David Sadler, *The International Steel Industry: Restructuring, State Policies, and Localities* (New York: Routledge, 1989).

6. Robert Benko, Governor's Office of State Planning and Development, "Analysis of the Impact of Selected Federal Programs on Large Pennsylvania Cities: A Background Paper on the Emerging National Urban Policy," March 1978, folder 4/13, box 4, files of Larry Hochendoner, Shapp.

7. Terry Nichols Clark and Lorna Crowley Ferguson, *City Money: Political Processes, Fiscal Strain, and Retrenchment* (New York: Columbia University Press, 1983), 201.

8. City of Pittsburgh, *Comprehensive Six-Year Development Program* (Pittsburgh: Office of the Mayor, 1969), 133–34.

9. City of Pittsburgh, *1977–1982 Proposed Program, City of Pittsburgh* (Pittsburgh: Office of the Mayor, 1976), 86.

10. James O'Toole, "Obituary: Pete Flaherty Dies at 80," *Pittsburgh Post-Gazette,* April 19, 2005.

11. Clark and Ferguson, *City Money,* 5.

12. Ibid., 184–87.

13. Wayne King, "Pittsburgh's Mayor Flaherty, a Source of Alienation and Affection, Entering 2nd Term," *New York Times,* January 7, 1974.

14. Clark and Ferguson, *City Money,* 200–202.

15. Pete Flaherty interview by Michael Snow, transcript, March 9, 1999, SLGA.

16. Roy Lubove, *Twentieth-Century Pittsburgh,* vol. 2, *The Post-Steel Era* (Pittsburgh: University of Pittsburgh Press, 1996), 73.

17. Robert Pease interview by Michael Snow, transcript, April 27, 1999, SLGA.

18. Pete Flaherty interview.

19. John Robin, interview by Michael Snow, transcript, October 6, 1998, SLGA.

20. Robert Pease interview.

21. O'Toole, "Obituary: Pete Flaherty Dies at 80."

22. Pete Flaherty interview.

23. Ibid.

24. Robert Pease interview.

25. City of Pittsburgh, *The 1976 Six Year Development Program of the City of Pittsburgh* (Pittsburgh: Office of the Mayor, 1975), 4; Gregory J. Crowley, *The Politics of Place: Contentious Urban Redevelopment in Pittsburgh* (Pittsburgh: University of Pittsburgh Press, 2005), 100.

26. Robert Pease interview.

27. City of Pittsburgh, *1972 Six Year Development Program of the City of Pittsburgh (Draft)* (Pittsburgh: Office of the Mayor, 1971), 23–29.

28. Joseph Cosetti interview by Michael Snow, transcript, January 24, 2000, SLGA.

29. City of Pittsburgh, *1976 Six Year Development Program of the City of Pittsburgh,* 28–31.

30. City of Pittsburgh, *1972 Six Year Development Program of the City of Pittsburgh (Draft),* 28.

31. Stuart Meck and Rebecca Retzlaff, "President Jimmy Carter's Urban Policy: A Reconstruction and an Appraisal," *Journal of Planning History* 11 (August 2012): 243.

32. Tracy Neumann, "Privatization, Devolution, and Jimmy Carter's National Urban Policy," *Journal of Urban History* 40, 2 (2014): 283–300.

33. President's Urban and Regional Policy Group, *A New Partnership to Conserve America's Communities: A National Urban Policy* (Washington, D.C.: HUD, 1978).

34. Roger Biles, *The Fate of Cities: Urban America and the Federal Government, 1945–2000* (Lawrence: University Press of Kansas, 2011), 237.

35. Meck and Retzlaff, "President Jimmy Carter's Urban Policy," 257.

36. Biles, *The Fate of Cities,* 237.

37. Ibid., 261.

38. On Carter's campaign, governing style, and worldview, see Jefferson R. Cowie, *Stayin' Alive: The 1970s and the Last Days of the Working Class* (New York: New Press, 2010); Laura

Kalman, *Right Star Rising: A New Politics, 1974–1980* (New York: Norton, 2010); Judith Stein, *Pivotal Decade: How the United States Traded Factories for Finance in the Seventies* (New Haven, Conn.: Yale University Press, 2010); Thomas J. Sugrue, "Carter's Urban Policy Crisis," in *The Carter Presidency: Policy Choices in the Post-New Deal Era*, ed. Gary M. Fink and Hugh Davis Graham (Lawrence: University Press of Kansas, 1998), 137–57.

39. Sugrue, "Carter's Urban Policy Crisis," 149–50.

40. President's Urban and Regional Policy Group, *A New Partnership to Conserve America's Communities*, 1.

41. Editorial, *North Hills News Record* (Allison, Pa.), November 15, 1977.

42. Edward K. Muller, "Downtown Pittsburgh: Renaissance and Renewal," in *A Geographic Perspective of Pittsburgh and the Alleghenies*, ed. Kevin J. Patrick and Joseph L. Scarpaci, Jr. (Pittsburgh: University of Pittsburgh Press, 2006), 7–20; Robert Pease interview.

43. City of Pittsburgh, *1977–1982 Proposed Program, City of Pittsburgh*, 7.

44. City of Pittsburgh, *1978–1983 Six Year Development Program* (Pittsburgh: Office of the Mayor, 1977), 3; City of Pittsburgh, *1982–1987 Six Year Development Program (Draft)* (Pittsburgh: Office of the Mayor, 1981), 15; City of Pittsburgh, *1983–1988 Six Year Development Program (Draft)* (Pittsburgh: Office of the Mayor, 1982), 15.

45. City of Pittsburgh, *1977–1982 Proposed Program, City of Pittsburgh*, 7.

46. Ibid., preface.

47. On Renaissance II, see especially Lubove, *Twentieth-Century Pittsburgh*, vol. 2.

48. City of Pittsburgh, *1977–1982 Proposed Program, City of Pittsburgh*, preface.

49. Ibid., 7.

50. Crowley, *The Politics of Place*, 102; Lubove, *Twentieth-Century Pittsburgh*, vol. 2, ix.

51. On urban renewal in New York, see Robert A. Caro, *The Power Broker: Robert Moses and the Fall of New York* (New York: Knopf, 1974); Jane Jacobs, *The Death and Life of Great American Cities* (New York: Random House, 1961); Christopher Klemek, *The Transatlantic Collapse of Urban Renewal: Postwar Urbanism from New York to Berlin* (Chicago: University of Chicago Press, 2011); Samuel Zipp, *Manhattan Projects: The Rise and Fall of Urban Renewal in Cold War New York* (New York: Oxford University Press, 2010).

52. Roger Dunstan, "Overview of New York City's Fiscal Crisis," CRB Note 3, 1, California State Library, March 1, 1995; Joshua Freeman, "If You Can Make It Here," *Jacobin*, Fall 2014, 131–37; Miriam Greenberg, *Branding New York: How a City in Crisis Was Sold to the World* (New York: Routledge, 2008), 126–29; Jason R. Hackworth, *The Neoliberal City: Governance, Ideology, and Development in American Urbanism* (Ithaca, N.Y.: Cornell University Press, 2007), chap. 6; Kim Phillips-Fein, "The Legacy of the 1970s Fiscal Crisis," *Nation*, April 16, 2013.

53. Dunstan, *Overview of New York City's Fiscal Crisis*; Phillips-Fein, "The Legacy of the 1970s Fiscal Crisis."

54. Joshua Freeman, *Working-Class New York: Life and Labor Since World War II* (New York: New Press, 2000), chapter 4.

55. Municipal Assistance Corporation, *1976 Annual Report* (New York: MAC, 1977).

56. Greenberg, *Branding New York*; Hackworth, *The Neoliberal City*; David Harvey, *A Brief History of Neoliberalism* (New York: Oxford University Press, 2005); Kim Moody, *From Welfare State to Real Estate: Regime Change in New York City, 1974 to the Present* (New York: New Press, 2007).

57. Timothy P. R. Weaver, *Blazing the Neoliberal Trail: Urban Political Development in the United States and the United Kingdom* (Philadelphia: University of Pennsylvania Press, 2015).

58. John Robin interview.

59. Summary information, Pease.

60. Roger S. Ahlbrandt and Morton Coleman, *The Role of the Corporation in Community Economic Development as Viewed by 21 Corporate Executives* (Pittsburgh: University of Pittsburgh, 1987), 24.

61. David L. Rosenberg, "Did the Collapse of Basic Industry Really Take the Allegheny Conference by Surprise?" *In Pittsburgh*, March 21, 1990, 18–20.

62. Charlie Humphrey, "Master Planners," *In Pittsburgh*, March 21–27, 1990, 17.

63. Rosenberg, "Did the Collapse of Basic Industry Really Take the Allegheny Conference by Surprise?"

64. On Pittsburgh's foundations and their roles in cultural development, see Sabina Detrick, "The Post Industrial Revitalization of Pittsburgh: Myths and Evidence," *Community Development Journal* 34, 1 (January 1999): 4–12; Lubove, *Twentieth-Century Pittsburgh*, vol. 2, chap. 9.

65. Crowley, *The Politics of Place*; Lubove, *Twentieth-Century Pittsburgh*, vol. 2; Muller, "Downtown Pittsburgh."

66. Crowley, *The Politics of Place*; Louise Jezierski, "Neighborhood and Public-Private Partnerships in Pittsburgh," *Urban Affairs Quarterly* 26, 2 (December 1990): 217–49; Lubove, *Twentieth-Century Pittsburgh*, vol. 2.

67. Jezierski, "Neighborhood and Public-Private Partnerships in Pittsburgh"; John T. Metzger, "Remaking the Growth Coalition: The Pittsburgh Partnership for Neighborhood Development," *Economic Development Quarterly* 12, 1 (1998): 12–29.

68. Jerry Vondas, "Historic North Side Lures Suburbanites," *Pittsburgh Press*, May 28, 1972.

69. City of Pittsburgh, *1977–1982 Proposed Program, City of Pittsburgh*, 10.

70. Lubove, *Twentieth-Century Pittsburgh*, vol. 2, 46.

71. Ibid., 44.

72. Barbara Davis, ed., *Remaking Cities: Proceedings of the 1988 International Conference in Pittsburgh* (Pittsburgh: Pittsburgh Chapter of the American Institute of Architects, 1988).

73. Sara Gonzalez, "Bilbao and Barcelona 'in Motion': How Urban Regeneration 'Models' Travel and Mutate in the Global Flows of Policy Tourism," *Urban Studies* 48, 7 (May 2011): 1409–10, 1405.

74. Summary information, Pease.

75. Michael Keating, "Commentary: Public-Private Partnerships in the United States from a European Perspective," in *Partnerships in Urban Governance: European and American Experiences*, ed. John Pierre (New York: Palgrave, 1998), 168.

76. James Purdue, "Hamilton Seeks New Balance of Industry, Commerce, Culture," *Globe and Mail*, May 19, 1972.

77. Hamilton and District Chamber of Commerce, *1970 Annual Report* (Hamilton: The Chamber, 1971).

78. Gonzalez, "Bilbao and Barcelona 'in Motion'," 1409.

79. On regional municipalities, see A. F. Burghardt, "The Move from County to Region," in *Steel City: Hamilton and Region*, ed. M. J. Dear, Lloyd George Reeds, and J. J. Drake (Toronto: University of Toronto Press, 1987), 156–69.

80. Ibid., 161–66.

81. Ibid.

82. Ibid., 166.

83. "Regional Study a Must to Hold Industry: Chamber," *Hamilton Spectator*, February 26, 1975.

84. "Mayor's One-Man Developing Show Is No Smash Hit," *Hamilton Spectator*, November 13, 1974.

85. Neil Bradford, "Public-Private Partnership? Shifting Paradigms of Economic Governance in Ontario," *Canadian Journal of Political Science* 36, 5 (2003): 1008.

86. Ibid., 1014. DREE-Toronto, "The Economic Development Strategy of the Ontario Government," May 25, 1981, File 101-1-8 Pt. 1, box 3, Files of the Deputy Minister, DRIE.

87. Ontario Economic Council, Press Release—Intergovernmental Relations, Toronto, April 14, 1977, RG 34-5-0-2 file, box 2, RG 34-5, OEC.

88. Ontario: Situation Analysis Report," ca. 1976, 2–3, 7, File 1410-3, Part 2, Vol. 153, MSUA.

89. Ibid., 7.

90. Ibid., 9.

91. J. B. Cullingworth, *Urban and Regional Planning in Canada* (New Brunswick, N.J.: Transaction, 1987), 42.

92. Donald J. Savoie, "The Toppling of DREE and Prospects for Regional Economic Development," *Canadian Public Policy* 10, 3 (1984): 330.

93. Herman Bakvis, "Regional Ministers, National Policies and the Administrative State in Canada: The Regional Dimension in Cabinet Decision-Making," *Canadian Journal of Political Science* 21, 3 (September 1988): 550–53.

94. "Stronger Voice Urged by New Chamber Head," *Hamilton Spectator*, March 4, 1975.

95. Planning and Development Department, *Economic Base: A Substudy of the Regional Official Plan* (Hamilton: Regional Municipality of Hamilton-Wentworth, 1978), 9.

96. Planning and Development Department, *Industrial Official Plan* (Hamilton: Regional Municipality of Hamilton-Wentworth, 1978), 16, 65.

97. Woods, Gordon & Co., *Hamilton-Wentworth Steel and Related Industries Substudy: Final Report* (Toronto: Woods, Gordon & Co., 1977), 9, 32.

98. Planning and Development Department and the Central Area Plan Advisory Committee, *Central Area Plan for the City of Hamilton* (Hamilton: Regional Municipality of Hamilton-Wentworth, 1981), 1.

99. Ibid., 8.

100. Planning and Development Department, *City of Hamilton Official Plan* (Hamilton: Regional Municipality of Hamilton-Wentworth, 1980), 55.

101. Joel Garreau, "The Nine Nations of North America," *Washington Post*, March 4, 1979.

102. Robert Magnuson and Larry Green, "The Best of Times, the Worst of Times," *Pittsburgh Press*, November 8, 1980.

103. Alan Toulin, "Hamilton-Wentworth Is Optimistic for the Future," *Hamilton Spectator*, December 11, 1980.

Chapter 3. Postindustrialism and Its Critics

1. Tri-State Conference on the Impact of Steel, "United States Steel Corporation 1980: Counter Annual Report," 1981, box 25, literature distributed by Tri-State, 1979–1984, Tri-State.

2. Bill Toland, "In Desperate 1983, There Was Nowhere for Pittsburgh's Economy to Go But Up," *Pittsburgh Post-Gazette*, December 23, 2012.

3. Frank Giarratani and David B. Houston, "Structural Change and Economic Policy in a Declining Metropolitan Region: Implications of the Pittsburgh Experience," *Urban Studies* 26 (1989): 549–58.

4. W. P. Anderson, "The Hamilton Steel Industry," in *Steel City: Hamilton and Region*, ed. M. J. Dear, Lloyd George Reed, and J. J. Drake (Toronto: University of Toronto Press, 1987), 210.

5. "Union Lays Off Staff," *Hamilton Spectator*, January 7, 1983.

6. Anthony C. Masi, "Structural Adjustment and Technological Change in the Canadian Steel Industry, 1970–1986," in *The New Era of Global Competition: State Policy and Market Power*, ed. Daniel Drache and Meric S. Gertler (Montreal: McGill-Queen's University Press, 1991), 190–91; L. Anders Sandberg and John H. Bradbury, "Industrial Restructuring in the Canadian Steel Industry," *Antipode* 20, 2 (1988): 116.

7. Steve Arnold, "1005: Glorious Past, Fear for Future," *Hamilton Spectator*, July 21, 2011.

8. Alan DiGaetano and Elizabeth Strom, "Comparative Urban Governance: An Integrated Approach," *Urban Affairs Review* 38, 3 (January 1, 2003): 356–95; Michael Keating, "Decentralization in Mitterrand's France," *Public Administration* 61, 3 (1983): 237–52.

9. For a brief overview of the decline of industry in European cities from Leipzeig to Torino, see Anne Power, Jörg Plöger, and Astrid Winkler, *Transforming Cities Across Europe: An Interim Report on Problems and Progress*, CASEreport (London: LSE, March 2008), 8–11. For detailed case studies of England, France, Wales, and Germany, see Ray Hudson and David Sadler, *The International Steel Industry: Restructuring, State Policies, and Localities* (New York: Routledge, 1989); Alistair Cole and Peter John, *Local Governance in England and France* (London: Routledge, 2001); Philip Cooke, ed., *Rise of the Rustbelt: Revitalizing Older Industrial Regions* (London: Routledge, 1995); Anthony P. D'Costa, *The Global Restructuring of the Steel Industry: Innovations, Institutions and Industrial Change* (New York: Routledge, 1999); Gert-Jan Hospers, "Restructuring Europe's Rustbelt: The Case of the German Ruhrgebeit," *Intereconomics* 39, 3 (2004): 147–56.

10. John Vinocur, "French Steel Town Tells Its Story with an SOS," *New York Times*, October 8, 1982.

11. In addition to her position at the University of Chicago, Pastora San Juan Cafferty had previously worked with HUD, the U.S. Department of Transportation, and the Chicago Transit Authority. Her research on race and ethnicity in cities led her frequently dissent from the panel's anti-urban, Sunbelt-focused, market-oriented recommendations. The other panels were science and technology; promises and dangers; the United States and the world community; government and regulation of corporate and individual decisions; government and the advancement of social justice; health, welfare, and civil rights; energy, national resources, and the environment; the electoral and democratic process; the American economy; employment, productivity, and inflation; and the quality of American life.

12. Panel on Policies and Prospects for Metropolitan and Nonmetropolitan America, *Urban America in the Eighties: Perspectives and Prospects* (Washington, D.C.: President's Commission for a National Agenda for the Eighties, 1980), 13, 24.

13. "UA Presidents and Chancellors: Charles Edwin Bishop University of Arkansas," Office of the Chancellor, 1974–1990, accessed December 12, 2015, http://chancellor.uark.edu/presidents-chancellors/bishop.php; "Charles Edwin Bishop (Death Notice)," *News & Observer*, January 17, 2012; Charles E. Bishop, "Underemployment of Labor in Agriculture in the Southern United States," Ph.D. dissertation, University of Chicago, 1952.

14. Robert Pear, "Panel on Goals Proposes U.S. Aid for Migration to Sunbelt," *The New York Times*, December 27, 1980; Clyde Haberman, "Koch's Office Criticizes the Idea of U.S. Aid in Moves to Sun Belt," *New York Times*, December 29, 1980.

15. Jimmy Carter, "President's Commission for a National Agenda for the Eighties Statement on Receiving the Commission's Final Report," January 16, 1981.

16. Roger Biles, *The Fate of Cities: Urban America and the Federal Government, 1945–2000* (Lawrence: University Press of Kansas, 2011), 283–84.

17. Timothy J. Conlan, "The Politics of Federal Block Grants: From Nixon to Reagan," *Political Science Quarterly* 99, 2 (Summer 1984): 260–64.

18. F. J. James, "President Carter's Comprehensive National Urban Policy: Achievements and Lessons Learned," *Environment and Planning C: Government and Policy* 8 (1990): 38.

19. Ronald Reagan, "Message to the Congress Transmitting Proposed Enterprise Zone Legislation," March 23, 1982, *American Presidency Project*, http://www.presidency.ucsb.edu.

20. Biles, *The Fate of Cities*, 325–30; Karen Mossberger, *The Politics of Ideas and the Spread of Enterprise Zones* (Washington, D.C.: Georgetown University Press, 2000).

21. Geoffrey Hale, *Uneasy Partnership: The Politics of Business and Government in Canada* (Toronto: Broadview, 2006), 21, 26.

22. See Kim Phillips-Fein, *Invisible Hands: The Making of the Conservative Movement from the New Deal to Reagan* (New York: Norton, 2009).

23. Hale, *Uneasy Partnership*, 26.

24. Ibid., 88.

25. William K. Carroll and Murray Shaw, "Consolidating a Neoliberal Policy Bloc in Canada, 1976 to 1996," *Canadian Public Policy* 27, 2 (June 2001): 197; Hale, *Uneasy Partnership*, 150–51; Gregory J. Inwood, *Continentalizing Canada: The Politics and Legacy of the MacDonald Royal Commission* (Toronto: University of Toronto Press, 2005), 33; Stephen McBride, *Paradigm Shift: Globalization and the Canadian State* (Halifax: Fernwood, 2005), 44–45.

26. Hale, *Uneasy Partnership*, 151.

27. Simon Enoch, "Changing the Ideological Fabric? A Brief History of (Canadian) Neoliberalism," *State of Nature: An Online Journal of Radical Ideas*, October 16, 2007, http://www.stateofnature.org/?p=6217; Inwood, *Continentalizing Canada*, chap. 10.

28. Inwood, *Continentalizing Canada*, 6–7, 98, 119, 139.

29. Ibid., 8, 83, 114.

30. Lorraine Eden and Maureen Appel Molot, "Canada's National Policies: Reflections on 125 Years," *Canadian Public Policy* 19, 3 (1993): 241.

31. Inwood, *Continentalizing Canada*, 9.

32. Richard Simeon and Ian Robinson, *State, Society, and the Development of Canadian Federalism* (Toronto: University of Toronto Press, 1990), 301–2.

33. Inwood, *Continentalizing Canada*, 322; Simeon and Robinson, *Development of Canadian Federalism*, 301–2.

34. Ross H. Munro, Jamie Murphy, and Frederick Ungeheur, "Canada: Hanging Out the Welcome Sign," *Time*, December 24, 1984.

35. Briefing Notes, Ontario Chamber of Commerce Brief to Cabinet, December 7, 1983, Ontario Chamber of Commerce: Presentation of Brief to Cabinet file, box 5, RG 9-88, IPB.

36. Simeon and Robinson, *Development of Canadian Federalism*, 267.

37. Neil Bradford, "Public-Private Partnership? Shifting Paradigms of Economic Governance in Ontario," *Canadian Journal of Political Science* 36, 5 (2003): 1008.

38. Elayne Rapping, "Irate in the Iron City," *Guardian*, April 20, 1983; Steven R. Weisman, "Reagan Jeered by 4,000 Protesters on Visit to Pittsburgh Job Forum," *New York Times*, April 7, 1983; Dale A. Hathaway, *Can Workers Have a Voice? The Politics of Deindustrialization in Pittsburgh* (University Park: Pennsylvania State University Press, 1993), 140.

39. Rapping, "Irate in the Iron City."

40. Quoted in Hathaway, *Can Workers Have a Voice?*, 98.

41. United States Steel, *1979 Annual Report* (Pittsburgh: U.S. Steel Corporation, 1980), 9–11.

42. Hathaway, *Can Workers Have a Voice?*, 94–98.

43. David Roderick, interview by Michael Snow, transcript, March 16, 1999, SLGA.

44. Gregory J. Crowley, *The Politics of Place: Contentious Urban Redevelopment in Pittsburgh* (Pittsburgh: University of Pittsburgh Press, 2005), 91.

45. Mike Stout, "Eminent Domain and Bank Boycotts: The Tri-State Strategy in Pittsburgh," *Labor Research Review* 1, 3 (Summer 1983): 15.

46. William Wylie, "Mellon Bank Defends Foreign Loan Policy," *Pittsburgh Press*, June 11, 1983; Mark Potts, "Pittsburgh's Mellon Bank Feels the Heat of Grassroots Rebellion," *Washington Post*, June 12, 1983.

47. Morton Coleman, interview by Michael Snow, transcript, October 27, 1999, SLGA.

48. MILRITE, "Partners in Progress: The Pennsylvania MILRITE Council Three-Year Report" (Harrisburg, Pa.: MILRITE, 1983); Walt Plosila to Rick Stafford, memo re: Background Materials—MILRITE Meeting, August 22, 1980, folder 2, box 306, Governor of Pennsylvania Series, Thornburgh; Gregg E. Robertson and David N. Allen, "From Kites to Computers: Pennsylvania's Ben Franklin Partnership," *Technovation* 4, 1 (1986): 30.

49. Dick Thornburgh, "State Strategies to Improve the Climate for Innovation and Economic Growth," presentation to the Joint Committee of Congress, August 9, 1984, Speeches and Testimony from the Papers of Dick Thornburgh, Pennsylvania Digital Library, University of Pittsburgh.

50. Introductory matter, Thornburgh FA.

51. See David L. Birch, *The Job Generation Process* (Cambridge, Mass.: MIT Program on Neighborhood and Regional Change, 1979); Robertson and Allen, "From Kites to Computers"; Richard Thornburgh, "State Strategies and Incentives for Economic Development," *Journal of Law and Commerce* 1 (1984): 1–17.

52. Harold Miller to Frank Wright and Terry Williamson, memo re: Governor's Remarks to the Pennsylvania Manufacturers' Association, April 21, 1986, folder 6, box 327, Thornburgh.

53. Pittsburgh Regional Planning Association, *Economic Study of the Pittsburgh Region, Vol. 2* (Pittsburgh: University of Pittsburgh Press, 1963), 4; Chet Wade, "How You View Decade May Depend on Whether You Kept or Lost Your Job," *Pittsburgh Post-Gazette*, December 31, 1989.

54. Introductory matter, Thornburgh FA.

55. Pennsylvania State Planning Board, *Choices for Pennsylvanians* (Harrisburg: Commonwealth of Pennsylvania, 1981).

56. Robertson and Allen, "From Kites to Computers," 29.

57. Hillard R. Hoffman, Director, Bureau of Statistics, Research & Planning to Jeffrey Stengel, Jr., Secretary of Commerce, memo re: Advanced Technology Progress Report, 1-14-1982, folder 5, box 233, Thornburgh.

58. Introductory matter, Thornburgh FA.

59. City of Pittsburgh, *Comprehensive Six-Year Development Program* (Pittsburgh: Office of the Mayor, 1969), 137.

60. On the formation of Tri-State, see Charles McCollester and Mike Stout, "Tri-State Conference on Steel: Ten Years of a Labor-Community Alliance," in *Building Bridges: The Emerging Grassroots Coalition of Labor and Community*, ed. Jeremy Brecher and Tim Costello (New York: Monthly Review Press, 1990), 106–13. On the idea of a community right to industrial property,

see Staughton Lynd, "The Genesis of a Community Right to Industrial Property in Youngstown and Pittsburgh, 1977–1987," *Journal of American History* 74, 3 (December 1987): 926–58.

61. On the origins of and conflict between Tri-State and DMS, see Hathaway, *Can Workers Have a Voice?*, chapters 2–3.

62. Ibid., chapter 3.

63. Ibid., chapter 2.

64. Ibid.

65. A. W. Calder to Thomas Flaherty, May 13, 1983, box 13, Tri-State.

66. Francis B. O'Neil to Thomas Flaherty, May 12, 1983, box 13, Tri-State.

67. Robert Dickey, III, to Thomas Flaherty, May 24, 1983, box 13, Tri-State.

68. Charles W. Parry to Thomas Flaherty, May 15, 1983, box 13, Tri-State.

69. Thomas F. Fought to Thomas Flaherty, May 27, 1983, box 13, Tri-State.

70. Leo R. McDonough, Letter to the Editor, *Pittsburgh Post Gazette*, May 27, 1983.

71. John W. McGonigle to Thomas Flaherty, May 19, 1983, box 13, Tri-State.

72. Richard Caliguiri to President and Members, City Council, July 5, 1983, box 13, Tri-State.

73. "Pittsburgh's Law Curbing Plan Closings is Upset," *New York Times*, August 21, 1983; Kevin C. Forsythe, "National, State and Local Perspectives on the Regulation of Business Dislocations: Smaller Manufacturers Council v. City of Pittsburgh," *University of Pittsburgh Law Review* 45 (1984): 439–79.

74. Slide Show Scrip[t], box 32, Tri-State.

75. Ibid.

76. Carol Hymowitz, "Mellon Bank Embarrassed in USW Protest," *Wall Street Journal*, June 10, 1983.

77. Potts, "Pittsburgh's Mellon Bank Feels the Heat of Grassroots Rebellion."

78. Hymowitz, "Mellon Bank Embarrassed in USW Protest."

79. Potts, "Pittsburgh's Mellon Bank Feels the Heat of Grassroots Rebellion."

80. Ken Fisher, "Big Stink: Mon Network Spreads Skunk Oil in Stores," *Pittsburgh Post-Gazette*, November 24, 1984.

81. William Robbins, "Bank and U.S. Steel Targets of Pittsburgh Protest," *New York Times*, July 23, 1984.

82. DMS, "An Open Letter to David Roderick, Chairman, United States Steel; J. David Barnes, Chairman, Mellon Bank," ca. 1984, Network to Save the Mon/Ohio Valley Documents 1983–1984 folder, box 1, DMS.

83. Barbara Hafer, interview by Michael Snow, transcript, April 25, 2000, SLGA. Hafer was a county commissioner with Tom Foerster in the 1980s. Philadelphia had success with a similar coordination effort, which is where Tom Murphy got the idea; both Foerster, the dominant force on the county commission, and Caliguiri had excellent relationships with the ACCD, but could not stand each other and had great difficulty working together on development initiatives.

84. University of Pittsburgh, *Recommendations for Southwestern Pennsylvania's Development Strategy for the 1980s and 1990s* (Pittsburgh: University of Pittsburgh Chancellor's Conference, June 1983); Allegheny Conference on Community Development, *A Strategy for Growth: An Economic Development Program for the Pittsburgh Region* (Pittsburgh: Allegheny Conference on Community Development, 1984).

85. Roy Lubove, *Twentieth-Century Pittsburgh*, vol. 2, *The Post-Steel Era* (Pittsburgh: University of Pittsburgh Press, 1996), 50–52, 67.

86. City of Pittsburgh, Allegheny County, the University of Pittsburgh, and Carnegie Mellon University, "Strategy 21: Pittsburgh/Allegheny Economic Development Strategy to Begin the 21st Century," proposal to the Commonwealth of Pennsylvania (Pittsburgh, June 1985).

87. Ibid.

88. Hathaway, *Can Workers Have a Voice?*, 107.

89. Coleman interview.

90. "Richard S. Caliguiri Dies at 56 in 3d Term as Pittsburgh Mayor," *New York Times*, May 7, 1988.

91. Bob Gradek, *The Root of Pittsburgh's Population Drain* (Pittsburgh: Carnegie Mellon University Center for Economic Development, November 2003), 1.

92. Wade, "How You View Decade May Depend on Whether You Kept or Lost Your Job."

93. Planning and Development Department, *City of Hamilton Official Plan* (Hamilton: Regional Municipality of Hamilton-Wentworth, 1980), 96, 101.

94. Mark Hallman, "Hamilton's Economy Shows Signs of Change," *Hamilton Spectator*, February 11, 1984.

95. Planning and Development Department, *City of Hamilton Official Plan*, 103–4.

96. Industry and Trade Analysis Branch, "Discussion Paper for an Industrial Development Policy for Ontario," May 1979, p. 3, box 3C, IPB.

97. DREE-Toronto, "The Economic Development Strategy of the Ontario Government," May 25, 1981, p. 1, 101-1-8 Pt. 1 file, box 3, Files of the Deputy Minister, DRIE.

98. Board of Industrial Leadership and Development, Building Ontario in the 1980s (Ottawa, January 27, 1981), 45, RG 9-85, box 1, Archives of Ontario. See also, "Economic Development Strategy of the Ontario Government," May 25, 1981, 2, DRIE.

99. Claire Hoy, *Bill Davis: A Biography* (Toronto: Methuen, 1985).

100. Robert MacDermid and Greg Albo, "Divided Province, Growing Protests: Ontario Moves Right," in *The Provincial State in Canada: Politics in the Provinces and Territories*, ed. Keith Brownsey and Michael Howlett (Peterborough, Ont.: Broadview Press, 2001), 175.

101. "Economic Development Strategy of the Ontario Government," May 25, 1981, 4, 12–13, DRIE.

102. Ibid., 12–13.

103. William G. Davis, "Ontario Takes Up the Challenge," paper presented at "Ontario and Canada: A Strategic Perspective," Toronto, February 25–26, 1981, Minister's Speeches file, box 1, IGP.

104. Hamilton-Wentworth Economic Development Department, *1981 Annual Report* (Hamilton: Regional Municipality of Hamilton-Wentworth, 1982), 2–4.

105. Ibid., 17.

106. Mike Pettapiece, "1005 Pushes for Nationalist Union Stand," *Hamilton Spectator*, May 30, 1984; Larry Moko, "Steelworkers Will Follow UAW Lead: Taylor," *Hamilton Spectator*, December 11, 1984; Michael Davie, "Stabbed in the Back: U.S. Petition Angers Local 1005 Members," *Hamilton Spectator*, May 11, 1993.

107. Pettapiece, "1005 Pushes for Nationalist Union Stand"; "U.S. Concessions Don't Pressure Us, Says Taylor," *Hamilton Spectator*, March 2, 1983.

108. Alan Toulin, "Chamber Putting Focus on Downtown," *Hamilton Spectator*, March 24, 1981.

109. "McCulloch Is Talkin' Proud About Businessmen's Blitz," *Hamilton Spectator*, June 2, 1982.

110. Ibid.

111. Max Wickens, Brian Christmas, and Paul Mitchell, "Another Nail in the Coffin," *Hamilton Spectator*, July 16, 1982.

112. Paul Mitchell, "The Pittsburgh Solution," *Hamilton Spectator*, September 4, 1982.

113. Ibid.

114. Hamilton-Wentworth Economic Development Department, *1983 Annual Report* (Hamilton: Regional Municipality of Hamilton-Wentworth, 1984), 1.

115. Mike Pettapiece, "The Hit List of the Recession Leaves Failures in its Wake," *Hamilton Spectator*, October 4, 1983.

116. Hamilton-Wentworth Economic Development Department, *1983 Annual Report*.

117. Florence Sicoli, "Promises, Talk Fail to Halt City's Loss of Jobs," *Hamilton Spectator*, August 3, 1985; Peter George, "Pushing Growth: Four Steps to Boost the Hamilton Area Economy," *Hamilton Spectator*, October 18, 1984.

118. Sicoli, "Promises, Talk Fail to Halt City's Loss of Jobs."

119. George, "Pushing Growth."

120. Paul Mitchell, "Businesses Can Do More, Says Murray," *Hamilton Spectator*, April 3, 1984.

121. Jerry Rogers, "Back from the Edge and Flying High: Hamilton Economy Shows Major Surge," *Hamilton Spectator*, October 24, 1986; Jerry Rogers, "Entrepreneurs," *Hamilton Spectator*, October 25, 1986; Jerry Rogers, "The Ambitious City: Mayor Says We've Only Just Begun; Critics Warn Bigger Projects Needed," *Hamilton Spectator*, October 29, 1986.

122. The Premier's Council, Executive Summary, n.d. (ca. 1986), Commissions/Councils, Premier's Council General file, box 1, RG 9-185, Ministry of Economic Development, TTPP.

123. Ministry of Industry, Trade and Technology, Speech from the Throne, n.d. (ca. 1986), 1, Commissions/Councils—Premier's Council General file, box 1, TTPP.

124. Speech from the Throne, n.d. (ca. 1986), 1, 3.

Chapter 4. The New Geography of Downtown

1. Robert McLean, *Countdown to Renaissance II: The New Way Corporate America Builds* (Pittsburgh: Urban Marketing Associates, 1984), cover flap and introduction.

2. William F. Buckley, Jr., "Foreword," to McLean, *Countdown to Renaissance II*, 3.

3. Carl Abbott, "Five Downtown Strategies: Policy Discourse and Downtown Planning Since 1945," *Journal of Policy History* 5, 1 (1993): 7.

4. Ibid., 7, 10–15.

5. See Bernard J. Frieden, *Downtown, Inc.: How America Rebuilds Cities* (Cambridge, Mass.: MIT Press, 1989); Arnold R. Hirsch, *Making the Second Ghetto: Race and Housing in Chicago, 1940–1960* (New York: Cambridge University Press, 1983); Alison Isenberg, *Downtown America: A History of the Place and the People Who Made It* (Chicago: University of Chicago Press, 2004); Clarence N. Stone, *Regime Politics: Governing Atlanta, 1946–1988* (Lawrence: University Press of Kansas, 1989); Jon C. Teaford, *The Rough Road to Renaissance: Urban Revitalization in America, 1940–1985* (Baltimore: Johns Hopkins University Press, 1990).

6. Abbott, "Five Downtown Strategies," 7, 15–19.

7. "City users" comes from Guido Martinotti, "A City for Whom? Transients and Public Life in the Second-Generation Metropolis," in *The Urban Moment: Cosmopolitan Essays on the Late-20th Century City*, ed. Robert A. Beauregard and Sophie Body-Gendrot (Thousand Oaks, Calif.: Sage, 1999), 155–83.

8. Anne Power, Jörg Plöger, and Astrid Winkler, *Transforming Cities Across Europe: An Interim Report on Problems and Progress*, CASEreport (London: LSE, March 2008), 48.

9. W. G. Peace and A. F. Burghardt, "Hamilton Today," in *Steel City: Hamilton and Region*, ed. M. J. Dear, Lloyd George Reeds, and J. J. Drake (Toronto: University of Toronto Press, 1987), 286–301; Brian Robick, "Blight: The Development of a Contested Concept," Ph.D. dissertation, Carnegie Mellon University, 2011; Margaret Rockwell, "The Facelift and the Wrecking Ball: Urban Renewal and Hamilton's King Street West, 1957–1971," *Urban History Review* 37, 2 (2009): 53–61.

10. Allegheny Conference on Community Development, *1977 Annual Report* (Pittsburgh: The Conference, 1978), 4.

11. Roy Lubove, *Twentieth-Century Pittsburgh*, vol. 2, *The Post-Steel Era* (Pittsburgh: University of Pittsburgh Press, 1996), chap. 9.

12. Department of City Planning, *Downtown Development Strategy: Progress Report* (Pittsburgh: City of Pittsburgh, August 20, 1979).

13. The executive was quoted anonymously. Based on his description of the headquarters building in question, it was likely PPG Industries chairman and CEO Vincent A. Sarni. Roger S. Ahlbrandt and Morton Coleman, *The Role of the Corporation in Community Economic Development as Viewed by 21 Corporate Executives* (Pittsburgh: University of Pittsburgh, January 5, 1987), 17–18.

14. Allegheny Conference on Community Development, *1981 Annual Report* (Pittsburgh: The Conference, 1982), 5.

15. McLean, *Countdown to Renaissance II*, 18.

16. Allegheny Conference on Community Development, *1976 Annual Report* (Pittsburgh: The Conference, 1977), 8.

17. McLean, *Countdown to Renaissance II*, 38.

18. Ibid., 38, 41.

19. City of Pittsburgh, *1977–1982 Proposed Program, City of Pittsburgh* (Pittsburgh: Office of the Mayor, 1976), viii.

20. Allegheny Conference on Community Development, *1981 Annual Report*, 5.

21. "A Proposal for a Joint Public-Private Development Effort," n.d., folder 7, box 37, ACCD.

22. City of Pittsburgh, *1983–1988 Six Year Development Program (Draft)* (Pittsburgh: Office of the Mayor, 1982), 180.

23. Allegheny Conference on Community Development, *1979 Annual Report* (Pittsburgh: The Conference, 1980).

24. David Nilsson, "Progress Building in City's Renaissance II," *Pittsburgh Post*, ca. 1980, folder 14, box 180, ACCD.

25. Ibid., 2.

26. Ibid.

27. David B. Houston, "A Brief History of the Process of Capital Accumulation in Pittsburgh: A Marxist Interpretation," in *Pittsburgh-Sheffield, Sister Cities*, ed. Joel A. Tarr (Pittsburgh: Carnegie Mellon University, 1986), 55.

28. City of Pittsburgh, *1983–1988 Six Year Development Program (Draft)*, 180.

29. Denominational Ministry Strategy, "Explosive: DMS Press Release," June 4, 1985, U.S. Steel folder, box 50, IUMSW.

30. City of Pittsburgh, *1983–1988 Six Year Development Program (Draft)*, 191.

31. Lubove, *Twentieth-Century Pittsburgh*, vol. 2, chapter 9.

242 Notes to Pages 118–122

32. Allegheny Conference on Community Development, *1986 Annual Report* (Pittsburgh: The Conference, 1987), 7.

33. Ibid.

34. Allegheny Conference on Community Development, *1983 Annual Report* (Pittsburgh: The Conference, 1984), 12.

35. Lubove, *Twentieth-Century Pittsburgh*, vol. 2, 198.

36. Allegheny Conference on Community Development, *1986 Annual Report*, 7.

37. City of Pittsburgh, *1987–1992 Six Year Development Program (Draft)* (Pittsburgh: Office of the Mayor, 1986), 1.

38. Lubove, *Twentieth-Century Pittsburgh*, vol. 2, 194–201; Edward K. Muller, "Downtown Pittsburgh: Renaissance and Renewal," in *A Geographic Perspective of Pittsburgh and the Alleghenies*, ed. Kevin J. Patrick and Joseph L. Scarpaci, Jr. (Pittsburgh: University of Pittsburgh Press, 2006), 15–16.

39. Allegheny Conference on Community Development, *1983 Annual Report*, 11; Allegheny Conference on Community Development, *1984 Annual Report* (Pittsburgh: The Conference, 1985), 12.

40. Donald Miller, "An Arts Angel: New Cultural Trust Promotes City as Regional Arts Center," *Pittsburgh Post-Gazette*, October 20, 1984.

41. Town meeting announcement, November 1, 1984, at Clairton Trinity Lutheran Church, folder 9—Documents, 1983–1986: Misc., box 1, Textual Records, DMS.

42. Ahlbrandt and Coleman, *Role of the Corporation in Community Economic Development*, 17. In 1986, Ahlbrandt and Coleman interviewed twenty-one high-ranking executives, most of whom were Allegheny Conference Executive Committee members. At the outset of their report, Ahlbrandt and Coleman identified their interviewees, but all quotes included in the report were done so anonymously. Interviewees included the presidents, CEOs, and/or chairmen of major manufacturing firms (including Alcoa, PPG Industries, Westinghouse, and U.S. Steel), financial institutions, and commercial enterprises; the presidents of Carnegie Mellon and the University of Pittsburgh; and the publisher of the *Pittsburgh Post-Gazette*.

43. City of Pittsburgh, *1987–1992 Six Year Development Program (Draft)*, 1.

44. City of Pittsburgh, *The 1976 Six Year Development Program of the City of Pittsburgh* (Pittsburgh: Office of the Mayor, 1975), vii.

45. Allegheny Conference on Community Development, *1978 Annual Report* (Pittsburgh: The Conference, 1979), 12.

46. City of Pittsburgh, *Comprehensive Six-Year Development Program* (Pittsburgh: Office of the Mayor, 1970).

47. David Nilsson, "Progress Building in City's Renaissance II," *Pittsburgh Post*, ca. 1980, folder 14, box 180, Allegheny Conference Records.

48. Gregory J. Crowley, *The Politics of Place: Contentious Urban Redevelopment in Pittsburgh* (Pittsburgh: University of Pittsburgh Press, 2005), 104.

49. Lubove, *Twentieth-Century Pittsburgh*, vol. 2, 218–19.

50. Crowley, *The Politics of Place*, 104.

51. The characterization was largely accurate, although a few dozen wholesalers remained active in the Strip District. City of Pittsburgh, *1978–1983 Six Year Development Program* (Pittsburgh: Office of the Mayor, 1977), 99.

52. Nilsson, "Progress Building in City's Renaissance II."

53. Ibid.

54. Mayor's Task Force on the Reuse of Downtown Buildings, "A Report," December 17, 1979, folder 1, box 8, ACCD.

55. McLean, *Countdown to Renaissance II*, 94.

56. David Morris and Peter Kelly, "Men of Steel Wage Guerrilla War for Survival," *Harrisburg Sunday Patriot*, October 21, 1984.

57. Charles J. McCollester, letter to the editor, *Pittsburgh Catholic*, January 9, 1981, 6.

58. John Robin, interview by Michael Snow, transcript, October 6, 1998, SLGA.

59. Victor Copps, quoted in John C. Weaver, *Hamilton: An Illustrated History* (Halifax: J. Lorimer, 1982), 191.

60. E. G. Faludi, *A Master Plan for the Development of the City of Hamilton* (Toronto: Town Planning Consultants, 1947), 40.

61. Hamilton Downtown Association, *Enrich Our Leisure Hours: Presentation to Vic Copps and Members of the Hamilton City Council* (Hamilton: Hamilton Downtown Association, June 1963).

62. Robick, "Blight: The Development of a Contested Concept," 312.

63. City of Hamilton Planning Department, *City of Hamilton General Background Information* (Hamilton: City of Hamilton, 1971), 22; Rockwell, "The Facelift and the Wrecking Ball," 54.

64. Hamilton Planning Department, *1968 Annual Report* (Hamilton: City of Hamilton, 1969), 5–6.

65. Arthur D. Little, Inc., *Commercial Development in Hamilton: A Report to the Hamilton Economic Development Commission* (Boston: Arthur D. Little, Inc., 1968), 1.

66. Ibid., 73.

67. Ibid., 13, 73, 89.

68. Ibid., 89.

69. James Carr, "A Solid Foundation for a Rosy Future," *Hamilton Spectator*, January 22, 1968.

70. "Goodbye, Stelco," *Hamilton Spectator*, November 1, 1968.

71. "A Telegram from the Hon. John Munro," *Hamilton Spectator*, November 1, 1968.

72. "Goodbye, Stelco."

73. James Carr, "Stelco Head Office to Toronto," *Hamilton Spectator*, November 1, 1968.

74. "Stelco Move in Hamilton Called Bigger Step than Toronto Plan," *Globe and Mail*, November 5, 1968.

75. "How Our Downtown Core Will Take Shape," *Hamilton Spectator*, September 12, 1970.

76. Ibid.

77. Ibid.

78. Weaver, *Hamilton*, 179.

79. Rockwell, "The Facelift and the Wrecking Ball," 53–54.

80. Ibid., 59. See also Kenneth B. Smith, "Hamilton Square Without Square a Heartache for Some Residents," *Hamilton Spectator*, May 6, 1969; Jane Coutts, "They're Remembering a Fighter," *Hamilton Spectator*, October 17, 1988.

81. Smith, "Hamilton Square Without Square a Heartache for Some Residents."

82. Ibid.

83. Hamilton and District Chamber of Commerce, *1968 Annual Report* (Hamilton: The Chamber, 1969).

84. Hamilton and District Chamber of Commerce, *1969 Annual Report* (Hamilton: The Chamber, 1970).

Notes to Pages 131–141

85. Hamilton and District Chamber of Commerce, *1970 Annual Report* (Hamilton: The Chamber, 1971).

86. Hamilton Planning Department, *Human Dimension in Downtown Hamilton* (Hamilton: City of Hamilton, 1974), 9–10.

87. Planning and Development Department and the Central Area Plan Advisory Committee, *Central Area Plan for the City of Hamilton* (Hamilton: Regional Municipality of Hamilton-Wentworth, 1981), 8–9.

88. Ibid., 13.

89. Arthur D. Little, Inc., *Commercial Development in Hamilton*, 75.

90. Planning and Development Department and the Central Area Plan Advisory Committee, *Central Area Plan*, 16–19.

91. Ibid., 13.

92. Ana María Guasch and Joseba Zulaika, *Learning from the Bilbao Guggenheim* (Reno: Center for Basque Studies, University of Nevada, Reno, 2005); John McCarthy and S. H. Alan Pollock, "Urban Regeneration in Glasgow and Dundee: A Comparative Evaluation," *Land Use Policy* 14, 2 (1997): 141–42; Peter Shapely, "Governance in the Post-War City: Historical Reflections on Public-Private Partnerships in the UK," *International Journal of Urban and Regional Research* 37, 4 (2013): 1288–1304.

Chapter 5. Spaces of Production and Spaces of Consumption

1. Tom Coleman, "A Paper Dream? An Unfulfilled Promise? Or Will the North End Regain Its Glory?" *Hamilton Spectator*, July 29, 1969.

2. Ibid.

3. Mark Hallman, "Funds in City's North-End Buy-Up Program Running Low," *Hamilton Spectator*, September 12, 1985.

4. Joyce Gannon, "South Side Experiencing Renaissance," *Pittsburgh Business Times*, March 5–11, 1984.

5. On immigration to Pittsburgh, see Nora Faires, "Immigrants and Industry: Peopling the 'Iron City,'" in *City at the Point: Essays on the Social History of Pittsburgh*, ed. Samuel P. Hayes (Pittsburgh: University of Pittsburgh Press, 1989), 3–32.

6. Hazelwood's population decreased by 58 percent and the South Side's by 54 percent, while the City of Pittsburgh as a whole decreased by 45 percent over the same period. Between 1990 and 2000, however, the rate of the South Side's population loss slowed dramatically, putting it at a pace with the city as a whole, with a net loss of 9.5 percent. Hazelwood's population loss, likely due to its more recent plant closure, was nearly double that rate at 17 percent. Campbell Gibson, "Population of the 100 Largest Cities and Other Urban Places in the United States: 1790–1990," Population Division Working Paper 27 (Washington, D.C.: U.S. Census Bureau, 1998); Department of City Planning, "Census 2000: Pittsburgh" (Pittsburgh: City of Pittsburgh, 2006).

7. The 1970 census showed that the white population declined by 33 percent between 1950 and 1970, while the African American population increased 31 percent, to 12 percent of neighborhood population. Bureau of the Census, *Decennial Census of Population and Housing* (Washington, D.C., 1970).

8. South Side Local Development Corporation, *The South Side Works: A Community-Based Planning Evaluation* (Pittsburgh: SSLDC, April 15, 1992), xi.

9. Roy Lubove, *Twentieth-Century Pittsburgh*, vol. 2, *The Post-Steel Era* (Pittsburgh: University of Pittsburgh Press, 1996).

10. City of Pittsburgh, *1978–1983 Six Year Development Program* (Pittsburgh: Office of the Mayor, 1977); City of Pittsburgh, *1988–1993 Six Year Development Program (Draft)* (Pittsburgh: Office of the Mayor, 1987).

11. City of Pittsburgh, *1982–1987 Six Year Development Program (Draft)* (Pittsburgh: Office of the Mayor, 1981).

12. Lubove, *Twentieth-Century Pittsburgh*, vol. 2, 142.

13. City of Pittsburgh, *1978–1983 Six Year Development Program*.

14. City of Pittsburgh, *1977–1982 Proposed Program, City of Pittsburgh* (Pittsburgh: Office of the Mayor, 1976).

15. On neighborhood activism and CDCs in Pittsburgh, see Gregory J. Crowley, *The Politics of Place: Contentious Urban Redevelopment in Pittsburgh* (Pittsburgh: University of Pittsburgh Press, 2005); Louise Jezierski, "Neighborhood and Public-Private Partnerships in Pittsburgh," *Urban Affairs Quarterly* 26, 2 (December 1990): 217–49; Lubove, *Twentieth-Century Pittsburgh*, vol. 2, chapters 5–7; John T. Metzger, "Remaking the Growth Coalition: The Pittsburgh Partnership for Neighborhood Development," *Economic Development Quarterly* 12, 1 (1998): 12–29; Shelby Stewman and Joel A. Tarr, "Public-Private Partnerships in Pittsburgh: A Study in Urban Government," in *Pittsburgh-Sheffield, Sister Cities*, ed. Joel A. Tarr (Pittsburgh: Carnegie Mellon University, 1986), 141–82.

16. Pete Flaherty, interview by Michael Snow, transcript, March 9, 1999, SLGA.

17. Jezierski, "Neighborhood and Public-Private Partnerships in Pittsburgh"; Lubove, *Twentieth-Century Pittsburgh*, vol. 2, chapters 5–7; Metzger, "Remaking the Growth Coalition"; Tracy Neumann, "Privatization, Devolution, and Jimmy Carter's National Urban Policy," *Journal of Urban History* 40, 2 (March 1, 2014): 283–300.

18. City of Pittsburgh, *1978–1983 Six Year Development Program*, 9–10.

19. South Side Chamber of Commerce, "Chamber History," www.southsidechamber.org, accessed November 17, 2011.

20. Tom Barnes, "Main St. USA? On South Side," *Pittsburgh Post-Gazette*, April 29, 1996.

21. Gannon, "South Side Experiencing Renaissance."

22. Ibid.

23. Lubove, *Twentieth-Century Pittsburgh*, vol. 2, 144.

24. South Side Local Development Corporation, *The South Side Works*, 4–5.

25. Donald I. Hammonds, "South Side Planners Aim to Blend Best of Old with New," *Pittsburgh Post-Gazette*, November 28, 1985.

26. Brochure, "Making Steel Again on the South Side!" n.d., box 24, Tri-State; Lubove, *Twentieth-Century Pittsburgh*, vol. 2, 149; South Side Local Development Corporation, *The South Side Works*.

27. Charles McCollester and Mike Stout, "Tri-State Conference on Steel: Ten Years of a Labor-Community Alliance," in *Building Bridges: The Emerging Grassroots Coalition of Labor and Community*, ed. Jeremy Brecher and Tim Costello (New York: Monthly Review Press, 1990), 108–9.

28. Reps. Tom Micholovic, Mike Dawida, Dave Levdansky, Tom Murphy, Ron Cowell, and Steve Seventy, Pennsylvania House to Linda Taliaferro, Chairman, Pennsylvania Public Utility Commission, March 18, 1987, Steel Retention Study folder, box 1, Tri-State.

29. McCollester and Stout, "Tri-State Conference on Steel."

30. Allegheny County Department of Planning, *Steel Retention Study—Executive Summary* (Pittsburgh: Allegheny County, February 1988); South Side Local Development Corporation, *The South Side Works*, xi.

31. McCollester and Stout, "Tri-State Conference on Steel," 110.

32. Brochure, "Making Steel Again on the South Side!"

33. Annmarie Draham, "Rekindling the Fires," *In Pittsburgh*, April 22–28, 1987; Margie Romero, "Eve of Destruction," *In Pittsburgh*, ca. 1988, Industrial Museums folder, box 53, Tri-State.

34. McCollester and Stout, "Tri-State Conference on Steel," 108–10.

35. Ibid.

36. Dale A. Hathaway, *Can Workers Have a Voice? The Politics of Deindustrialization in Pittsburgh* (University Park: Pennsylvania State University Press, 1993), 111–12.

37. Lubove, *Twentieth-Century Pittsburgh*, vol. 2, 147.

38. South Side Local Development Corporation, *The South Side Works*, i.

39. Letter of transmittal for SSLDC South Side Works report, quoted in Lubove, *Twentieth-Century Pittsburgh*, vol. 2, 147.

40. Flora's comment was in the context of the possible construction of a warehouse and maintenance facility near Seventeenth Street.

41. South Side Local Development Corporation, *The South Side Works*, v, 27, 31–33, 37.

42. Joyce Gannon, "Controlling Influence," *Pittsburgh Post-Gazette*, March 6, 1994.

43. Suzanne Elliott, "Development Group, Soffer, Work to Blend SouthSide Works into Neighborhood," *Pittsburgh Business Times*, February 14, 2003.

44. Chris Swaney, "Redevelopment Advances on Pittsburgh's Waterfront," *New York Times*, March 17, 2002.

45. Ruth Walker, "A Retail Lease on Life in Germany's 'Rust Belt,'" *Christian Science Monitor*, December 11, 1996.

46. Charles M. Unkovic, *Hazelwood Neighborhood Survey* (Pittsburgh: Duquesne University, 1962).

47. Jeffrey Fraser, "Philanthropic Field," *H Magazine* 4, 4 (Fall 2004): 24.

48. Pete Flaherty interview, March 9, 1999.

49. City of Pittsburgh, *1977–1982 Proposed Program, City of Pittsburgh*; City of Pittsburgh, *1982–1987 Six Year Development Program (Draft)*.

50. City of Pittsburgh, *1977–1982 Proposed Program, City of Pittsburgh*; City of Pittsburgh, *1982–1987 Six Year Development Program (Draft)*.

51. City of Pittsburgh, Allegheny County, the University of Pittsburgh, and Carnegie Mellon University, "Strategy 21: Pittsburgh/Allegheny Economic Development Strategy to Begin the 21st Century," Proposal to the Commonwealth of Pennsylvania (Pittsburgh, June 1985)

52. Joyce Gannon, "New Owner to Resurrect Strip Mill," *Pittsburgh Business Times*, April 16–22, 1984; Joyce Gannon, "City Hopes to Transform Mill into High Technology Park," n.d., LTV/J&L Early Information, 1970s–1980s folder, box 18, Tri-State.

53. Barbara Davis, ed., *Remaking Cities: Proceedings of the 1988 International Conference in Pittsburgh* (Pittsburgh: Pittsburgh Chapter of the American Institute of Architects, 1988), 64–68.

54. "A Park for High Tech," *Pittsburgh Post-Gazette*, November 2, 1984.

55. R. C. Longworth, "Software Stepping in Where Steel Left Off," *Chicago Tribune*, August 18, 1985.

56. Ibid.

57. "A Phoenix Rising," *Pittsburgh Post-Gazette*, October 13, 1986.

58. Press release, October 10, 1986, FF1—Economic Development, memoranda, news releases, correspondence, clippings 1984–1986–, box 327, Thornburgh.

59. "Editorial: Better with Coke," *Pittsburgh Post-Gazette*, July 17, 1998.

60. Jan Ackerman, "Farewell to the City's Last Big Steel Plant," *Pittsburgh Post-Gazette*, July 12, 1999.

61. Cindi Lash, "Neighbors, City Clash at Forum on Coke Plant," *Pittsburgh Post-Gazette*, August 6, 1998.

62. Ibid.

63. "Editorial: Closing, not Closure," *Pittsburgh Post-Gazette*, February 18, 1998.

64. "Editorial: Better with Coke."

65. Ackerman, "Farewell to the City's Last Big Steel Plant."

66. On citizen participation in Canada, see Tom Coleman, "A Paper Dream?"

67. Garry Smith, "People Power Planning: Hamilton's Official Plan Is Losing Ground to Neighborhoods," *Hamilton Spectator*, April 17, 1973.

68. "Area Plan Project Unique in Canada," *Hamilton Spectator*, May 16, 1972; "People Do the Planning," *Hamilton Spectator*, June 29, 1973.

69. Garry Smith, "People Power Planning."

70. "Planning No Longer Joke, It's Top Job," *Hamilton Spectator*, January 13, 1973.

71. "Residents Protest Industrial Area Plan," *Hamilton Spectator*, November 25, 1971.

72. "Beach Strip Residents Fear Deal," *Hamilton Spectator*, November 13, 1971.

73. Paul Palango, "Industrial Park Fight Upsets Alderman," *Hamilton Spectator*, August 10, 1976.

74. On immigration and early settlement patterns in Hamilton, see Harold A. Wood, "Emergence of the Modern City: Hamilton, 1891–1950," in *Steel City: Hamilton and Region*, ed. M. J. Dear, Lloyd George Reeds, and J. J. Drake (Toronto: University of Toronto Press, 1987), 119–37.

75. On the history of the North End urban renewal project, see Brian Robick, "Blight: The Development of a Contested Concept," Ph.D. dissertation, Carnegie Mellon University, 2011, chapter 4. On North End building conditions, see Murray V. Jones and Associates, *North End Urban Renewal Scheme, City of Hamilton, Ontario* (Toronto: Murray V. Jones, 1968), 23, A.29.

76. Murray V. Jones and Associates, *North End Urban Renewal Scheme*.

77. Ibid., 9.

78. Ibid., 3, A.42–A.43.

79. Robick, "Blight: The Development of a Contested Concept," 240–41.

80. Ibid., 243.

81. Coleman, "A Paper Dream?"

82. Robick, "Blight," 243–44.

83. Murray V. Jones and Associates, *North End Urban Renewal Scheme*, A.43–44.

84. Ibid., 17–18.

85. Hamilton Planning Department, *1969 Annual Report* (Hamilton: City of Hamilton, 1970), 17, 31.

86. Murray V. Jones and Associates, *North End Urban Renewal Scheme*, 6, 10, 18.

87. Ibid., 8, 57, 43. See also Coleman, "A Paper Dream?"; John Gibson, "The North End—A Planner's Dream," *Hamilton Spectator*, September 18, 1969; and Jim Travers, "North-End Nightmare," *Hamilton Spectator*, October 15, 1977.

88. Coleman, "A Paper Dream?"

89. Travers, "North-End Nightmare."

90. Coleman, "A Paper Dream?"; "City May Intervene to Get Bay Area Development Land," *Hamilton Spectator*, March 6, 1970.

91. "City May Intervene to Get Bay Area Development Land."

92. Coleman, "A Paper Dream?"

93. Planning and Development Department, *North End Neighborhoods: Household Questionnaire and Survey Report* (Hamilton: Regional Municipality of Hamilton-Wentworth, ca. 1972).

94. Travers, "North-End Nightmare."

95. Ken Campbell, "North-Enders Hit at Urban Renewal," *Hamilton Spectator*, August 29, 1977.

96. Ibid.

97. Travers, "North-End Nightmare."

98. Ibid.

99. Gibson, "The North End—A Planner's Dream."

100. Travers, "North-End Nightmare."

101. Planning and Development Department, *Industrial Official Plan* (Hamilton: Regional Municipality of Hamilton-Wentworth, 1978), 52.

102. Hamilton Planning Department, *1969 Annual Report*, 17–18.

103. Planning and Development Department, *[Draft] Official Plan for Hamilton Harbor* (Hamilton: City of Hamilton, 1976), 24; "City Approves Dofasco Sale," *Hamilton Spectator*, July 29, 1981.

104. Planning and Development Department, *Industrial Official Plan*, 63–64.

105. Ibid., 64.

106. "200 Homes in North End Escape Threat," *Hamilton Spectator*, March 4, 1974.

107. "City Accused of Block-Busting," *Hamilton Spectator*, April 1, 1976.

108. "Residents Need Help in Moving," *Hamilton Spectator*, April 30, 1977.

109. Ibid.

110. "Look at Land-Banking, Alderman Asks," *Hamilton Spectator*, September 27, 1977.

111. Planning and Development Department, *City of Hamilton Official Plan* (Hamilton: Regional Municipality of Hamilton-Wentworth, 1980), 100.

112. Jerry Rogers, "Zone Changes Threaten Us, Firms Tell City," *Hamilton Spectator*, October 12, 1984.

113. Rogers, "Zone Changes Threaten Us, Firms Tell City."

114. Mark Hallman, "Dilemma of Industry Versus People," *Hamilton Spectator*, November 26, 1984.

115. Rogers, "Zone Changes Threaten Us."

116. "Impact Report on Zoning Requested," *Hamilton Spectator*, October 18, 1984; Hallman, "Dilemma of Industry Versus People."

117. Hallman, "Dilemma of Industry Versus People."

118. Tami Paikin Nolan, "Real Solution to Hamilton's North End Is to Move Residents," *Hamilton Spectator*, February 16, 1988.

119. Jane Coutts, "Heavy-Industry Ban Rejected by Council," *Hamilton Spectator*, February 10, 1988.

Chapter 6. Marketing Postindustrialism

1. Rand McNally's ranked cities based on climate, terrain, housing, health care, transportation, education, art and recreation, and economic outlook. "Pittsburgh Rated Most Livable City," *Los Angeles Times*, February 28, 1985.

2. Gary Rotstein, "'Most Livable City' Took Its Lumps over Tag," *Pittsburgh Post-Gazette*, February 27, 2010.

3. Ibid.

4. Paul Mitchell, "The Pittsburgh Solution," *Hamilton Spectator*, September 4, 1982.

5. Stephen Ward, *Selling Places: The Marketing and Promotion of Towns and Cities, 1850–2000* (London: Routledge, 1998), 2.

6. On urban boosterism in the United States since the 1850s, see Carl Abbott, *Boosters and Businessmen: Popular Economic Thought and Urban Growth in the Antebellum Middle West* (Westport, Conn.: Greenwood Press, 1981); Carl Abbott, *How Cities Won the West: Four Centuries of Change in Western North America* (Albuquerque: University of New Mexico Press, 2010); James Charles Cobb, *The Selling of the South: The Southern Crusade for Industrial Development 1936–1990* (Urbana: University of Illinois Press, 1993); John R. Gold and Stephen V. Ward, *Place Promotion: The Use of Publicity and Marketing to Sell Towns and Regions* (New York: Wiley, 1994); John R. Logan and Harvey Molotch, *Urban Fortunes: The Political Economy of Place* (Berkeley: University of California Press, 1987); Gerard Kearns and Chris Philo, *Selling Places: The City as Cultural Capital, Past and Present* (New York: Pergamon, 1993); Bruce J. Schulman, *From Cotton Belt to Sunbelt: Federal Policy, Economic Development, and the Transformation of the South, 1938–1980* (Durham, N.C.: Duke University Press, 1994); Elizabeth Tandy Shermer, *Sunbelt Capitalism: Phoenix and the Transformation of American Politics* (Philadelphia: University of Pennsylvania Press, 2013); and Ward, *Selling Places*. On Pittsburgh in particular, see Laura Grantmyre, "Selling Pittsburgh as America's Renaissance City," *Journal of Urban History* 41 (2015): 5–13.

7. Miriam Greenberg, *Branding New York: How a City in Crisis Was Sold to the World* (New York: Routledge, 2008); Kearns and Philo, *Selling Places*; Ward, *Selling Places*; Sharon Zukin, "Postcard-Perfect: The Big Business of City Branding," *Guardian*, May 6, 2014.

8. Logan and Molotch, *Urban Fortunes*; Eugene McCann, "Policy Boosterism, Policy Mobilities, and the Extrospective City," *Urban Geography* 34, 1 (2013): 6.

9. Greenberg, *Branding New York*, 10; Zukin, "Postcard-Perfect."

10. Greenberg, *Branding New York*. See also David Harvey, *A Brief History of Neoliberalism* (New York: Oxford University Press, 2005).

11. Sociologist Sophie Watson uses the term "gilding the smokestack." Sophie Watson, "Gilding the Smokestacks: The New Symbolic Representations of Deindustrialised Regions," *Environment and Planning D: Society and Space* 9, 1 (1991): 59–70.

12. On Sydney, Australia, see ibid. On other cities, see Andy Pike, *Brands and Branding Geographies* (Cheltenham: Edward Elgar, 2011), 231.

13. Rebecca Madgin and Richard Rodger, "Inspiring Capital? Deconstructing Myths and Reconstructing Urban Environments, Edinburgh, 1860–2010," *Urban History* 40, 3 (August 2013): 507–29.

14. Pike, *Brands and Branding Geographies*, 238–46.

15. Patrick Horsbrugh, interview by Yana R. Owens, January 13, 2009, Lew Clarke Oral Histories collection, North Carolina State University, Raleigh, N.C.

16. Patrick Horsbrugh, "Pride of Place: An Argument in Favor of Visual Diversity in the Urban Scene," paper presented at "The Canadian City: A Symposium," Canadian Federation of Mayors and Municipalities, 1961, 47.

17. Ibid., 45.

18. Patrick Horsbrugh, *Pittsburgh Perceived: A Design Image of Pittsburgh* (Pittsburgh: University of Pittsburgh Center for Regional Economic Studies, February 1964).

19. Ibid., 10.

20. Pittsburgh Regional Planning Association, *Economic Study of the Pittsburgh Region*, vol. 2 (Pittsburgh: University of Pittsburgh Press, 1963); Regional Economic Analysis Policy Group, *Policy Statement Based on the Economic Study of the Pittsburgh Region* (Pittsburgh: Allegheny Conference on Community Development, 1964).

21. Regional Economic Analysis Policy Group, *Policy Statement*, 8.

22. Ibid., 8–9.

23. Ibid., 10.

24. Horsbrugh, *Pittsburgh Perceived: A Design Image of Pittsburgh*, 25–26.

25. On Lorant, see Michael Hallett, *Stefan Lorant: Godfather of Photojournalism* (Lanham, Md.: Scarecrow Press, 2006). On marketing Renaissance I, including the publication of *Pittsburgh*, see Laura Grantmyre, "Selling Pittsburgh as America's Renaissance City," *Journal of Urban History* 41, 1 (January 1, 2015): 5–13.

26. Stefan Lorant, *Pittsburgh: The Story of an American City* (New York: Doubleday, 1964), 6–7.

27. Ibid., chap. 10.

28. Ibid., 388–89.

29. Ibid., 373.

30. *Pivot Point* (Pittsburgh: Duquesne Light Company, 1966).

31. Douglas E. Kneeland, "Pittsburgh: A Brawny City Puts on a Silk Shirt," *New York Times*, October 3, 1970.

32. Ibid.

33. Lawrence Maloney, "Pittsburgh's Old Image Goes onto the Slag Pile," *U.S. News & World Report*, January 12, 1981, 55.

34. Steve Massey, "Jay Aldridge to Leave Penn's Southwest," *Pittsburgh Post-Gazette*, December 19, 1996.

35. Penn's Southwest Association, *1976 Annual Report* (Pittsburgh: The Association, 1977); and *1977 Annual Report* (Pittsburgh: The Association, 1978).

36. Penn's Southwest Association, *1976 Annual Report*, 7.

37. Ibid.

38. John Eyles and Walter Peace, "Signs and Symbols in Hamilton: An Iconology of Steeltown," *Geografiska Annaler. Series B, Human Geography* 72, 2/3 (1990): 75.

39. Quoted in ibid., 73.

40. Arthur D. Little, Inc., *Commercial Development in Hamilton: A Report to the Hamilton Economic Development Commission* (Boston: Arthur D. Little, Inc., 1968), 2, 62–63, 66.

41. Ibid., 2, 72, 78.

42. James Carr, "Business & Finance—Review & Forecast," *Hamilton Spectator*, January 2, 1969.

43. David Proulx, *Pardon My Lunch Bucket* (Hamilton: Corporation of the City of Hamilton, 1972).

44. Ibid.

45. Ibid.

46. Hamilton and District Chamber of Commerce, *Hamilton, Ontario* (Hamilton: Chamber, ca. 1974).

47. Hamilton and District Chamber of Commerce, *Hamilton, Canada: A Place for All Reasons* (Hamilton: The Chamber, ca. 1979); Hamilton and District Chamber of Commerce, *Hamilton: An Adventure in Good Living* (Hamilton: The Chamber, 1983).

48. Ministry of Industry and Tourism, Industrial Development Branch, memo re: Activities of the Industrial Development Branch, August 12, 1981, box 3, IGP.

49. Ministry of Industry and Tourism, Policy and Priorities Division, "A Comparison of the Tax & Incentive Structure, Canada and the U.S.," January 5, 1978, 11–12, Mr. Fisher 79/80 file, box 3, IGP.

50. Ministry of Industry and Tourism, "Industrial Development Advertising: United States, a Report on Expenditures and Budgets," 1979, box 3, IGP.

51. Ministry of Industry and Tourism, Industrial Development Branch, "Ontario's Competitive Position with Respect to International Industrial Development Promotion," September 27, 1979, 6, 1979/1980 Competitive Advertising File #2, box 3, IGP.

52. Ministry of Industry and Tourism, "Industrial Development Advertising: United States," August 14, 1979, 2, Federal Department of Industry file, box 80, RG 9-10, MI&T; Remarks by the Honorable Larry Grossman, Ministry of Industry and Tourism, to the Ontario Industrial Commissioners' Seminar, Hotel Ontario, January 23, 1980, Minister's Speeches file, box 3, RG 9-65, IGP.

53. Remarks by the Honorable Larry Grossman, January 23, 1980.

54. Economic Development Branch, Ministry of Treasury and Economics, "Ontario in Comparison with Selected U.S. States," August, 1979, 2, RG 9-65, Box 3, Ontario folder, IGP.

55. *Living in Pittsburgh* (Pittsburgh: Duquesne Light Company, 1977).

56. Greenberg, *Branding New York*, chap. 7.

57. Ibid., 10–11.

58. Ibid., 35–36.

59. John Heeley, *Inside City Tourism* (Bristol: Channel View, 2011), 6–7; Ronan Paddison, "City Marketing, Image Reconstruction and Urban Regeneration," *Urban Studies* 30, 2 (1993): 339–49.

60. *Seven Pittsburghs: Discoveries by Some Younger Settlers* (Pittsburgh: Duquesne Light, ca. 1980); Richard L. Florida, *The Rise of the Creative Class, and How It's Transforming Work, Leisure, Community and Everyday Life* (New York: Basic, 2002).

61. *Seven Pittsburghs*.

62. Ibid.

63. Ibid.

64. On Pittsburgh's post-1945 African American history, see Joe W. Trotter and Jared N. Day, *Race and Renaissance: African Americans in Pittsburgh Since World War II* (Pittsburgh: University of Pittsburgh Press, 2010).

65. The first ad ran May 28, 1981, and continued every other week into early 1982. Penn's Southwest Association, "Dynamic Pittsburgh," ca. 1981, Dynamic Pittsburgh.

66. Ibid.

67. Ibid.

68. Penn's Southwest Association, *1981 Annual Report* (Pittsburgh: The Association, 1982), 5–6.

69. Michael Sorkin, *Variations on a Theme Park: The New American City and the End of Public Space* (New York: Hill and Wang, 1992); Zukin, "Postcard-Perfect."

70. "Pittsburgh, A Place Worth Investing In," 1981, folder 6, box 216, ACCD.

71. William E. Geist, "Pittsburgh Gives a Luncheon to Try Out a New Civic Image," *New York Times*, February 29, 1984.

72. Allen Dieterich-Ward, *Beyond Rust: Metropolitan Pittsburgh and the Fate of Industrial America* (Philadelphia: University of Pennsylvania Press, 2015); John P. Hoerr, *And the Wolf*

Finally Came: The Decline of the American Steel Industry (Pittsburgh: University of Pittsburgh Press, 1988); William Serrin, *Homestead: The Glory and Tragedy of an American Steel Town* (New York: Times Books, 1992).

73. "A Tale of Two Cities," *Pittsburgh Magazine*, March 1984, 3.

74. Jack Markowitz, "Roderick Says Radicals Scaring Jobs Away," *Pittsburgh Tribune Review*, July 22, 1984.

75. Marginalia on a copy of Markowitz, Misc Network to Save the Mon/Ohio Valley Documents 1983–1984 folder, box 1, Denominational Ministry Strategy (DMS) Papers, 1983–1989, DMS.

76. Editorial, "Misguided Mellon Boycott," *Pittsburgh Post-Gazette*, June 16, 1983.

77. Editorial, "A Strategy for Chasing Jobs Out of the Area," *Pittsburgh Business Times*, May 21–27, 1983.

78. Roger S. Ahlbrandt and Morton Coleman, *The Role of the Corporation in Community Economic Development as Viewed by 21 Corporate Executives* (Pittsburgh: University of Pittsburgh, January 5, 1987), 52.

79. Editorial, "Saving the Valley," *Pittsburgh Business Times*, January 21–27, 1985.

80. Geist, "Pittsburgh Gives a Luncheon to Try Out a New Civic Image."

81. William K. Stevens, "Pittsburgh Bemused at No. 1 Ranking," *New York Times*, March 31, 1985.

82. "Celebrate Pittsburgh," ca. 1985, folder 2, box 216, ACCD.

83. Christopher H. Marquis, "When Cities Shun Their Roots," *Christian Science Monitor*, December 26, 1985, 12.

84. Vince Rause, "Pittsburgh Cleans Up Its Act," *New York Times*, November 26, 1989.

85. Rotstein, "'Most Livable City' Took Its Lumps over Tag."

86. Currie, Coopers & Lybrand Ltd., *The Regional Municipality of Hamilton-Wentworth: An Action Plan for Economic Growth* (Toronto: Currie, Coopers & Lybrand Ltd., 1978).

87. C. T. C. Armstrong to the Chairman and Members of the Economic Development Committee, memo re: Goals and Objectives, February 16 1979, file # 548/EC DEV 16-79 #2, Hamilton Clerk.

88. Ibid.

89. John Morand, *Marketing Plan: 'A Plan for Economic Growth' for the Regional Municipality of Hamilton-Wentworth* (Hamilton: Regional Municipality of Hamilton-Wentworth, October 2, 1979), 2.

90. Ibid., 4–5, 8.

91. Bill Johnston, "If You Can Help Improve Our Image, You'll Win $500," *Hamilton Spectator*, May 19, 1982.

92. Wayne MacPhail, "Steel City—Is It Even on the Map?" *Hamilton Spectator*, October 6, 1984.

93. Ibid.

94. Ibid.

95. Ibid.

96. "Ad Captures Image," *Hamilton Spectator*, October 11, 1984.

97. *Talk About a Great Place* (Hamilton: Regional Municipality of Hamilton-Wentworth, ca. 1985); *Look at Us Now* (Hamilton: Regional Municipality of Hamilton-Wentworth, ca. 1987).

98. *Talk About a Great Place.*

99. *Look at Us Now.*

100. "A Lot of Good News on the Home Front," *Hamilton Spectator*, May 26, 1986.

101. Jerry Rogers, "Back from the Edge and Flying High: Hamilton Economy Shows Major Surge," *Hamilton Spectator*, October 24, 1986; Jerry Rogers, "Entrepreneurs," *Hamilton Spectator*, October 25, 1986.

102. Jerry Rogers, "The Ambitious City: Mayor Says We've Only Just Begun; Critics Warn Bigger Projects Needed," *Hamilton Spectator*, October 2, 1986.

103. Regional Planning Branch, Hamilton-Wentworth Planning and Development Division, *Building on Strength – Realizing Opportunity: An Economic Strategy for Hamilton-Wentworth* (Hamilton: Regional Municipality of Hamilton-Wentworth, 1986).

104. Regional Municipality of Hamilton-Wentworth Economic Development Department, memo to Economic Development and Planning Commission, re: Pittsburgh Marketing Campaign, April 28, 1988, Hamilton Clerk.

105. Regional Municipality of Hamilton-Wentworth Economic Development Department, memo to Economic Development and Planning Commission, re: Pittsburgh In-Coming Trade Mission, May 16, 1990, Hamilton Clerk; Regional Municipality of Hamilton-Wentworth Economic Development Department, memo to Economic Development and Planning Commission, re: IDAC/External Affairs Trade and Investment Seminar; Pittsburgh Business Mission, May 2, 1991, Hamilton Clerk.

Epilogue. Cities for Whom?

1. Steve Arnold, "Hamilton's Steel Industry from Birth, to Boom and Beyond," *Hamilton Spectator*, February 11, 2012; Greg Keenan, "U.S. Steel Ends an Era in Hamilton," *Globe and Mail*, October 29, 2013.

2. "In the Shadow of Steel," *Ideas with Paul Kennedy*, CBC Radio One, January 3, 2014.

3. Meredith MacLeod, "Envision Hamilton as It Could Be, Not as It Was," *Hamilton Spectator*, September 14, 2013.

4. Gary Rotstein, "30 Years of Change: A New Direction for Pittsburgh," *Pittsburgh Post-Gazette*, October 6, 2013.

5. The ranking excluded state and federal employees. Bill Toland, "30 Years: Pittsburgh Moves from Heavy Industry to Medicine, Tech, Energy," *Pittsburgh Post-Gazette*, October 13, 2013.

6. Rotstein, "30 Years of Change."

7. Sally Kalson, "30 Years: 'Hell with the Lid Off' to Most Livable—How Pittsburgh Became Cool," *Pittsburgh Post-Gazette*, October 20, 2013.

8. "Hamilton: The Comeback Kid of Canadian Cities," *Ontario Business Report*, 2012.

9. MacLeod, "Envision Hamilton as It Could Be, Not as It Was."

10. Neil Bradford, "Public-Private Partnership? Shifting Paradigms of Economic Governance in Ontario," *Canadian Journal of Political Science* 36, 5 (2003): 1017; Dave Snow and Benjamin Moffitt, "Straddling the Divide: Mainstream Populism and Conservatism in Howard's Australia and Harper's Canada," *Commonwealth & Comparative Politics* 50, 3 (July 1, 2012): 271–92.

11. "Hamilton: The Comeback Kid of Canadian Cities."

12. Barbara Davis, ed., *Remaking Cities: Proceedings of the 1988 International Conference in Pittsburgh* (Pittsburgh: Pittsburgh Chapter of the American Institute of Architects, 1988).

13. "Remaking Cities Congress Program," http://www.remakingcitiescongress.org/, accessed October 25, 2013.

14. Ibid.

15. Creative Class Group, "Richard Florida: About Richard," http://www.creativeclass.com/richard_florida/about_richard, accessed January 5, 2014.

16. Richard L. Florida, *The Rise of the Creative Class, and How It's Transforming Work, Leisure, Community and Everyday Life* (New York: Basic, 2002).

17. Dan Fitzpatrick, "Pittsburgh Image-Makers Battling to Get Message Out, Negate Bad PR," *Pittsburgh Post-Gazette*, June 30, 2002; Florida, *The Rise of the Creative Class*, 305.

18. Richard L. Florida, "Pittsburgh: The 'Base Case' Turns the Corner," in "Visions of Pittsburgh's Future," *Pittsburgh Quarterly*, Fall 2013.

19. Jamie Peck, "Struggling with the Creative Class," *International Journal of Urban and Regional Research* 29, 4 (December 2005): 766.

20. Ibid., 741.

21. Zach Mortice, "2013 Remaking Cities Congress: Cities Remade, But for Whom?" *AIArchitect* 20 (October 2013).

22. Ibid.

23. Ontario Common Front, *Falling Behind* (Toronto: Ontario Common Front, 2012).

24. Sarah Mayo and Deirdre Pike, *The Rich and the Rest of Us* (Hamilton: Social Planning and Research Council of Hamilton, 2013).

25. Mark Price and Stephan Herzenberg, *State of Working Pennsylvania 2013* (Harrisburg: Keystone Research Center, 2013).

26. U.S. Census Bureau/American FactFinder, "Individuals Below Poverty Level," 2008–2012, American Community Survey 5-Year Estimates, U.S. Census Bureau American Community Survey Office, 2012.

27. Mary Niederberger, "Pittsburgh Suburbs Suffering Poverty at High Rate," *Pittsburgh Post-Gazette*, November 17, 2013.

28. Harold D. Miller, "Regional Insights: High Black Poverty a Shame," *Pittsburgh Post-Gazette*, July 4, 2010.

29. Louis Uchitelle and David Leonhardt, "Men Not Working, and Not Wanting Just Any Job," *New York Times*, July 31, 2006.

Flaherty, Tom, 91–92
Florida, Richard, 190, 212–14. *See also* creative class; Creative Class Group
Foerster, Tom, 54, 94, 153, 238n83. *See also* Allegheny County
Ford Foundation, 142
Ford, Gerald (president), urban policies of, 43, 57. *See also* Nixon, Richard
France, 9, 16, 19, 76. *See also* North Atlantic
free markets, 18, 19, 82. *See also* BILD; Macdonald Commission; privatism
free trade, 81–84
Frick Museum of Art. *See under* museums

Gans, Herbert, 18
General Development Agreements (GDAs), 39, 69. *See also* Canada; DREE; Special Areas program
general revenue sharing, 41–43, 44, 47, 80. *See also* decentralization; New Federalism; Nixon, Richard
gentrification: of blue-collar neighborhoods, 59, 145; and urban redevelopment, 167–68, 213. *See also* neoliberalism
Germany, 2, 9, 16, 18, 19, 21; East, 149. *See also* North Atlantic; Ruhr Valley
Glasgow, 5, 63; marketing of, 190; redevelopment partnership of, 135. *See also* North Atlantic
Golden Horseshoe, 6, 22, 24. *See also* Hamilton
Golden Triangle, 27, 29, 45; in marketing, 193, 197; as model, 125; redevelopment of, 116, 123, 180–81; relationship to neighborhoods, 50–52, 93, 111, 120, 182. *See also* Pittsburgh
Greater Pittsburgh Chamber of Commerce, 107, 200
Great Migration, 25
Great Society, 36, 41, 142–43. *See also* Johnson, Lyndon
growth coalitions, 3, 6–7: challenges of, 35, 37, 106, 135–36; and downtown redevelopment, 29, 111–14, 118, 120, 122–24, 135; forms of, 19–22, 56, 58; and free market, 59, 108; and high-technology industry, 152, 156; and marketing, 175–76, 180–84, 188–95, 200, 204, 207; opponents of, 9, 90, 100, 197–99; and postindustrial transition, 75–77, 87, 95, 138, 157, 159, 170, 172–73,

213–14; relations with city residents, 89, 139, 109–10, 199–200; and state/provincial and national governments, 15, 44, 64, 85, 88, 104–5, 187. *See also* Allegheny Conference; CAPAC; community development corporations; corporate welfare; growth partnerships; Hamilton; Pittsburgh; privatization; redevelopment partnerships; Strategy 21; urban renewal
Grove, John J., 1, 32–33, 64
growth partnerships. *See* growth coalitions
Gulf Oil, 55, 97, 193, 227n43

Hamburg, 20. *See also* North Atlantic
Hamilton, 4, 6–7, 15, 22–26, 83, 210–11, 220n14; branding of, 183–87, 201; and city planning, 29–30, 45–46; and downtown renewal, 31, 98, 109–10, 124–36; federal and provincial relations with, 33–35, 37–40, 64–65, 85, 100, 187–88, 201; growth coalition of, 32–33, 64–73, 77, 100–106, 204; neighborhood redevelopment in, 137–38, 157–73; marketing of, 174–77, 202–7; Pittsburgh as model for, 44, 63; poverty in, 214. *See also* Bay Area Council; Beach Strip neighborhood; Canada; Central Area Plan Advisory Committee; Copps, Vic; corporate welfare; cultural development; Dofasco; Economic Development Commission; Economic Development Department; Faludi, E. G.; Hamilton and District Chamber of Commerce; Hamilton and District Labor Council; Hamilton-Wentworth Regional Municipality; Hess Village; H. H. Robertson; Jackson, Lloyd D.; Jackson Square; James Street; Lunchpail Report; MacDonald, Jack; McMaster University; Mohawk College; Moore, Jack; Morrow, Bob; Mountain neighborhood; North End neighborhood; Ontario; *Pardon my Lunch Bucket*; postindustrialism; public-private partnerships; service sector; slums; *Steeltown*; Stelco; Stoney Creek; Toronto; U.S. Steel; Westinghouse
Hamilton and District Chamber of Commerce, 32; and business activism, 171–72, 206; and city marketing, 186–87, 202–3, 204, 207, 210; as development partner, 7, 64, 101, 135, 157

ACKNOWLEDGMENTS

The seeds of *Remaking the Rust Belt* were planted on a 2006 road trip from Brooklyn to my hometown, Traverse City, Michigan, to introduce my then-boyfriend to my grandmother. We stayed with family friends in Pittsburgh and Hamilton along the way. Ray and Sheila Karolak showed me around Pittsburgh and Tom and Marion Bryner did the same in Hamilton. They told me remarkably similar stories about the pasts and presents of the two cities, and I returned to New York eager to get to work on the project that, over many years, developed into this book. Along the way, I have accumulated no shortage of intellectual and personal debts of gratitude. The greatest is to Tom Bender. He has read as many drafts of the book as I have written, and each iteration was substantially better for his insights. Perhaps more important, Tom's wide-ranging interests and exceptional generosity offer the best model I have seen for how to be in the academy.

My research could not have been successful without the assistance of the wonderful archivists, librarians, and staff members at the National Archives, the Library and Archives of Canada, the Gerald Ford Library, the Jimmy Carter Library, the Pennsylvania State Archives, the Archives of Ontario, the Archives Service Center at the University of Pittsburgh, the Senator John Heinz History Center, the Carnegie Library of Pittsburgh, and the Hamilton Public Library. Nancy Watson and David Rosenberg at the Archives Service Center, in particular, helped guide my inquiries.

I received substantial financial support to research and write *Remaking the Rust Belt*. NYU provided me with a McCracken fellowship, a Margaret Brown fellowship, and smaller grants for conference travel to present my work. A CLIR/Mellon fellowship and a term as a Scholar in Residence at the Pennsylvania State Archives funded my research in Pittsburgh, Harrisburg, Washington, D.C., and Hamilton. Fellowships from the Canadian Government and the International Council for Canadian Studies underwrote my research in Toronto and Ottawa. A Residency Research Fellowship at the University of Michigan's Eisenberg Institute for Historical Studies, a Faculty

Fellowship from Wayne State University's Humanities Center, and a Wayne State University Research Grant supported me as I wrote the book. The Canada Program of Harvard University's Weatherhead Center for International Affairs, where I was a fellow as the book went into production, generously provided the funds that paid for the book's index. Portions of Chapters 2 and 6 have appeared in articles in the *Journal of Urban History*, and I thank Sage Publications for allowing me to reprint them here.

Elizabeth Tandy Shermer, who recruited my manuscript for this series, and Robert Lockhart, my editor at Penn Press, have nurtured the project for several years. Both Bob and Ellie have read multiple drafts, offered incisive critiques, and helped me structure and restructure the manuscript. They were far more hands-on and supportive than I ever dreamed possible, and I am immensely grateful for their encouragement and enthusiasm. Bob likes to make connections between his authors, and I would like to thank him especially for introducing me to so many great people and their wonderful work. Thanks, too, to Alison Anderson at Penn Press, who prepared the manuscript for production. I also owe a debt of gratitude to Stephanie Inson, who created the first drafts of the lovely maps that appear in the book, to Timothy Pearson, who crafted the index, and Andrew Hnatow, who helped me track down image permissions and proofread multipledrafts (any errors that made it past him are, of course, are my own).

A dizzying number of readers have shaped this project over the years. Critiques from the anonymous readers for Penn Press were vital to my manuscript revisions. At NYU, Daniel Walkowitz, Andrew Needham, Kim Phillips-Fein, and Guy Ortolano provided incisive feedback on early drafts, and they have continued to encourage and support me to far more than I had any right to expect. The book has benefited from careful readings of earlier drafts by the members of Tom Bender's dissertation seminar, Wayne State University's Spaces and Places working group, the Metropolitan History Workshop at the University of Michigan, and the Pittsburgh History Roundtable. The graduate students in Andrew Needham's urban history course at NYU read the penultimate draft and their comments helped guide my final revisions. Dan Amsterdam and Allen Dieterich-Ward read the manuscript in its entirety and offered criticism and encouragement in equal measure. Dan and Allen are outstanding storytellers, and this book is infinitely better for their suggestions on everything from chapter organization to crafting narrative arcs. I have especially valued my Skype conversations and frequent email exchanges with Allen as we negotiated the publishing process—I've benefited tremendously from his experience and willingness to share it. Patrick Vitale, who started off as my archive buddy in Harrisburg and has since become a great friend and co-conspirator, has pushed me to think more critically about space, scale, and political economy. Allen and Patrick also write about post-war Pittsburgh, and along with Ted Muller and Sabina Detrick at the University of Pittsburgh, they have been incredibly generous with their knowledge of the city and region, which far surpasses my own.

Many friends, classmates, mentors, and colleagues have supported me personally and professionally as I worked on this project. Stephanie Carpenter and Megan Rupnik have sustained me in my highest and lowest moments. Jenifer Witt and Meagan Belden reappeared in my life just as I started to write the book, and our renewed friendship has brought me great joy. In Pittsburgh, Ray and Sheila Karolak (and Maggie and Kayley) always welcomed me with a good meal, a stiff drink, and a warm bed. I like to call them as my "fake parents," a label they (seem to) have accepted with good humor. Tom and Marion Bryner (and Gracie) did the same in Hamilton. I am also grateful to Maureen Madden-Kershaw and the rest of the Madden clan for their generosity and good company.

My cohort at NYU and my comrades from GSOC shaped my expectations for collegiality, solidarity, and life in the academy; I want to thank Bekah Friedman, Jay Diehl, Atiba Pertilla, and Lilly Tuttle in particular for their friendship over the years. Jenny Shaw and Sarah Cornell have always made time to patiently advise me at every step of my career. At Wayne State University, my colleagues in the history department have been unfailingly encouraging and unstinting with their time and wisdom. I am indebted to my faculty mentors Elizabeth Faue and Liette Gidlow for their guidance and exceptional good humor, and to Janine Lanza and Kidada Williams for their informal mentorship. My (too frequent) lunch and coffee dates with Janine and Liz, in particular, kept me laughing and made me feel supported personally as well as professionally. John Bukowczyk, Jennifer Hart, Marc Kruman, Gayle McCreedy, and Andrew Port have been especially generous with their support and advice. Abdullah Al-Arian and Alex Day, who left Detroit for warmer climates, helped keep me sane my first two years on the tenure track. John Pat Leary and Lara Cohen defy categorization—they are friends and colleagues, part of my NYU crew and my life in Detroit—but I am so glad to have had them, and Louisa, in my life for the past several years.

Wednesday writing sessions with Elena Past at Pinwheel Bakery in Ferndale have been one of my greatest pleasures as I finished the book. Elena's unfailing encouragement and her superior discipline kept me on track and off the internet. I also thank Pinwheel's staff for letting us linger for hours and supplying us with tasty treats.

My grandmother, Joan Neumann, and my late grandfather, Raymond Neumann, made the life I have today possible. I owe them everything. My grandmother, in particular, is a source of boundless love, support, and patience, and of a fluffy little dog, Benji, who always makes me smile. Finally, I thank Paul Kershaw, that boyfriend (now husband) I took home to meet my grandmother a decade ago. He's been my sounding board for this project from its inception to its completion, and the resulting book is far stronger for our conversations about it. When I decided to write about Pittsburgh and Hamilton, I joked that it meant that we would never be able to break up. He took me at my word, and I am grateful for him every day.